OUR FRIEND MANSO

Benito Pérez Galdós

OUR FRIEND MANSO

Translated from the Spanish
by ROBERT RUSSELL

New York
COLUMBIA UNIVERSITY PRESS
1987

*Columbia University Press is grateful for a grant from the
Program for Cultural Cooperation Between the Spanish Ministry of
Culture and North American Universities to aid
in the publication of this book*

Library of Congress Cataloging-in-Publication Data
Pérez Galdós, Benito, 1843–1920.
Our friend Manso.
I. Title
PQ6555.A745E5 1987   863′.5   86-14758
ISBN 0-231-06404-7

Columbia University Press
New York   Guilford, Surrey
Copyright © 1987 Columbia University Press

Printed in the United States of America

TRANSLATOR'S NOTE

Benito Pérez Galdós (1843–1920) wrote *El amigo Manso* in 1882. It was the second novel to be published in Galdós' great series of *Novelas Españolas Contemporáneas,* which occupied his creative energies between 1881 and 1897.

The translation has required only the barest minimum of footnotes. Names and honorifics (Manuel, señora) have been left in their Spanish forms; titles (duchess, Cabinet Minister) have been put into English.

R.R.

CONTENTS

I

I DO NOT EXIST

I DO NOT EXIST. And just in case some untrusting, stubborn, ill-meaning person should refuse to believe what I say so plainly, or should demand some sort of sworn testimony before believing it—I swear, I solemnly swear that I do not exist; and I likewise protest against any and all inclinations or attempts to consider me as being endowed with the unequivocal attributes of real existence. I declare that I am not even a portrait of anybody, and I promise that if one of our contemporary deep-thinkers were to start looking for similarities between my fleshless, boneless being and any individual susceptible to an experiment in vivisection, I should rush to the defense of my rights as a myth, demonstrating with witnesses called forth from a place of my own choosing that I neither am, nor have been, nor ever will be, anybody.

I am—putting it obscurely in order for you to understand it better—an artistic, diabolical condensation, a fabrication born of human thought (*ximia Dei*) which, whenever it grasps in its fingers a bit of literary style, uses it to start imitating what God has done with material substance in the physical world; I am one more example of those falsifications of a man which from the dawn of time have been sold on the block by people I call idlers—and by so doing I fail in my filial duties—though an undiscerning and overgenerous public confers on them the title of artist, poet, or something of the sort. I am a chimera, dream of a dream, shadow of a shade, suspicion of a possibility: I enjoy my nonexistence, I watch the senseless passing of infinite time, which is so boring that it holds my attention, and I begin to wonder whether being nobody isn't the same as being everybody, whether my not possessing any personal attributes isn't the same as possessing the very attributes of existence itself. This is a matter which I haven't clarified as yet, and I pray God I never may, lest I be deprived of that illusion of pride which always alleviates the frigid boredom of these realms of pure thought.

Here, ladies and gentlemen, in the home of all that does not exist, we too have our vanity (can you believe that?), our social classes, and all sorts of

1

intrigues . . . ! We have long-standing animosities, special privilege, uprisings, soup kitchens, and pronunciamientos. Many of us entities who live here, if we were really alive, might say that we live by a miracle. But I shall make a quick retreat from such labyrinthine speculations and take the path of plain talk to explain how, having no voice, I speak, and having no hands, I scribble these lines which will come to be—if there's a living soul who'll read them—a book. Have a look at me now, in human guise. Somebody is calling me forth, and by some unknown magical skill is giving me a sort of bodily shell, turning me into a mimicry or mask of a living person, with all the look and movements of one such. The one who is jolting me out of my routine and sending me down the garden path is a friend . . .

But order, we must have order in our narration! I have a friend who, for his sins—which must be as numberless as the sands of the sea—has fallen under an infamous curse: he writes novels; and others, by reading them, complete the cycle of divine punishment or damnation. This fellow came to me a few days ago, spoke to me of his labors, and when he told me that he had already written thirty volumes, I took such pity on him that I was unable to remain insensitive to his urgent pleadings. Having fallen once again into the heinous crime of writing, he begged my complicity in adding another volume to the thirty aforementioned outrages. That virtuous convict, that hardened innocent, explained that he was quite taken with the notion of perpetrating a lengthy novelistic crime, dealing with the great subject matter of Education. He said he'd worked out the plan, but in the absence of certain data necessary to carry it forward with all the crafty dispatch he characteristically employs in his misdeeds, he had determined to postpone this opus so that he might take it on again with real spirit once he had in his hands all the weapons, tools, stepladders, lock-picks, dies, and other valuable objects appropriate to the matter. Meanwhile, not wishing to remain idle, he desired to undertake a trivial bit of work, and knowing that I was the owner of a simple and pleasant story, he had come to buy it from me. He offered me four dozen literary genres, payable in four installments; a bushel of outmoded ideas—all-purpose ideas, neatly packed; ten gallons of sentimental syrup, tightly corked to stand up to export; and finally a great ration of expressions and set phrases, ready-made and all cut to size, along with more than one pot of glue for sticking, fitting, mounting, joining, and assembling. It didn't look like a bad deal, so I said yes.

2

I can't say what inept movements he performed before my eyes in his guileless perversity; I can't say what diabolical magic he worked . . . I think he plunged me into a drop of ink; set fire to a sheet of paper; and then the fire, the paper, and I were put into a little bottle which had an awful stench of pitch, sulfur, and other infernal concoctions . . . A bit later I emerged from a flash of red flame, transformed into mortal flesh. The pain I felt told me I was a man.

II

I AM MÁXIMO MANSO

AND I WAS thirty-five years old when that business happened. And if I add that it happened recently and that many of the occurrences included in this true story happened in less than one year's time, that should satisfy even those readers who are most demanding in matters of chronology. I must disappoint the sentimentalists right from the outset by informing them that I have two Doctor's degrees and hold a professorship in the Institute,* a post I earned in open competition. The subject I teach is a most important one but I choose not to mention it by name. I have dedicated my small intelligence and my time totally to philosophical studies, for in them I have found the purest joys of my life. I don't see how most people can profess to find this delightful study dry; it's always old and yet always new, this mistress of all wisdom who governs human existence, visibly or invisibly.

Perhaps those who reject philosophy have done so out of a failure to study her methodically, for that is the only fashion in which to navigate her tortuous secrets. Or perhaps in superficial study they have seen only her external harshness, and never gone deep enough to taste the remarkable sweetness and gentleness of what she holds within. As a special gift in my nature, I showed from early childhood a particular fondness for speculative labors, and for the investigation of truth and the exercise of reason. To this privilege was added, by great good fortune, that of coming under the tutelage of a skillful teacher, who from the very beginning put me on the right path. How true it is that the happy achievement of difficult undertakings results from a good start; and that a first step, correctly taken, leads to the swift and sure completion of a long journey.

Let it be said of me, then, that I am a philosopher, though I consider myself undeserving of that title, applicable only to the great masters of think-

*A prestigious preparatory school in Madrid.

4

ing and of living. I am but a disciple, or if you wish, a humble aide of that phalanx of noble builders who, age after age, have worked at carving the beautiful image of divine man out of the rude slab of the human beast. I am the apprentice sharpening a tool, holding onto a fragment. But active penetration, fruitful boldness, the strengths of power and of creation—these are denied me, as they are to all mortals of my time. I am one more teacher in the ranks, fulfilling my duty by teaching what was taught to me, working without surcease; uniting in my wholehearted and methodical way the things around me, be they solid theory or fleeting event, indubitable phenomenon or bold hypothesis; moving every day, with slow and careful step, beyond mediocrity; building my own wisdom with the wisdom of others; and finally making every effort to assure that the ideas I've acquired and the system I've so laboriously worked out may not be empty constructions of wind and smoke, but instead a solid structure of reality for my life, strongly grounded in my conscience. The preacher who doesn't practice what he preaches is no preacher at all; he's a talking pulpit.

Turning now to my outward nature, I may say that my general appearance, so I've been told, offers the aspect of a sedentary man, one given to study and meditation. Rather than a professor, many people take me for a court clerk or lawyer; and others, observing that I don't have a good growth of beard and thus go clean-shaven, have imagined that I was an actor or a liberal priest, two remarkably similar types. I think I have by now lost a bit of this appearance; at least several persons have expressed such an idea directly or indirectly. I am of middle height, such that, in view of the continuing trend toward shortness in the human race, I might pass as one of noble stature. I am well-fed, strong, muscular, but neither heavy nor obese. Indeed, as a result of well-organized gymnastic exercises, I am quite agile and enjoy perfect health. Myopic from birth, and addicted in childhood to nighttime reading, I am obliged to wear glasses. For a long time I wore a pince-nez, a practice more preventive than it is convenient. But finally I adopted gold-rimmed spectacles, whose comfort I cannot praise enough, though I realize they make me look a bit older.

My hair is vigorous, dark, and abundant, but I've always taken special care not to go long-haired, and I have it barbered military-fashion, sacrificing in the interests of simplicity a decorative element not usually disparaged by men who, like me, have no others. I dress unaffectedly, eschewing alike gaudy novelty and ridiculous antiquity of style. I get good wear out of my clothes, with the help of a mender-tailor, a friend of mine; and I've become

5

so accustomed to my stovepipe hat (which common folk pun on by calling it a *chistera**) that I cannot get along without it, nor am I able to replace it with any other family or class of head-covering. So I wear it even in summer, and I'd be very happy to wear it while traveling, if I weren't afraid of being outlandish. My cape never drops from my shoulders all winter long; I even wrap up in it to study in my sitting room, since I abhor braziers and stoves.

I've already said that my health is splendid; to that I'll now add that I can't remember ever having sat down to a meal without a good appetite. I am no epicure, nor do I have the least understanding of exquisite or overrefined dishes. I eat everything that is put before me, without asking the dish about its family tree or scrutinizing its components. As regards favorites, I have but one; I openly declare it, although to do so is to name an ordinary thing, the *cicer aretinum*, which in plain language we call the chick-pea, and which, to believe the tiresome nutritionists, is an indigestible food. If it is, I have not noticed it. Those delicious pellets of vegetable flesh have no possible substitute; such is the view of my own palate, a great authority in these matters. I should be disconsolate were I to be without them, and all the more so if their disappearance were accompanied by that of Lozoya Valley water, † which is my wine. I need not add that I am completely untroubled by the ravages of phylloxera, since my wine cellar is stocked only by the fresh springs of our nearby mountains. Nothing but red wine of low alcoholic content do I sparingly imbibe, and that only after it has been well baptized by the wine merchant and confirmed by me. But not a drop of those treacherous southern wines enters my body. One more detail: I don't smoke.

I am an Asturian. I was born at Cangas de Onís, at the very gates of Covadonga and Mount Auseba. Spanish nationality and I are brothers, for we were both born in the shelter of those towering mountains, covered in green the year round, and in winter bearing a snowy headdress, their skirts a carpet of grass, their heights thick with oak and chestnut trees bent forward as if scaling the slopes; their deep, labyrinthine, mysterious forest glades so densely wooded, a promenade for the bears; their steep rocky summits a resting place for the clouds. My father, the town pharmacist, was a great hunter and knew every palm's breadth of the region, from Ribadesella to Ponga and

---

*A comon colloquialism for stovepipe hat, close in form to *chiste,* or joke.
†The salubrious water of Madrid's first municipal system, inaugurated in 1858.

Tarna, from Las Arrondas to Los Urrieles. When I was old enough not to get tired on these outings, he would take me and my brother José María with him. We went up to the High Passes, we hiked through Cabrales and Peñamellera, and at Liébana, that magnificent spot, we walked through the very clouds.

By myself or in the company of boys my age, I often went toward evening to the monastery of San Pedro de Villanueva. On its stones is sculpted the story, as short as it is sad, of that king, the one who was eaten by a bear.* I used to shinny up the worn columns of the Byzantine portico to have a close look at the terrified faces of the Everlasting Father and saints. They were rough sculptures, infused with a strange sort of religious terror. I would put my arms around them and, with the help of other mischievous boys, would paint eyes and moustaches on them with shoe-blacking, which made them look even more terrified. This made us laugh; but when I reached home I would recall the figure I had touched up and would go to sleep in fear of it, and dream about it. In my dreams I would see the stubby, symmetrical hand, the feet like ferules, the contorted bodies, the eyes popping from their sockets, and I'd begin to cry out and not stop until my mother took me to her bed to sleep.

I did not do what other, perverse boys did: take a big stone and knock off an apostle's nose or the Everlasting Father's fingers; or remove the tails of the dragon-gargoyles, or put indecent signs over the votive slabs whose writing we did not understand. For playing bounce-back we always preferred the Byzantine portico to the other sides of the poor monastery, because it seemed as if the Everlasting Father and His Court returned the ball more quickly. The boy who was leader of our gang is today one of the most respectable personages in Asturias and sits as chairman—how ironic life is!—of the Commission on Monuments. The character of the places where I spent my childhood has left such a deep and lasting imprint on my spirit that I am always aware of something in me that springs from the melancholy and the amenity of those valleys, the grandeur of those mountains and hollows whose echoes repeat the first stammerings of our history as a nation; of those heights where the traveler thinks he's walking above the air on a stone skylight. All of this, and the resounding, picturesque river, and sad Lake Nol, a hermit sea, and the lonely monastery of San Pedro have in them something of me, or

*King Favila of Asturias reigned from 737 to 739. Legend says he was devoured by a bear while hunting.

perhaps I share with them a blood relationship in a formal sense—certainly not in terms of content. Something like a casting and its mold. I must also say that I carry a deep mark of pity for that king who was eaten by the bear. I feel imprinted or retraced in my own brain-mass the capitals of the columns where that dreadful story is told. On one of them the young sovereign says farewell to his young wife; on another, he is taking on the wild creature and, farther along, the creature is eating him for lunch. When I was a naughty boy my father would threaten to have the bear come and eat me as he did King Favila. On many such nights I had a nightmare where I saw passing before me the frightful figures of the capitals. I wouldn't have gone into the woods alone for anything in the world; and even today when I see a bear I imagine for an instant that I am a king. Or if I manage to see a king, I seem to have a bit of bear in me.

My father died before reaching old age. My brother and I were thus left orphans, José María at twenty-two and I at fifteen. My brother had an ambition more for money than for glory and he went off to Havana. I seemed to show a certain scorn for empty worldliness, and felt a spur toward fame. At my tender age I was unsurpassed in learning by anyone in town. I passed as a savant; I had a lot of books, and even the priest would consult me on matters of natural philosophy and science. I took on a certain pedantic presumption and an aroma of authority, of which, thank God, I later cured myself entirely. My mother was out of her head with pride, and whenever some distinguished gentleman would visit her she would make me come into the parlor and then trick me into showing off my learning in history or literature by steering the conversation in the direction of those subjects. Most of the time she had to drag them in by the hair.

As we had more than enough to live on, my mother brought me to Madrid with the notion that here the paths to glory would easily be opened to me. Indeed, after unlearning what I knew, so that I could study it afresh, I saw more attractive horizons and made friends with young persons of merit and with renowned teachers. I frequented literary circles, I broadened the scope of my reading and achieved notable advancement in my career. I soon found myself ready to occupy a modest academic post and to aspire to better ones. My mother had some good friends in Madrid, among them García Grande and his wife, who were active for a long time in the Liberal Union. But these connections had little effect on my life, since my eagerness for study kept me isolated from everything except the university treadmill. I didn't go out in society; nor did I like it or need it at all.

I am eager to tell about my moral character and my devotion to my favorite subject of study. Willy-nilly, my pen pushes on, at the impulse of this special predilection of mine, and I allow it to do so, even permitting it to treat this point squarely and honestly, not scrimping in its praises of me when I think I deserve them. It may appear boastful to say that where principles are concerned I am so strict as to produce laughter in some of my fellow inhabitants of this planet. But what's said is said and no one can erase it from this paper. I am constantly congratulating myself on my temperate personality and on the secondary place which fantasy has in my character. Secondary, that is, to my observant, practical spirit, which permits me to see things as they really are, and never to be mistaken about their true size, extent, and importance. I am thus enabled always to keep a tight rein on myself.

As soon as I began to control these difficult matters of study, I set out to establish reason as the absolute mistress and guide of my actions, the most important ones as well as the most trivial; and this beautiful plan has turned out so well for me that I am amazed that all men don't follow it faithfully, and employ the logic of facts, in order for the chainlike succession thereof to become the efficient and prudent rule of their lives. I have been able to stifle petty passions which would have brought me unhappiness, and appetites whose immoderate indulgence has led others to degradation. These laborious reformations have made me skillful and strong, and I have won in the area of everyday morals a series of victories, all of great importance. I have achieved a regularity of life which many envy in me, a sobriety which brings with it more delights than the unchecked exercise of all the appetites. Budding vices like smoking and going to cafés have been utterly uprooted.

Method rules me and orders my actions and movements with a solemnity which is something akin to the laws of astronomy. This plan, these battles won, this sobriety, this regimen, this clocklike movement which makes each minute a tooth on a gear wheel and turns into a carefully groomed spiral spring—all this, I say, could have had no other effect, as it was projected on my life, than to trace that straight line called celibacy, a state of life on which it is otiose to pronounce any final judgment: it may be highly imperfect or relatively perfect, as determined by the accumulation of the facts, *i.e.*, all those physical and moral elements drawn in by the currents of life, and deposited in the hardening strata or sediments we call habits, concerns, or the routine characterizing both slavery and freedom.

My dear mother lived for twelve years with me in Madrid, the whole length of time I spent studying at the University and in giving private classes, and in making a name for myself with various articles in newspapers and magazines. I would fall far short in anything I might say about the heroic endurance with which that unique woman helped my efforts forward. She infused me with courage and patience, and took exquisite care of my material wants, in order that I not be distracted from my studies even for a moment. All that I am, I owe to her: first, life itself; my social status, and then other greater gifts, such as my stern principles, my work habits, my sobriety. I am even more in her debt in the sense that she preserved part of the little fortune my father left, defending it with her thrift, never spending more than what was strictly necessary to live on and to give me such a university education as a poor boy can get. We thus lived in genteel poverty; but that scarcity of things gave my spirit a temper and a vigor worth all the treasures in the world. I won my professorship and my mother fulfilled her mission.

As if her life were contingent and had no other object than to put me into my professorial chair, once I had won it she passed away—she who had been my guiding light along the toilsome way I had just trod. My mother died at peace and fulfilled. I knew I'd be unable to walk alone; but how *very* awkward I was in my first periods of solitude! Accustomed as I was to consult my mother about even the most insignificant matters, I couldn't take a single step, and felt my way along, timid and scared. My grand apprenticeship with her was not enough, and the only way I could overcome my clumsiness was to remember, even on the least weighty occasions, her words, her thoughts, her behavior, all of which were prudence itself.

After this great misfortune, I lived for some time in boardinghouses; but that turned out so badly for me that I took a small house, where I lived six years. It was scheduled for demolition, however, and I then moved to my present home. An admirable Asturian woman, a friend of my mother's, possessed of the finest character and ability, offered to be my housekeeper. Bit by bit her diligent attentions put my household on a footing of comfort, order, and cleanliness. My bachelor's life was thus made eminently agreeable and at present I have not the slightest reason to complain. Indeed I would not exchange my Petra for all the ladies who have kept house for priests or waited on canons all through history.

For three years now I've lived in the Calle del Espíritu Santo, where one may hear every unpleasant noise. But I have become accustomed to work within range of the market's noisy disorder—it even seems as if the shouts of the green-groceresses encourage me to meditate. I hear the street noise as one hears the sound of the sea, and I believe—how powerful habit is!—that if I were deprived of my "Escarole, only two *cuartos*!" I wouldn't be able to prepare my classes as well as I do.

III

I WILL NOW SPEAK OF A WOMAN
WHO IS MY NEIGHBOR

AND I WILL DISCUSS no other neighbors because they have no connection with my story. The one I mention is of great importance, and I beg my readers not to skip over this chapter for any reason whatever, even though it should take some effort. Still, I must warn them not to generate any enthusiasm on the basis of the fact that it's a *woman* neighbor, lest they believe that this is the start of an *affair* or that I'll be getting into a sentimental tangle. Sweet nothings whispered from window to window are not part of my plan, and what I have to tell is just one more of life's very ordinary events which gives rise to others perhaps less ordinary.

On the street floor of the building where I live there was a butcher's shop, one of the oldest such establishments in Madrid. It bore the name of the Rico dynasty. This well-reputed shop was owned by one Doña Javiera, who was well known in this neighborhood and in the next one over. She was the daughter of a Rico, and her deceased husband had been a Peña, another sausage dynasty which has celebrated several alliances with the Ricos. I first met Doña Javiera one night in the summer of 1878, when we had a fire alarm in the house and all the inhabitants were running up and down stairs and back and forth between flats. Doña Javiera seemed to me like a fine lady, and I must have appeared to her to be a serious person, worthy of her esteem on all counts, for one day she showed up in my flat (third floor, right-hand door) without being announced, and straightaway heaped praises upon me, calling me a model man and a mirror for youth.

"I don't know another one like you, Señor de Manso," she said. " A man who doesn't get into scrapes, hasn't a single bad habit, spends the whole blessed morning at home; a man who goes out only twice a day: bright and early to class; and then in the late afternoon for a stroll; a man who spends so little, looks after his health, and doesn't do foolish things! There just aren't any like that left, Señor de Manso. You should be put up on an altar . . .

12

Blessed Mother! But no, it's the truth, why not say it? I talk about you every day to anybody who'll listen, and I point you out as a model . . . Men like you aren't born every day."

Beginning from that day I called on her, and when I would enter her flat (main floor, left-hand door) she received me with something approaching pomp and circumstance.

"I oughtn't to open my mouth in your presence," she'd say, "because I'm such a *dummy*, a real clot, and you know everything. But I can't keep quiet. You'll let my foolish talk go right past you and pretend not to hear it. But don't you think I'm not aware of how ignorant I am, no sir, Señor de Manso. I don't pretend to be smart or educated, because that would be ridiculous, don't you see? I say what I feel, whatever comes from my heart, that's to say my mouth . . . I'm just that way—straight, natural, clear as running water; you see I'm from near Ciudad Rodrigo . . . Better to be like this than talk ever so nice and purse up your mouth, going after fancy words that I don't even know the meaning of."

The honest friendship between that good matron and myself grew rapidly. When I would go down to her flat she would show me her sumptuous *charra* finery from Ciudad Rodrigo: the cloak, the velvet jerkin with shaped sleeves, the capelet or shawl, the kerchief embroidered with sequins, the purple satin, the knotted mantilla, the silver hairclips, the filigree eardrops and necklaces, all of it splendid and absolutely genuine. To cap off my wonderment she would then show me her embroidered silken Chinese shawls, a real treasure. One day, when I visited her I noticed that she had placed in a frame hanging on the sitting-room wall a picture of *me* which had been published in some illustrated newspaper or other. This made me laugh; and her self-congratulation about having done it made me laugh all the more.

"I took down St. Anthony and put you up. Out with the saints, and in with the professors . . . Why, the other day when I read what the papers said about you, it gave me such a thrill . . . "

On important holidays or on my own saint's day, I could always count on her gift of pickled pork, ham, or other appetizing things from the abundant and excellent stocks of her shop. There was always so much of it that, as I was unable to eat it all myself, I passed around a good bit of it among my faculty colleagues, some of whom, devoted pork-eaters, would twit me about my neighbor lady.

But Doña Javiera's exquisite attentions concealed no amorous intention, nor yet were they totally disinterested. She made this plain to me one day when she came up to my flat on her way back from St. Ildefonso's church. She sat down with her accustomed unceremoniousness in the big chair in my sitting-room-study, and began contemplating my bookshelves, surmounted by plaster busts. I was busy that morning with some notes and a preface for a translation of Hegel's *System of the Fine Arts*, done by a friend of mine. My head was filled with ideas about beauty, fairly spinning with them to such a confusing degree that the vision of that lady was a welcome rest for my thoughts. I looked at her, and my head felt clear, in complete order again, the way it happens when a schoolteacher enters a classroom full of mischievous and prankish youngsters. My neighbor was the aesthetic authority, and my ideas—why not admit it?—were the imprisoned rascals who, bereft of reality, had yielded to disorderly games and acrobatics.

I had always counted Doña Javiera a good-looking person; but that day she seemed to me positively resplendent. Her black mantilla, her great Chinese silken shawl, yellow and worked with embroidery—she had just been to church to stand godmother for the coal-merchant's youngest child—her jewelry, out of style but all real treasures and solid silver, showy, with emeralds and heavy touches of filigree: all of it together set off beautifully her white complexion and her black, neatly coiffed hair. Blessed be Hegel!

Doña Javiera was still a woman in her prime, and though her sedentary life had made her a bit stouter than the Master prescribes in his chapter on proportions, her whole stature, its fine conformation and distribution of fleshiness and hollows and prominences, came just *that* close to turning her defect into a virtue. As I sat there looking at her, in strong relief against the background of bookcases, I found the contrast so amusing that right then and there I got the idea of adding to my commentary a new section on *Irony in the Fine Arts*.

"I'm having a look at your Wise Old Owls," she said, glancing toward the top of the wall.

The "Wise Old Owls" were four busts purchased by my mother in a plaster-cast shop. She had chosen them without any set idea, with an eye only for their size. They were Demosthenes, Quevedo, Marcus Aurelius, and Julián Romea.

"They are the masters of everything there is to know," averred the lady, filled with the deepest respect. "And look at all these books! Just think of all the letters in them! Blessed Mother! And to think you've got it all in

14

your head. That's what makes you so wise. But let's get down to cases. Listen to me."

There was no need for her to say it, for all my attention was fixed upon her.

"I set great store by you, Señor de Manso; there aren't many men like you . . . to be perfectly truthful, there aren't *any*. Right from the start I took a liking to you, and you made a real impression on me and found a place in my heart . . . "

At this last she burst out laughing, and added: "Well, I *do* seem to be starting a courtship, and that's not it at all, Señor de Manso. Not that you're unworthy of that kind of attention, Blessed Mother! You *do* look a little like a priest, though—no offense meant, no sir . . . But let's get down to business . . . You've gone quite pale: you look as stern as a dish of beans."

I was, in fact, a bit perturbed, not knowing quite what to say. At last, Doña Javiera made her point clear. What did she want from me? A very natural and simple thing, but one I wasn't expecting at such a moment, because the little demons inside my head, making a great hash of the aesthetic ideas I was dealing with, had quite separated me from reality; and those very same little demons were the reason I was so confused and stunned when I heard Doña Javiera put forth her proposition, which was that I should take on the education of her son.

"The boy is a perfect rascal," she went on, letting her shawl fall back. He'll soon turn twenty-one. He's made of good stuff, no doubt of that, the kindest lad in the world, and a heart of gold. Nobody could drive an evil thought into his head, not even with a hammer. But not a soul on earth can get him to study. *His* textbooks are pretty girls' eyes, and his library is a box seat at the theater. He sleeps through the morning, and spends the afternoon at the riding class or the gym, doing what they call SKATTIN or something like that, you know, rolling around on shoes with wheels. One of these days he'll come home with a broken leg. He spends a fortune on clothes and as much again on treats for his sponging friends. He's wild about young bulls and amateur bullfights and calf-tryouts; all brave and fierce he is. He's so full of himself that nobody had better even try to come close. Blessed Mother! . . . Well, at any rate, with his good qualities and even with his nonsense, I think there's material for a perfect gentleman; but the gentleman has to be worked on, my friend Don Máximo, because if that doesn't happen, my son will turn out to be a silly goose . . . I love him so, I can't seem to set him straight, because I get angry, d'you see? I get it into my head to scold him and

15

beat him. I work myself into a lather, I set my teeth so he won't make me give in; but then he shows up with that naughty angel-face of his, and kisses me and I just go silly again . . . I fairly drool over the boy, Manso my friend, and I can't refuse him a thing. I realize I'm ruining him—I don't seem to have the strength of character to be a good mother . . . So just hear me out: I've got the idea that to set my boy straight and turn him in the right direction and make a man of him, a great man, a gentleman, it's no good fighting him or holding him down by force. It'd be better, let's see if I can put it right, to *nudge* him along a bit at a time, lead him ahead, first some flattery, then a shove, hold on tight and let up once in a while, get him to change his pastimes bit by bit, try to get him interested in new things, pretend to let him have his way so you can come down hard later on, yes to this, no to that, put a silken brake-rope on him, and if you can manage it, find some amusements that will teach him something or get the lessons themselves to amuse him. If I hand him over to some dry-as-dust tutor, he'll just laugh at him. What we need is a teacher who's still a teacher but a good friend too, a companion who on the sly and without seeming to, can get some good ideas into his head, make learning seem attractive and pleasant; not an old nagger, or dull. Just a kind man, a good soul with a lot of horse sense. Somebody who'll laugh once in a while, and be shrewd enough to talk about heavy things with some wit, using his eyes and his heart in the process."

I was left astounded to see how admirably a woman with no learning at all had understood the great problem of education. Delighted by her chatter, I said nothing, and with expressive nods alone signified to her my acquiescence, narrowing my eyes a bit too. That's a habit I've picked up in class when a student gives an especially good answer.

"My son," added the butcher-woman, "has—and always will have—enough to live on. Let's be plain about it: I'm from the country near Ciudad Rodrigo. That's why I want him to learn to be economical, thrifty but not stingy. I'm not ashamed to have spent my life behind a butcher block. Blessed Mother! But I'd rather not, Manso my friend, have my son be a butcher, nor deal in livestock, nor touch horns or hides or tripe. But I'm not content to have him be a loafer or a rascal or a lamebrain, like the ones who graduate from the University without even knowing how to make the sign of the Cross. I want him to know everything necessary for a gentleman who lives on his income. I don't want him yawning wide open when serious matters are mentioned in from of him. And just look how God and Our Lady of Mt. Carmel have provided me the teacher I need for my young sprout. That teacher, that wise man, that wise old owl is you, Señor Don Máximo. No, no, don't be modest or roll your eyes! Just to make things perfect, my Manolo has taken such a shine to you! Once he starts talking about *our neighbor*, he never stops. And I tell him 'Well you just try to be like him, even from a distance.' Yesterday I told him: 'I'm going to start you studying three or four hours every day in our friend Manso's house,' and wasn't he pleased!! I've got him enrolled in the University, but he misses class seven days out of eight. He says he's bored by the professors and gets sleepy during the lectures. Anyway, Señor Don Máximo, either you take him on for me or we'll have a falling out, you and I. As for the fees, you'll have to set them . . . Thanks be to God for bringing you to roost on the third floor of my building. I'll say it, my friend Manso, you've come down from seventh heaven."

I was very pleased by the trust the good lady had put in me. Given the pleasant character of my mission, and the honor she did me by it, I accepted. I caviled at accepting fees; but Doña Javiera put up such resistance to my generosity and became so angry that she was on the point of striking me. I even think she did strike me once or twice. It was all settled that very day, and the lessons began the next day.

IV
MANOLITO PEÑA, MY DISCIPLE

ONA JAVIERA WAS A WIDOW. (I'm troubled by all those *w*'s but I can't do anything about it.) Her establishment had had a great prosperity under the management of her deceased husband, a man of much probity who was very clever in matters having to do with horn and hide. He was a shrewd businessman, a Castilian of the old school; a man who could hold his liquor and was a wildly passionate devotee of the bullfight. He died at fifty of an intestinal blockage. When I first met Doña Javiera four years had passed since that misfortune, and she must have been about forty. About that same time neighborhood gossip had her linked illicitly with Señor Ponce, who had been a comic-opera baritone; a fellow of a certain flash and good figure but by then quite past his prime. He was a complete idler, though he boasted of certain mechanical skills that were of no use to anyone, unless one counts the man's own eager impatience and everybody else's complete boredom. The fellow would spend the whole blessed day at Doña Javiera's house, working either on a great cardboard palace to raffle off, or on a huge complicated wire cage that he would never finish. It was a *copy* of the Escorial, made of wire. He was good at making repairs, and had a mechanical jigsaw that he used to put together all sorts of trinkets made of wood or veneer or ivory, all very fussy and in bad taste, useless and never finished.

But let's leave Ponce and move on to my disciple. Manuel Peña was of such good character and such clear intelligence that I saw right off that it wouldn't be an onerous task to get rid of his bad habits, which in any case were the result of his hot-bloodedness, his generosity and noble instincts, that impulse toward the ideal which shows such a strong profile in the character of young people. His bad habits resulted, too, from his temperament, somewhere between strong-nerved and sanguine; from his spendid health and good humor, which kept him safe from depression; and, finally, they came

18

from that youthful vanity which was awakened in him by his very handsome physique and his charming countenance.

My pleasure was the same as that felt by a sculptor who is given a perfect slab of the finest marble to create a statue. From the very first day I could see that I was earning not only his respect but his affection as well. A fortunate circumstance, since he who does not succeed in having his students love him is no real teacher. Indeed no learning is possible without the blessing of friendship, which is the best conductor of ideas between one person and another.

I was quite careful at the start not to speak to Manuel of weighty subject matters, and not even in passing did I mention any science, much less philosophy, fearful lest he run fleeing from my study. We spoke of ordinary things, things which at the same time he liked and I was bound to fight against; I insisted that he speak spontaneously, to show me all facets of his thinking. At the same time, and while giving to such things their true worth, I sought to show him the serious and transcendent side of all human affairs, no matter how frivolous they might seem.

In this fashion, the hours rolled by, and sometimes Manuel would pass the greater part of the day in my flat. Among the powers of his mind, it seemed to me that the weakest were conceptualization and volition. On the other hand I did notice that his varied basic impulses came together with vigor and harmony in the realm of feelings, and I could see what profit I might obtain by cultivating that tendency on aesthetic terrain. An excellent plan. With no hesitation, I attacked the fortress of his ignorance through the breach-point of art, certain that my victory would be aided by his imagination, that quality which always betrays us and ill resists the hardships of a long siege.

I began my undertaking with the poets. What a great pity that the boy knew not a word of Latin, thus keeping me from opening to him the treasures of antique poetry! Limited to our own tongue, we took on the Spanish Parnassus, with such good fortune that my disciple took genuine delight in our interchanges. I observed him go pale, or turn red, showing plainly on his face his sadness or enthusiasm, according as we might be reading or discussing one lyric poet or another, Fray Luis de León, St. John of the Cross, or the bombastic, clangorous Herrera. It took but a few early signals from me to make him understand good verse, and very soon he began anticipating my own analyses with astonishing accuracy. He was an artist, he had an ardent sense of beauty, and even seemed to value the excellence of style, this in spite of his almost complete ignorance of grammar.

Later on we studied poets of the present day, and he became familiar with them in no time at all. His memory was utterly felicitous, and I might well come upon him reciting—with admirable understanding—snatches of modern poems, famous legends, or compositions of both light and grave character. There was reason to hope that my disciple, who empathized so closely with poetry, might himself turn out to be a poet. One day he very mysteriously put some stanzas into my hands. I read them; but they seemed to me so awful that I commanded him never again to invoke the Muses on a familiar basis, but rather to maintain that respectful yet affectionate distance which makes intimacy impossible. I convinced him that he was not one of the family, that feeling beauty and giving expression to it are two quite different things. And he, without the slightest injury to his self-esteem, promised never again to be concerned with any poems except those written by other people.

At the beginning of our sessions, he ingenuously admitted to me that he found *Don Quixote* boring; but when we took up that book, having studied our poets well, he found himself so charmed by the reading that he would sometimes weep with laughter, and other times showed such vehement compassion toward the hero that he almost wept out of grief and pity. He told me that he went to sleep at night thinking about the sublime boldness and bitter misfortunes of the great knight, and that as he awoke in the morning he would get it into his head to emulate him, going out into the world with a plate on his head. It was simply that out of his own nobility of spirit, he had discovered the profound meaning of that one book in which are most perfectly expressed both the grandeur and the weakness of the human heart.

One of the chief ends of my lessons was necessarily to teach Manuel to express himself in writing, for though in conversation he did so with grace and skill, his written style was a disaster. His letters made one laugh. He would use the strangest turns of phrase, the most bedeviled syntax imaginable; and his poverty of vocabulary was matched by his lack of correctness in spelling. Realizing that grammatical theory would do him no good without practical application, I combined the two, making him copy passages selected not from the classics—to imitate them is harmful—but from the moderns, such as Jovellanos, Moratín, Mesonero, Larra, and others.

And, all the while, to round out the morning's studious activity, we would go out for walks in the afternoon, exercising both body and spirit, for we walked and learned at the same time. This is the effective method of *teaching as you walk*, which deserves its name of *peripatetic* not for its Aristotelian content, but for its ambulatory character. We would discuss everything, we saw, whatever occurred to us. On Sundays we'd go to the Prado Museum, and he went into ecstasies before so many wonders. At first I noticed a certain bewilderment in my disciple's artistic appreciation. But very quickly his discernment took on an amazing clarity, and his taste in the plastic arts underwent a powerful development, just as it had in the area of poetry. He'd say: "I'd *been* to the Museum many times before; but I'd never *seen* it until now."

I enjoyed teaching him everything in a practical way, using examples whenever I didn't have reality itself handy. For reality is the consummate teacher whose lecture-room is the world and whose library an infinity of phenomena. In the moral sphere, experience has made more converts than sermons, and misfortune has made more Christians than the Catechism. If I wanted to instill in him some artistic principle, I sought to do it in front of a work of art. In the moral realm, I used apologues, parables, and even physical demonstrations, explaining phenomena of this kind, whenever I could, in the face of the phenomena themselves. This was the flimsiest part of my teaching, for, since I know only the rudiments, my lessons were limited to meteorological events, and to rapid descriptions (as if I were walking on burning coals): the nature of lightning, rain, snow, a bit about rainbows and a few passes at the Aurora Borealis. I didn't much like getting into that sort of investigation.

I was contented with that pattern of life, and took real joy in seeing my disciple's growing regard for me. What grand victories I had won over his willfulness, and the rebelliousness and harshness of his nature! But I'll say more about this later. Now, lest you think my life was just a bed of roses, I'll speak of certain annoyances and unpleasant matters, giving first place to a person, a gadfly or mosquito who often interrupted the peace of my studious pursuits with her visits, and sucked the blood—coin, that's to say—from my pockets, not without first having buzzed me and bored me with unbearable chatter and a sharp stinger. I refer to the wretched Señora de García Grande, always linked in my mind to the tender memory of my mother, who out of her inexhaustible generosity, left me this legacy, this tax, this tiresome burden, to be paid off in blood, money, time, and patience.

21

V

WHO COULD EVER PAINT
DOÑA CÁNDIDA'S PORTRAIT?

NOBODY. Absolutely nobody. But since a heroic attempt is itself heroism, I shall be the hero of this pictorial undertaking, reserved for me ever since the aforementioned gadfly traced her first graceful curve in the air and cajoled human ears with the C-sharp of her stinging trumpet. Doña Cándida was the widow of García Grande, a personage who had held second- or third-rank posts in the political period called the Liberal Union. He was that sort of man who wearies neither posterity nor fame, men whose death merits only the tepid homage of the partisan press, which refers to them as *worthy, energetic, zealous, conscientious, intelligent,* or some such. García Grande had been a man of affairs, the sort who have one hand in petty politics and the other in big business deals, a double-face of that inextinguishable and ever-so-fruitful race of men who are reproduced and thrive in the fungoid sediments of Parliament and the Stock Exchange. A man with no ideas, but gifted with a good manner which made up for the other; eager for easy riches; a sort of petty sergeant in the factions which align themselves with parliamentary subdivisions; a polished nonentity, a stock-trader without genius, an orator without style, and a politician without political feel. He did not *participate* in situations: he *adorned* them. He was anthropomorphic substance which under the active influence of politics might appear crystallized into different forms, first as a provincial governor, then as administrator of patronage, then as a director general, and after that as manager of a bankrupt bank or a rail-less railway.

In all these chores, García Grande's psychophysical detersion took on two forms, lymphatic hypertrophy and vanity. He squandered his own fortune, his wife's as well, and no mean portion of several others, since a life insurance company of which he was managing director whisked away the savings of half a generation, and poured them all down the hole. They used to say that García Grande was honest, but weak. What a joke! Weakness and honesty are never good partners, just as evangelical humility and love for one's neighbor are always at odds with that toughness of character demanded by the management of one's own and others' private funds.

Let it stand to García Grande's credit, though certainly not to the comfort of those who bought life insurance from him, that his eminent wife was a providential being, specially created and sent by God upon stock companies (God moves in mysterious ways!) to devour any and all capital that might be placed before her, and even behind her. That confounded woman could turn her destructive hands in any and all directions. Madrid has never seen such a spendthrift, such a passionate devotee of luxury, such a maniac for all the ruinous vanities of the present age.

My mother, who met her in her good era, back in those times—blissful or adverse?—when Consolidated was at 50 points, during the war in Africa, when Negrete said *no*, when fortunes were made from the sale of government properties, when they widened the Puerta del Sol, the times of Mario and la Grissi, of the all-powerful O'Donnell and of the Long Ministry.* My mother, as I have said, was a close friend of this lady, and told me that she lived in the relative opulence of those who are rich by fits and starts. Her house (one of the ones they pulled down behind the Almudena church to lengthen the Calle de Bailén) was the scene of large dinner parties, soirées and "evenings," teas, great hors d'ouevre affairs and improvised card-parties. Cándida's aristocratic pretensions were so extreme that she never gave García Grande a moment's peace all his life about getting himself a title . . . But he stood his ground on this matter, and reserving for the aristocracy that respect which has latterly been lost (now that all the rich have entered the nobility in droves), he refused to acquire a title, not even one of the Papal kind which, I'm told, are quite inexpensive.

While her money lasted, Cándida's vanity and dissipation far exceeded the extravagance of the Marchioness of Tellería. But in adverse fortune the marchioness had a knack for heroically fending off poverty and for masking her needy state in dignity. In contrast, my mother's old friend played the role of poor woman most pitiably, and once she had started her way down the staircase, she made her descent rapidly, approaching an extreme not far from degradation. The Tellería woman had certain ways, a certain innate delicacy which helped her conceal her pecuniary losses; but Doña Cándida, whose upbringing must have been perverse, had no ability to cloak her difficulties in

*A way of saying "long, long ago." All these references are to events of the 1850's.

the gauze of nobility and distinction which were the hallmark of the other woman. Twenty years after her husband's death, when Doña Cándida had lost her youth, her beauty, her house, and her income, she lived virtually on alms. Her bombastic pride was unendurable, as was her very conversation, filled as it was with pompous lies. She was always waiting for the price to rise so she could sell some bonds . . . ; she was always in negotiations for the sale of some land or other located on the far side of Zamora . . . ; she was about to find herself in the painful situation of having to sell (for a pittance) two of her paintings: one by Ribera, the other by Paul de Voss, an apostle and a hunt scene . . . Rubbish! The bonds, the land, the paintings existed only in the fantasy of her mind. She would never open her mouth for any purpose, serious or trivial, without trotting out the names of marquesses or dukes.

Her dignity was on view at all times; she made a ridiculous comedy of her unhappy state, and what she referred to as her decorum was a veil of lies which failed to conceal the most pitiful tatters. The veil was so transparent that even the blind could see through it. She wheedled money out of people by elaborate artifice and deceitfulness, thus descending to the level of actionable mendicancy. I could tell who it was just from the way she yanked on the bell-pull when she came here. She would ring in an imperious way; she'd say to the maid: "Is *he* at home?" and she would slither directly into my room, interrupting me just at the most untimely moments, for it seemed as if the devil of a woman had the knack of choosing those times when I was most eager for solitude and peace. Aware of my weakness for collecting bric-à-brac, my enemy always brought with her a piece of porcelain, some print or bauble, and she's show them to me and say: "Say, how much do you think I can get for this? It's a lovely piece. I know the Marchioness of X_____ would give me 50 or 60 pesetas; but if you'd like it for your little collection, it's yours for 20, and you can thank me for that. You can see that I'm sacrificing my own interests for you . . . perfectly dreadful!"

I had a strong urge to throw her out; but then I remembered my sainted mother and the solemn trust she had given me before she died. Doña Cándida, in her prosperous days, had really been quite kind to Mother. Besides, while García Grande himself was Director of Local Administration in 1859, he got my father out of some mess or other involving ballot-box irregularities. My mother, whose memories turned especially syrupy when it came to gratitude—she was reluctant for such a favor to be forgotten even from beyond the grave—my mother, as I say, charged me in her final hours that on no account should I fail to succor the poor widow as best I might. So I bought her trinkets from her. But, with her ingenious trickiness, she always managed to take away both my money *and* the things I had just bought. With unbelievable inventiveness, she varied the tactics of her ferocious depradations. One day she might come in and say:

"D'you know what? My business manager in Zamora has written me that by next week he'll send the first payment due on that land . . . Oh . . . didn't I tell you that I *did* find a buyer at last? Yes, my friend, you're quite behind on the news . . . And what a good deal it is, too! The Duke of X_____, whose land is alongside, is buying mine to round out his estate—el Espigal . . . At any rate, I've got to send an authorization and fill out several documents, perfectly dreadful . . . Lend me 250 pesetas, I'll return them next week without fail."

And then, to conceal her eagerness to get the cash, she adopted a lighthearted, high-society voice, exclaiming:

"How dreadful! It's unbelievable what I've spent, doing over my drawing-room furniture . . . Upholsterers these days are just bandits! Perfectly dreadful, my boy! . . . Oh! Haven't I told you about it? Yes, I think I have."

"About what, madam?"

"My niece and I are embroidering a large pillow-cover together. It's just dreadfully pretty. The Countess H and her daughter the Viscountess M saw it yesterday and were enchanted. As a matter of fact they'd like to meet you. And I just have to tell them that you never go out anywhere, and spend all your time thinking about your books and your pupils. Well, good-bye, my boy; I wish you well."

Feigning a well-bred distractedness, she made a move to leave, and Heaven seemed to open for me as I saw her on her way, but she turned back at the doorway and said:

"Oh, how absent-minded of me! Will you let me have the 250 pesetas or not? Next week I could pay you ten thousand, if you need them for any business purpose . . . No, don't try to thank me . . . You're doing me a favor; where else could I invest my money more safely?"

"I really don't need anything," I said.

These other words were rising to my lips: "Go to the devil, madam"; but, as I reckoned that she was begging the money to pay her rent or some other pressing necessity, my selfish impulses gave way to my flabby generosity and the memory of my mother, and I gave her half of what she'd asked me for.

25

Not a month would go by after such an episode without a return visit, when she'd bring me an old watch or an antique miniature of very slim value.

"I beg you a favor: please accept this in memory of me. If you only knew how ill I am; it's perfectly dreadful! It's a nervous condition . . . I can't explain it to you. I don't even understand it myself, and neither do the doctors. When I walk down the street the walls of the houses seem to be collapsing on top of me . . . It's been ever so many nights since I've slept! I don't eat anything but a breast of woodcock now and then, a bit of toast with foie-gras, and sometimes half a wine-glass of Chablis."

I couldn't suppress my laughter, for I knew what sort of food the poor thing really did eat.

"Just to forget my troubles," she went on, "I went to the Opera House last night. I climbed up to the top gallery—I didn't feel like dressing. From up there I saw the Duchess of So-and-So in her box. She's just come back from Paris . . . So then, to go back to that other subject: I'm making you a gift of these precious objects, because I'm dying, my boy, dying without reprieve, and I want to leave you a memento; they're pieces of such unusual merit that the antique-dealer in the Carrera de San Jerónimo offered me five hundred pesetas for them."

"Well take them to the dealer then, and collect the five hundred pesetas; they'll come in handy."

"Don't rebuff me that way; really . . . How dreadful! Remember your dear mother, who loved me so." She made a real point of displaying her afflictions, and did so well at it that she finally managed to reward me with one tear.

"As I get closer to the grave," she said in her pathetic voice, "my feelings for you grow more ardent and I care for you more; it's perfectly dreadful . . . Good-bye, my boy."

She rose laboriously; but after only a couple of steps toward the door, she put her hands into her purse and said:

"My word! How forgetful! How dreadful! I've gone and forgotten my coin purse! . . . And I *did* have to stop in at the pharmacy. I'll have to go home again and climb those ninety stairs . . . Good Lord, I'm not at all well! Say— do you have fifteen pesetas there? I'll send them back this afternoon with young Irene."

And I'd always give her the money. What could I do? But one day when she attacked with this particular strategem, I wasn't able to hold back my anger, and said to my gadfly:

"Madam, when you are in need, just ask without all this play-acting, for I take it as a duty not to let you die of starvation . . . I prefer the truth in all things, and made-up stories really do bother me."

She laughed it off, saying that she was amused by my little jokes, that her dignity . . . perfectly dreadful! And a whole lot more.

After I had let loose this philippic on her, I felt that I had been a bit severe, and really felt sorry about it. For poverty does, after all, have certain rights to use even the strangest means to conceal itself. Indigence is the Earth's great propagator of untruth, and hunger furnishes people with the imagination for their deceptions.

Doña Cándida had once been beautiful. During the first phase of her penury she had defended her features from the ravages of time; but by the time of these visits and her attacks on my ill-defended purse, old age had excused her from the obligation of caring for her looks. Indeed, not only had she put away all her cosmetics; she had given up that care of her person which belongs more to plain decency than to vanity. Only the most deplorable care-lessness could be seen in her dress and also in her coiffure, made of *crêpés* of different colors, switches and woolenlike balls, all of it aspiring to emulate the latest fashion. Just as her conduct was bereft of the dignity of poverty, so also her clothing was utterly lacking in that cleanliness and neatness which are the luxury, or better yet the decorum of poverty. The style might be up-to-date, but the cloth, rumpled and soiled, bespoke the infinite metamorphoses through which it had passed before reaching its present state. She would rather wear elegant-looking tatters than a new percale skirt or woolen shawl. She had a raisin-color dress, which went back at least to the Pronunciamiento of 1854. Through many transformations and so much wear it had turned a sort of mahogany color, with a certain iridescence or tint or reflection which made it pass for a rare and miraculous fabric.

She wore a heavy veil which in sunlight seemed to offer all the tones in the rainbow; this was due to the particles of dust which had lodged in its weft. In the shade it looked like a mass of cobwebs veiling her forehead, as if the woman's ancient head had been left alone and untended in an attic for half a century. Her two hands, in ashen-colored gloves, produced in me the effect of a pair of claws when I saw them turned in my direction, for the kid leather was all unsewn at the finger-ends and let her sharp fingers show through. I always felt a certain sense of relief when I saw her hands tucked out of sight into the two ends of a muff, whose fur appeared, I may say, to have been used to wash the floor.

In profile Doña Cándida had something of a Roman face. My gadfly was very like the plaster Marcus Aurelius who was one of the group of Wise Old Owls on top of my bookshelves. Looked at full-face, she gave fewer signs of her former beauty. There shone in her eyes some indescribable, wild eagerness, and she had a series of disagreeable smiles—like those of a thief, actually. She also had a way of nodding her head, always in affirmation, which to me (I can't say why) only revealed her incorrigible urge to deceive other people. The echo of fine manners was another leftover that made her bearable, even agreeable sometimes, though not to the point of making one look forward to her visits. The resemblance to Marcus Aurelius, which I pointed out to my disciple one day, induced him to use that Roman name for her. But later, in a malicious confusion with another emperor, he started calling her *Caligula*.

Affected no doubt by the philippic I had delivered that day, she changed her tactic. A long time passed without visits from her—or very few, at any rate; but she ceased making verbal requests for money. To hit me up she made use of her niece, whom she would send to my house bearing a bit of paper with a request for a sum of cash, in the following form: "Be kind enough to lend me 15 or 20 pesetas, and I'll return them next week."

Doña Cándida's weeks, like those of the prophet Daniel, were seventy times seven years, or nearly that long.

The tactic of placing the sponge in the guileless hands of a young girl gave clear proof of the old woman's astuteness and sagacity. For she knew my great love for children, and reckoned that it would be impossible for me to refuse. And she was right, damn her. For the moment I saw the petitioner come in, holding out the note to me with directness and candor, I would put my hand into my pocket or my cash drawer, anticipating the action of the poor child, and sparing her the torment of handing me the tiresome message.

VI
HER NAME WAS IRENE

HER PALLOR and her slightly wandering, anxious glance—probably the result of malnutrition; her inhibited and shy demeanor, as if she were extremely uncomfortable doing the errands her aunt entrusted to her; all this awakened in me a great pity for her. So it was that, besides the alms for Doña Cándida, I got into the habit of keeping a supply of sweets in my desk. Supposing that the urgent appetites of childhood were rarely satisfied in her, I gave her those treats without making her wait, and she would take them with unconcealed eagerness, thanking me shyly, and start to eat them immediately. I suspected that this haste in the enjoyment of my little gifts derived from her fear that, if she reached home with candies or sweets in her bag, Doña Cándida would want to share in them. Later on I learned that I had not been mistaken in that opinion.

I can see her now, beside my desk, peering over books, manuscripts, papers, reading some of each thing that she found. She was twelve then, and in little more than three years she had overcome the obstacles of primary education in some private school or other. I used to have her read aloud, and I was amazed at her intonation and her confidence in reading, as well as her ability to understand the ideas. She was never stopped by an unusual word or an obscure phrase. When I asked her to write for me, so that I could see her penmanship, she would write my name in the elegant strokes of English calligraphy, and add underneath: *Professor*.

As she talked with me and answered my inquiries about her studies, her life, and her probable career, she revealed to me a grade of discernment beyond her years. She bore the outline, already, of a lovely, decent, intelligent woman. What a pity if, by harmful influences, her proper development should be twisted or ruined before reaching its appropriate maturity! But I could see in her spirit some admirable resources for defense and an embryonic sort of will-power, constituting a foundation for great rectitude of character. Her ability to see beyond the obvious was remarkable indeed, and she even showed a more than superficial knowledge of the weaknesses and follies of Doña Cándida. She used to relate to me, in an amusing style—childishly naïve but yet sparked with irony—some of the adventures of the poor old woman, all of it without losing the respect and love she bore her.

The compassion which this child inspired in me was greater when I realized how ill-clad—and worse-shod—she was. Throughout many long months, which seem now like years, she wore a cheap straw hat, a sort of deformed, ball-shaped basket, with a ribbon as pale as her own face. It hung to one side in the most graceless way that one could imagine. All the rest of her attire was faded, rumpled, old, third- or fourth-hand, with cover-ups here and there which only made it uglier. It displeased me so much to see her wearing her great twisted, heelless boots that I determined to replace those horrible barges with a pair of elegant high shoes. It would have been useless to give her the money for them, since Doña Cándida would have taken it for herself. My diligent housekeeper took it upon herself to go with Irene to a bootery, and after a bit returned her to me, perfectly shod. When I saw her weeping, I thought the stiff new shoes were pinching her cruelly; but she said no, no. And in order to convince me she started to jump and run about my room. Her tears dried up as she laughed.

On certain days the *little note,* after its request for money, bore an addendum such as: "Please give Irene a grammar-book."

Or on another occasion: "Irene is too timid to ask you for a pretty book to read. For me you can send along an interesting novel, or if you have it, a collection of *causes célèbres*."

It gave me great pleasure to attend to the matter of books for Irene. But her pallor, her strained look, gave evidence of another kind of need, one not satisfied by books nor placated by sophistry of the mind: it was organic need, the stern law of animal life. Those of us who live in plenty obey it unthinkingly, and we have no concern for those in need who try to outwit or avoid it. A very sad state of affairs indeed! Irene was hungry. I became convinced of it one day when I made her stay to dinner with me. It seemed as if the poor child had gone a month without any food, to judge by the way she went at the different dishes. Without ever losing her composure, she ate with the appetite of a bear, and we had no difficulty in getting her to take home the dessert leftovers, wrapped up in paper. After the meal she seemed almost ashamed of her voraciousness; she spoke but little, petted the cat, and then asked me for a picture-book to pass the time.

She was not a very boisterous girl and she didn't enjoy mischief. Except for the episode of her new shoes, I never saw her jumping in my room or making a racket. As a rule, she would sit quiet and composed like a grown-up woman; or she would look, in order, at the prints on the wall, or review the labels on the bookshelves, or pick up (after asking my permission) some volume of pictures, or a travel book, to enjoy their engravings. She bore me such great respect that she dared not even ask, like other children: "What's this, what's that?" Either she guessed it all, or simply contained her curiosity.

On my saint's day she brought me a watch-case she had embroidered herself, and, wonder of wonders, that day, by the special favor of my gadfly, she brought no little note. On other special days she gave me several little handwork things and a tiny hemp-paper box, which I no longer have because one day the cat got hold of it and smashed it to peices. I repaid these fine offerings of Irene—and the compassion she inspired—by buying her a nice little dress.

This intelligent, unfortunate child was not the niece of Doña Cándida herself, but of her late husband García Grande. Her parents had been quite well-off. She was orphaned while Doña Cándida's husband was still living, and he treated her as a daughter. Disaster struck when the life-insurer died; but luckily Irene was not of an age to notice the abrupt passage from prosperity to adversity. My gadfly kept her at her side, since the child had no other family. And it makes me wonder: was it bane or blessing for Irene to have been born amid want, to have learned life in that somber school of misfortune which brutalizes some people and strengthens and refines others, according to the character of each one? I used to ask her if she was content with her lot in life, and she always said she was. But her lovely eyes radiated sadness, almost as an innate or intrinsic quality. Sometimes I thought it must be only an aesthetic phenomenon produced by light and the color of the pupils. At other times it seemed rather an aspect of her self-expression, in which the hidden things of inner experience are revealed. Her sad eyes might thus be revealing one of those cardinal deceptions under which we all live for long periods of time—all our lives perhaps—unaware.

As time moved on and Irene grew up, her visits became less and less frequent. This in no way signified an improvement in Doña Cándida's fortunes, but simply Irene's revulsion at carrying out ignoble errands, begging-note in hand. As her age advanced, so did her self-respect, and she came to my house only for the extraction of larger sums; smaller ones were taken care of by their maid. At length, as time sped by unnoticed, the day arrived when the maid ran all the errands for money. I no longer got to see my gadfly's niece, although I always had news of her through Doña Cándida and the maid. I learned, after a long time, and to my unjustified surprise, that Irene now wore long dresses, something quite natural, though strange to me. We routinely forget that our very lives depend upon the growth of all things and upon the march of time. I was very pleased to learn that Irene had enrolled in the Female Normal School, not at the suggestion of her aunt but on her own initiative, desiring to carve out a place for herself and not be dependent on anyone. She had performed brilliantly in her exams and had won some awards. Irene's talents were praised to the skies by Doña Cándida, who told me her niece was the marvel of the whole School, a sage, a philosopher, in short "just dreadfully bright."

This part of my story brings me up to about 1877. In that year I moved from the peaceful Calle de Don Felipe to the raucous Calle del Espíritu Santo. It was shortly later that I met Doña Javiera and undertook the education of Manuel Peña and all the rest, which by sacrificing chronological order to logical order (this latter much more my style), I have already related. Time, a veritable clock, still has arbitrary movements; logic, though having none, is still the key to knowledge and the clockmaker of time itself.

VII
I WAS PLEASED WITH
MY DISCIPLE

BECAUSE SOME OF his brilliant faculties were developing admirably as he studied, revealing new riches to me each day. He was enchanted by history and could find in it those beautiful syntheses which are the chief joy and greatest profit of studying it. The thing that always came hard for him was the expression of his thoughts in writing. What a pity, when he could think so clearly—at times even with acuity and originality—and being so gifted at assimilating the ideas of good writers, that he should prove so rebellious when obliged to put things in proper written form! I would assign him compositions on some point of history or eonomics. He would write them quickly, and as I read them I marveled at the solid judgment while despairing at the awkward, pedestrian style. I wasn't even able to get him to spell with complete correctness, though by constant effort I did make considerable progress in that area.

There is but one detail lacking for an understanding of the intellectual character of my disciple, and it's this: I assigned him for oral presentation the same work he had so admirably thought through and so atrociously written. The change in the man was something to behold; in full command of himself, free, comfortable, like one casting off the chains of oppression. He'd stand before me, and with perfect clarity deliver me a speech surprisingly marked by abundant thought, successful transitions, gradations, warm persuasiveness. At the same time it was utterly smooth, captivating, full of agreeable sonorities.

"Now then," I said to him enthusiastically one day, "it's perfectly clear that you're an orator, and if you apply yourself you'll reach heights not scaled by many."

Then it came to me that his real verbal strength lay in conversation, and that thus his thoughts were not aptly to be expressed except in oratory. He had already begun to show a sparkling wit in dialogue, tending toward the paradoxical and contentious. He was captivated by *burning questions* and *vital issues,* and showed a very evident revulsion toward speculative matters. I saw this more clearly when I tried to teach him something about philosophy. A vain labor! My fine young Manuel yawned, understood not one word, paid no attention, folded paper birds, and finally at the outer limits of boredom, begged me for the love of God, to stop those dissertations because it made him sick, yes, nervous and feverish.

So vigorously did his mind reject this kind of study that, as he said, my first lesson on the *determination of a principle of certainty* had produced in his understanding an effect like that of an emetic on the body. I urged him to reflect upon the *real unity of being and knowledge,* assuring him that once he got used to speculative exercises he would find untold delight in them; but there was just no way. He argued that each time he had started thinking about this or about the *essential conformity of thought and its object,* his mind clouded over completely, and he got such a devilish stomach-ache that he stopped thinking and closed his book automatically.

Resistant to philosphy, a rebel against proper style! Poor Manolito Peña! If concurrently with his revolt against philosophical studies he had not also amazed me by his progress in other branches of learning, the master's opinion of his disciple would have dropped considerably. The best I could get from him in the area of philosphy was some short attention to its history. But he viewed it more as a matter of curiosity and erudition than as the object of rigorous systematic learning. It angered me to have Manuel being trained that way as a skeptic. I made great efforts to overcome it, but everything I did served only to increase his aversion to what he called a *theology without God.* By that time he had come to enjoy condemning or praising things with a biting, epigrammatic sentence. At times they were most opportune, and usually paradoxical. But this practice of judging even the gravest matters with epigrams has become so prevalent lately that my disciple, once in possession of that ability, seemed only to be placing a weathervane at the crest of the handsome edifice of his talents. As I considered these talents, and took stock of what Manuel lacked and what he had in great abundance, I would ask myself: "What will this boy turn out to be? Will he be a featherbrain, or the most solid of men? Will we have in him one more celebrity without principles, or the personification of a practical and effective spirit?" In utter confusion, I was unable to answer my own questions.

Manolito was also beginning to show a personal charm and magnetism such as I have never seen in a young man his age. He had the knack of getting everyone he met to like him. His grace and ease and aptness of expression gave his speech a convincing strength, and a winning way that opened the doors of every heart. He could place himself at the intellectual level of whomever he might be talking to, and speak the language most appropriate to each one. But his most praiseworthy trait was his great heart, whose outpourings often went beyond the prudent limits imposed by generosity. I was at some pains to regulate his noble impulses and charitable spirit, setting him some judicious limits and rules. I also sought to correct his pernicious habit of spending money foolishly; he would spend it on trifles that were no sooner bought than forgotten. I was utterly unable to uproot the vice of smoking, since he had practiced it for so long. But I did win the battle against his accursed habit of always sucking on sweets. He always had a pocketful of them. This, together with his smoking, took away his appetite. The worst of it was that during our lessons he would give me candy, too; and habits take hold so fast and the treacherous appetites so easily overcome our weak good sense that the one day when—by my own order—there were no sweets, my tongue yearned for them, and I came very near to feeling mortified in my flesh by their absence.

It is unnecessary to record the great thankfulness Doña Javiera felt toward me for having achieved a reformation of her son's behavior. The declarations of her gratitude came to me at Christmas, and other festivals, in the form of hams, and *morcilla* and *butifarra* sausages, all of them of the best quality and in great abundance, but the restrictions I had placed on the filial purse had resulted in such large savings to Señora de Peña, that she might have given me half the shop and still come out ahead.

Manuel dressed with elegance and variety, and I never tried to change him much in this respect, for a person's care in dress is a guarantee of good manners, and an axiom of proper rearing. He was a rich lad and would be expected to play a somewhat resplendent role in the world. He must then prepare for it, cultivating and developing right from the start the proper forms, a good appearance and a personal style. For personal style gives to one's character the same virtues that a good sentence gives to one's thoughts: tone, profile, vigor, personality. One thing that *did* displease me however, was to see him occasionally adopt, as a kind of elegant whim, the mannerisms and dress of people connected with bullfighting. In such a getup he would go off to a roundup, a jaunt to the country, or a visit to a bull-breeding ranch. We had strong and rather bitter arguments about this. He would fight back with flattery. But I realized that to each age one must grant most if not all of

35

what belongs to it, and that it's madness to fight against the environment and local influences. So I gave in, waiting for time and life's serious demands to cure my disciple of that puerile vanity.

I thought ceaselessly of the obstacles Manolito would have to overcome in order to make his way in society and occupy a position suited to his excellent endowments. A vexed question! It is abundantly obvious that social democracy has put down deep roots in this country, and no one is asked who he is or where he comes from before being admitted anywhere, being lauded and applauded, just so long as he has money or talent. We are all acquainted with a number of persons of the humblest origins who have attained the highest rank, and even married into the historic nobility. Money and wits, or even their stand-ins, speculation and skullduggery, have broken down all the barriers here, bringing about a mixture of all the classes to a much greater degree and with more telling effects than in the "European" countries, where democracy, having no place in daily intercourse, is provided for in the laws. From this perspective, and leaving aside the great political differences, Spain is becoming, strange though it seems, more and more like the United States of America. Like that nation, we are becoming a skeptical and utilitarian country where everything is dominated by the spirit of the melting pot, and of social leveling. History has less and less applicability every day here in Spain; it has passed entirely into the hands of archeologists, collectors, and curious, erudite, dried-up monomaniacs. Improvised fortune and rank are now the general rule; and tradition, perhaps having become hateful because of the forcefulness of its adherents, has lost all prestige. Freedom of thought is flying high and the ruling forces of our era, wealth and talent, are expanding their immense empire.

But the transformation, advanced as it already is, has not yet reached the point of eliminating a certain circumspection, a certain reluctance regarding the admission of low-born persons into the inner circle, so to say, of our society. If one's low origins are far from view, even though separated from the present moment by only a decade or so, that's fine, just fine. Our democracy has a short memory, but it's not blind; thus when one's vulgar origins are still there and easy to see, it's hard for money alone to conceal them. Who would deny that on certain noble escutcheons there could well be painted a leg of mutton, a little fish, or any other emblem of a humble trade? The origin of these noble houses is now so remote that nobody takes notice of it, but in the case of my disciple the plebeian shop was still open and doing business, and Manolito Peña, with all his wit, all his discretion and good looks and distinguished bearing, all his nobleness within and without, was still habitually called by his University chums, *the butcher-boy.*

I didn't talk with him about such matters, but I thought about them a great deal and feared there might be painful reverses. One day when we were speaking of his future and his plans, he confessed to me that he was slightly enamored of the daughter of the bull-ring impresario, a pretty and lively girl. Doña Javiera found out about this also, and didn't seem displeased. The young Vendesol girl was from a decent family, and would inherit a great fortune; her moral character seemed irreproachable, and she was of a higher social grade than Manuel, for though the Vendesols had been butchers, the shop had been shut down thirty years ago. Then they became cattle merchants, large-scale suppliers. Doña Javiera viewed her son's inclinations with pleasure, and said to me good-humoredly:

"It's like Providence, Manso my friend. The girl has *boodle,* and as for rank, well it's horns against horns."

With all due respect for this practical and horn-based argument, I thought Manuel's age (he was only 23), was not yet suitable for matrimony, but Doña Javiera argued back that any age is a good one for getting married. I realized that it was a matter I should not intrude upon and said no more. It seemed to me that Doña Javiera was terribly eager for an alliance with Vendesol, a person of very low birth indeed. As a child he had run and romped barefoot through the bloody gutters of Candelario, but his lowly origin was now made up for by thirty years as a wealthy, honored, respected man. Vendesol's wife and sisters lived in a world of elegance and high-placed contacts which were beyond the reach of Doña Javiera, since her butcher's block was still present and visible. Doña Javiera knew these ladies only by name and by sight. But she was dying to know them personally and rise to their level, something she thought would be very easy as long as she had money. Through Ponce I learned one day that she was seeking to negotiate the sale of the butcher-shop, thus getting out of trade once and for all.

Manuel became daily more ensnared in his courtship, scrimping on the time and concentration devoted to his studies. We had been having lessons together for two and a half years by then, and, although his respect and kind feelings for me had not cooled, our intellectual comradeship was not as close as it had been, and our sessions together became shorter. We saw each other every day, talked of all manner of things, and while I tried to turn his mind

37

toward general principles, he liked to talk only of facts and individual phenomena, with a special preference for anything recent and visible. Our discussions were sometimes vigorous, and we discussed the newest books; but we no longer took walks together. He went riding every afternoon and I took my walks alone. At length, we even stopped seeing each other at the Ateneo* in the evenings, for he was now attending the theater very often or going to the Vendesols' house.

I noticed within me a kind of loneliness, the sad emptiness left by cutting off an old habit. We had come to a place at which I had to consider the intellectual guidance of my disciple as completed. He was now capable of learning on his own all there was to learn, and even to surpass me. I said so to Doña Javiera, and she expressed her deep gratitude in return. The good woman had the habit of coming up to my flat at nightfall for a visit with me and her conversation was beginning to show a certain pretentious vanity which contrasted with her earlier straightforwardness. The idea of becoming related to the Vendesols had begun to warp her good judgment, and since she felt financially able to embark upon a life of luxury, her vanity didn't seem entirely without justification. There was, by the way, an ironic contrast between her grandiose plans and the language she used to express them: out of ancient custom, she still said *boodle* for money, and *making a splash* for moving in society. On more than one occasion her son had tried, with little success, to put some standardizing correctness into his mother's way of talking.

Doña Javiera confided some of these things to me very clearly, and others she merely intimated with graceful discretion. In very plain words she announced to me the idea of closing the shop and washing her hands forever of calves' blood. I indicated my approval, thinking to myself at the same time that if the lady kept on using the language she did, she would have as much trouble washing her hands as Lady Macbeth had had. In an indirect fashion she declared her intention to legitimize her relationship with Ponce, and to acquire for him something which might adorn him in high society and give him the aura of a respectable person. For example, a medal or cross from some Order, even the easily-gotten Beneficence Cross, or perhaps a job or appointment of the honorary sort.

About that time—it was the spring of 1880—Doña Cándida resumed the personal delivery of her stings. She and Doña Javiera would meet in my

*Madrid's venerable literary society was founded in 1834.

study, and I don't need to tell you what happened when two such different natures brushed against each other. They both gave free rein to their feelings, each according to her character. Doña Javiera was all naturalness and spontaneity; Señora de García Grande was all pretense, deception, and feigning. She was in the most delicate health, her nerves ruined. She had been examined by Federico Rubio, Olavide, and Martínez Molina, and by order of these doctors, she was going to Spa for the waters. Doña Javiera prescribed sherry and bitter orange-leaf-water for her. Doña Cándida just laughed at these home remedies and proclaimed the virtues of mineral waters. From here she went on to the subject of her travels, her contacts, the dukes and marquesses she knew. Finally even I, who knew her as she really was, concluded that her name must be printed in the *Almanach de Gotha*.

When my gadfly and I were alone, she set aside the bugle of vanity for the sharp stinging trumpet of the mosquito, and amid lies and tears she let me know of her need. It was perfectly dreadful! She was waiting for the rents from Zamora, . . . and that rascally manager! Oh, what a rascal that manager was! In the interim, she didn't know how she could get along and meet Irene's considerable expenses at Normal School. Why, just on books she spent half of her income. But she considered it all money well spent. Young Irene was a prodigy, the wonder of the professors and the glory of the School. To her greater good fortune, she had come under the tutelage of some foreign ladies (Doña Cándida couldn't quite remember whether they were English or Austrian), who had taken a great liking to her. They were teaching her all kinds of lovely things about good taste and shaping her posture as a schoolmistress. They were teaching her those refinements of upbringing and that cultivation of good form and appearances which are the chief adornment of Saxon women. She was now nineteen.

I had not seen her in quite some time, and wanted to so that I might assess her progress for myself. But out of some mistaken notion of delicacy, and of self-esteem, or some other reason I couldn't imagine, she never came to my house. One morning I met her in the street, beside a green-grocer's stall. She was doing the marketing, with the maid. I was taken aback by her graceful carriage and by her humble but immaculate dress, revealing in every way the virtue of good order which I was certain had not been imparted by her aunt. One could see clearly in her the noble model of poverty, a poverty accepted with valor and even affectionate good will. My first impulse was to greet her; but she seemed embarrassed and turned away, pretending not to see me, and resumed her chat with the greengroceress. Respecting her shyness, I went on to my class and as I turned the corner of the Calle del Tesoro I had already forgotten Irene's always pale and expressive countenance, her slender figure. I was thinking only of my lecture for that day, which dealt with *The Reciprocity Between Moral Consciousness and the Will.*

VIII
AH, WRETCHED ME!

O MOST UNHAPPY MAN! Mortal man, miserable a hundred times over, wretch among all the wretched, cursed be the hour when you fell from your paradise of tranquillity and methodical order into the hell of the most frightful confusion and chaos! Folk of this world, I implore you to submit your lives to a regimen of suitable work and satisfying regularity. Find a comfortable cocoon, like the skillful larva. Arrange all your duties, all your pleasures, your times of leisure and of work in a careful balance and measure, only then to have someone from the outside come and upset the whole thing, forcing you into the mainstream, upsetting, chaotic, hurried . . . Curses upon you, *life out there,* you are fatal a thousand times over! You yank us out of the joys of pure reflection, the enjoyment of the Ego and its felicitous projections. You steal from us the agreeable shadow of ourselves, that's to say our routine, our fixed and regular schedule, and the comfortable order of our home! . . ." But these outcries, though issuing from the depths of my soul, are not really a sufficient explanation of the great and radical change which overtook my way of life.

Listen and tremble! My brother, my only brother, the one who had left for the Antilles at the age of twenty-two, seeking his fortune, sent word that he was planning to return to Spain with his whole family. He had spent twenty years in America trying out different vocations and jobs, undergoing great hardships first, then completely ruined by the Cuban uprising, and finally made rich all of a sudden by the very war which threatened him, but which proved to be the infamous ally of his good fortune.

At Sagua la Grande he married a rich woman. Their combined assets came to several millions. What could be more prudent than to leave the Pearl of the Antilles to get along as best she might, and to bring back all the money and the family to Europe, where both would be more secure? The matter of the children's upbringing, the eagerness to be safe from fright and fear, the itch to move in society and to satisfy a certain vanity; all worked together to

41

bring about my brother's decision. Two months had gone by since he had notified me of his plans when I received a telegram from Santander announcing, oh! . . . just what I had feared.

My heart told me that the coming of that enormous family would upset my existence, and the normal joy at embracing my brother again was made bitter when I thought of the extremely annoying disorder which was about to afflict my way of life. It was September of 1880. One morning I went to the North Station to meet José and all his baggage, *viz.*: his wife, his three young children, his mother-in-law, his sister-in-law, plus a young black boy about fourteen years old, a mulatto girl, and in addition eighteen trunks, large and small, which had been checked through, fourteen suitcases, eleven smaller bundles and four armchairs. The animal kingdom was represented by a parrot in his cage, a mockingbird in his, and two tropical birds in yet another cage.

I had already had the better part of an inn made ready for the accommodation of this squadron. I settled my people the best I could, and my brother expressed from that very first day the need to take a house, a large, spacious, first-floor apartment where the whole family might have as much elbowroom as in an American house. José María is six years older than I, but he looked as if we were separated by twenty. When he arrived I was surprised to see how much of his hair had gone white. His face was the color of tobacco, wrinkled and rough, but with a certain pitchlike transparency that allowed one to see the yellow tegument beneath the resinous tint of the epidermis. He was clean-shaven like me. He wore a fine alpaca suit, a fine-quality Panama hat with a very narrow black band and a necktie just as narrow. His shirt had an embroidered front, diamond buttons, and a loose collar. He wore patent-leather boots with squared-off toes. Lica (this was the way they addressed my sister-in-law) was wearing a green and pink dress; her sister a blue one, and a straw hat. The two of them seemed to me to represent the flora of those cheerful lands, the charm of those forests filled with great lovely birds and insects clad in every color of the rainbow.

All José María could speak of the first day was our beautiful, poetic Asturias. He told me that the night before landing at Santander he had burst into tears when he saw the lighthouse at Ribadesella. Having paid this sentimental tribute to our motherland, we set about finding a house. It was quite a job that had fallen on me! Burdened with the September exams, I had to be in several places at once and break up my time in a way that caused me unutterable annoyance. Finally, we found a magnificent first-floor apartment in the Calle de San Lorenzo, renting for something above eleven thousand pesetas; it had livery stables, nine balcony windows on the street, and an enormous amount of room inside: it was the Noah's Ark they needed. I calculated the expenses of moving in and acquiring furniture and carpets at two thousands pesetas, and José María didn't find that out of line. The achievements (and the invoices) of the upholsterers proved later on that my estimate was a bit low, and that my knowledge of abstract and transcendent things did not include the possession of clear ideas on carpeting and carriages.

The family occupied the inn somewhat over a month longer, using that time to transform their clothing and to outfit themselves according to the style of this side of the great ocean. A horde of seamstresses invaded the rooms, and at all hours one could see fittings taking place, and observe the selection of fabrics, ribbons, and decorations. The dressmakers acted as if they were in their own house. The three ladies supplied themselves with winter coats bulging with fur and padding, for nothing was too great a precaution against the terrible cold they expected, and against pneumonia. At the end of two weeks all of them, from my brother to the youngest, looked like different people.

Lica, her mamma, and her sister were quite satisfied with the metamorphosis they had achieved—not without heated arguments, consultations, and some torture of their waistlines. All three gave exaggerated praises of the skill of the seamstresses and corsetières, and especially of the low price of everything, both of materials and labor. They were so thrilled by the low prices that they went from shop to shop buying odds and ends, and came home every afternoon laden down with all sorts of things, fake jewels and cheap trinkets. Then the shop assistants would appear bringing packages of everything created by God and perfected by industry in patterns, molds, and looms. The dozens of gloves, the reams of engraved paper, the knickknacks, the fans, the artificial flowers, the jewel-cases, the hand-painted fire-shovels, the lampshades and novelties in crystal and porcelain, all gave a feeling of fantasy to the tables and consoles of the house. Frankly, I thought they were going to open a shop of their own.

They also made frequent raids on the confectioners' shops, and there was always a box of candy in the sitting room, given Lica's need to regale herself constantly with sweets, varying the candy with fruit or sometimes a pastry or cold meats. Since she was *expecting* (and quite far along, too), it was just one whim after another. One must admit that her sister, without being—far

43

from it!—in a like condition, also had the same whims, and every little while they'd say, the two of them: "I feel like grapes, I feel like meringue." The call-bells of the rooms rang as if there were little playful demons walking on the wires, and the servants went back and forth with plates and trays, so much so that I was moved to pity when I saw how overworked these poor folk were.

Meanwhile, the little girls and the lad were left to their own devices in a room set aside just for them and their raucous rompings. They were looked after by the mulatto girl Remedios and young Rupertico, the black boy. You could hear their shouting from the street; they played wagons, dragging chairs about, and not a day went by without their breaking something or ripping a curtain from top to bottom or crippling a piece of furniture. Shortly after they came to Madrid they romped almost naked on the carpets; later, as the weather grew colder, one saw them playing dressed in the costly fur-trimmed broadcloth garments that had been made for them to wear on their outdoor walks.

The three ladies would spend hours stretched out indolently in their rocking chairs, without having changed out of their street clothes, fanning themselves furiously when it was warm, and all wrapped in blankets when it was cold. At night they'd go to the theater and then have some hot chocolate and go to bed. They slept right through the forenoon, and when the hair-dresser came they were still so dead asleep that there was no earthly way to get them out of bed. Lica, overcome by a crushing sloth and wishing neither to get up nor to go without a coiffure, would stick her head out from the pillows and sleep right on while her hair was being done, uncomfortable though that might be.

Rupertico was so mischievous that there was no way to set him straight. From morning till night he did nothing but play or put his face to the window to watch the carriages go by. When his mistresses called him to get something for them (which occurred about every two minutes), Rupertico had to be tracked down all through the house, and when we found him, we dragged him back by the ear. I undertook this painful mission, so totally at odds with my abolitionist views, because the cries of the black boy were less of an annoyance than the unbearable screechings of the ladies, who were constant-ly saying: "You black rascal, bring me my shoes; come tighten my corset; fetch me some water; find me a hairpin," etc. One day we searched fruitlessly for him all over the house. "Where can that damn boy have got to?" my brother and I were saying as we went through all the rooms. Finally we found him in a dark inner room. His little ebony face appeared to me like an anthropomorphism of the darkness, which gave off the white light of his two globular eyes, the ivory glint of his teeth, and the deep red glow of his lips. A hoarse low voice kept saying these words: "It's so co'd; it's so co'd." We took him out of there, and it was like pulling him out of an inkwell, for he was all wrapped up in one of his mistress's black blankets. That day they brought him a red Bayona vest, which put him very much in character. He was a good boy, an innocent soul, loyal and kind. He made me think of the good angels of African fetishism.

Nearly every day I had to stay for dinner with the family. This was cruel martyrdom for me, for there was more uproar at the table than on the docks of Havana.

The festivities would begin with disputes betwen my brother and Lica over what she would eat.

"Lica, have some meat. It's what you need. Take care of your health, for Heaven's sake."

"Meat? How revolting! . . . I'd like some cherry jam. No soup either."

"My dear, have some meat and wine."

"Oh, how tiresome you are! I want some melon."

Meanwhile *Niña Chucha* (for thus they called my brother's mother-in-law), who from the start of the meal had done nothing but make bitter criticisms of Spanish cookery, opened her eyes wide, exclaimed and sighed, expressing her longing for sweet potatoes, yucca, yams, malanga root and other vegetables which make up the Cuban diet. Suddenly the good woman, dizzy from the uproar at the table, filled a plate and went off to eat in her room. Distracted by all of this, I had failed to notice that one of the girls, seated next to me, was putting her hand on my plate and was grabbing what she found. Then she rubbed her hand over my face, calling me *pretty unkie*. The little boy dragged his napkin across a great platter of gravy and then dropped it, sopping, on the carpet. The other little girl was crying at the top of her voice for everything that at the moment was *not* on the table, while Papa and Mamma continued their discussion concerning what might be the best food for Lica's delicate temperament and critical condition.

"Sweetie, have some wine."

"Wine? How revolting!"

"Say, don't drink all that water!"

"Good Lord, but you're tiresome! Have them bring me some spun sugar sticks."

"Meat, woman, have some meat."

And the little boy came out in favor of Mamma, saying:

"Daddy is a dummy."

"Boy, if I get my hands on you . . . "

"Daddy is a pig."

"I'd like some spaghetti and sugar," screamed a little voice from farther down the table.

"I feel like some chick-peas."

"Quiet, everybody be still!" shouted José María, striking the table heavily with his knife-handle.

A cutlet soaked in tomato sauce flew down the table, landing precisely on Papa's white shirt-front. José María stood up in a rage and went and gave the boy a drubbing; the child bounded out of the room and set the inn a-thunder with his wailing. Lica got angry; her sister grumbled; *Niña Chucha* reappeared angrily objecting to the boy's punishment, and sat down at the table to continue eating. They called for Rupertico and for the mulatto girl. While all this was going on, I was at a total loss for a set of ideas or a philosophy to which I might appeal for some serenity of spirit.

Since she spent the whole day eating tidbits, Lica just picked at each course and drank glasses of water. Finally, at dessert time she would satiate her appetite for sweet, cool things. Coffee was served, blacker than ink; but I eschewed the imbibing of that devilish brew for fear it might deprive me of my sleep. Impatient, I counted the hours, waiting for the happy one when I might escape to the street.

Then it was time to smoke, and there I was among those pestiferous chimneys. For it wasn't just my brother who smoked: Lica lit up her cigarette and *Niña Chucha* put a small cigar into her mouth. The smoke and the rocking of their chairs turned my head a-spin like a windmill. I endured and fed my brother's conversation, which had now veered toward politics, until with the arrival of the time of my emancipation from slavery, I said my good-byes and withdrew, angry at my wretched life and sighing for my lost freedom. I turned my sad eyes back on history, and was unable, yes, unable to forgive Christopher Columbus for having discovered the New World.

IX

MY BROTHER WISHES TO DEVOTE HIS LIFE
TO THE SERVICE OF THE NATION

THEY SETTLED INTO their rented house at mid-October and lit fires in the fireplaces the first day, for they were all dying from the cold. Lica had the *catarrh,* her sister Chita (short for Merceditas) something nearly as bad, and *Niña Chucha*, in a sudden attack of nostalgia, begged in plaintive elegiacs to be taken back to her beloved Sagua, for in Madrid she was dying of grief and cold. The house, cramped and not well-lit, was a tedious confinement to her, and ceaselessly she recalled the spacious, bright, open houses of the warm country where she was born. Falling victim to the same malady, the expatriate mockingbird died during the first rainy spell, and his sorrowing mistress uttered such sighs of grief that we thought she might follow after him. One of the tropical birds got out of the cage and was never seen again. No one could get the good lady to believe anything but that the poor bird had flown off like a shot to the perfumed forests of his native land. If only she could do the same! Poor Doña Jesusa! How pitiable she seemed to me! Her only amusement was to tell me things about her blessed homeland, to explain how chili sauce is made. She would describe for me the dances of the black people, the rhythm of the maracas and the gourds, and she came close to teaching me to play the mouth-harp. She never went out in the street for fear of catching pneumonia; she didn't stir from her armchair even to eat her meals. Rupertico served them to her and on his way back to the kitchen he would gobble up whatever she'd left on the plate for him.

By contrast, my brother and his wife and sister-in-law were making an astonishingly good adjustment to the new life, to the harsher climate, and to the bustle and tumult of our way of doing things. José María, especially, was without nostalgia for anything he had left behind in Cuba. It was very obvious that he took pleasure in being so well treated, so much the object of flattery and attention, all of which made clear that he was a moneybags of the first order. He made frequent visits to Parliament, and I was amazed to see how he sought the friendship of deputies, journalists, and politicians, even those of fifth or sixth rank. His talk began to turn on the well-worn axis of public affairs, especially overseas matters, which are the most embroiled and subtle ones ever to weary human understanding. One didn't need to be a clairvoyant to see in José María a man eager to play a role and be important in some trivial political party of the sort that are formed every day at the whim of somebody who has nothing better to do. One day I found him in his study, in great distress, talking to himself, and he answered my questions by saying that he honestly felt himself to be a public speaker, that his mind was over-flowing with ideas, lines of argument, plans. He said he had in his head an endless number of phrases and a thousand combinations of words which, in his judgment, were worthy of being shared with the nation.

When I heard *nation*, I told him that he had better start off by getting a good knowledge of the one he had fallen so ardently in love with, for there exists a purely hypothetical nation-on-paper—referred to in all our electoral campaigns and political rhetoric. It's a being whose reality consists solely of the eager personalities and light-weight heads of our eminent leaders. One has to distinguish this apocryphal nation from the real one, which must be sought in its very palpitating flesh. To do that, in my view, one has to turn a deaf ear to all those deceptive forces around us, pay no heed to the roar of press and parliament, shut one's eyes to this whole decorative theatrical apparatus, and only then give one's self, body and soul, to rigorous thinking and to the unflagging observation of reality. One must bring down this empty catafalque of painted cloth and lay new foundations, resting on the staunch heart of the authentic Spain, thus enabling us to build a new and solid State. José María said he didn't understand my way of thinking, and proved it by calling me a destructive influence. I had to explain to him that the use of an architectural metaphor, which always comes to mind when you're thinking of politics, did not mean I had any destructive or demagogic leanings. I pro-fessed my indifference to the *forms* of government, adding that for me politics was and always would be a body of doctrine, a wise methodical combination of scientific principles and rules of the art of governing, that it was an organism, really; and that as a result my system left no room for personal con-tingencies, pernicious subjectivity, passing fads, abuses in word or in deed, all of which seem to sum up the current art of government among us.

Bored by my explanation about as quickly as he was amused by it, my brother yawned as he heard me out, and then he laughed. With commonness in his ironic laugh, he called me *metaphysical,* and suggested I study the wisdom of the angels in Heaven since human beings, he felt, were not made for such lofty and totally impractical things. Then he discussed with me very earnestly the question of which party he should join, and I said any one at all, since they're all the same in their behavior. Whether or not they are the same in their doctrines is a moot point, since it's never been put to a careful analysis. Nobody cares anyway. Then, giving him a lesson in practical common sense, I advised him to join the freshest and most recently formed party. He found the idea very appropriate, and said delightedly: "Metaphysician, you've hit it."

The circle of the family's acquaintance widened every day, a perfectly natural thing given the smell of money the house gave off. A month after moving in, my brother had the doors open and the table set for any and all notables who might wish to honor him. Visit followed visit, and introductions came one on top of another. It took the head of the family only a short time to realize that he had to uproot certain table manners which were harmful to his reputation, and thus when there were guests at table, which was almost every day in the year, there now reigned the most perfect order, unruffled by disputes over meat and wine or *Niña Chucha*'s quirks, or the unbridled license of the children. They lured a good chef, and a *maître* or waiter: it seemed like a different place. Good taste was gradually winning out all through the house itself, and in their ways as well. Not least in the persons of Lica and Chita could one observe the transformation, the rapid triumph of European manners. My sister-in-law managed to curb a bit her passion for egg-sweets, hard candy, and chocolates. The children, banished from the family table, ate separately and alone, under the supervision of the mulatto girl. Realizing how poor their upbringing was, their father made haste to put an end to this serious fault, for really they knew nothing, not how to eat, nor dress themselves, nor speak, nor walk properly. Lica also deplored the negligent way her children were being reared, and as she was talking to her husband about it one day he turned to me and said:

"You've got to find me a governess, and quickly too."

X
INSTANTLY I THOUGHT OF IRENE

WHO, FOR THE CASE AT HAND, would be ideal. A valuable acquisition for my family and an admirable opportunity for the orphaned Irene! Very pleased with myself for having thought of this doubly beneficial arrangement, I spoke with Doña Cándida that very afternoon. Good God, you should have seen the woman carry on when she found out that my brother and all his retinue were in Madrid! I was afraid that the shock, and the blow to her already shattered nervous system might send her into an epileptic seizure, for I saw lightning-bolts of joy issue from her eyes. She was all frisky, feverish, on the verge of going into a dance. But soon those signs of joy changed to rage, which she turned loose on me, shouting:

"Why, you dolt, you clot, why didn't you tell me sooner? Where is your mind? You've been off star-gazing."

In her glance I could see the sparkle of her supreme cleverness, an admirable blend of the swiftness of Bonaparte, the audacity of a highwayman, and the inventiveness of a French serial-fiction writer. Woe to her victims! Like a vulture on his naked summit, espying from an incredible distance the dead carcass down in the valley, so Doña Cándida, from the summit of her poverty, caught sight of the rich harvest to be reaped at my brother's house and the sumptuous flesh ready for her beak and claws. Laughter played on her trembling lips, and her whole expression revealed a state similar to artisitc inspiration. Wild with joy, she said:

"Oh Máximo, I do love you so! You're my guardian angel."

I didn't realize what I was doing by putting the bloodthirsty Caligula in touch with my brother's unsuspecting family. It was already too late when it struck me that my charitable impulse had brought down on my relatives a curse worse than the seven plagues of Egypt put together. I was the one responsible for this curse, and yet I laughed, I couldn't help it, I laughed when I saw her come into the house for her first visit. She was the representation of

50

Divine wrath, put together with twenty-five pins, radiant, threatening, a look of wild majesty on her face, something like Attila's, I suppose. I don't know where she got the clothes she wore on that tragic occasion. I believe she rented them at a pawn-shop owned by some friends of hers, or that they lent them to her, or who knows what? There are always impenetrable mysteries in the ways and wiles of certain people, and not even the sharpest observer can see through their marvelous machinations. What she was wearing, without really being good, was passable, and since the rascal had a certain way of acting the great lady, she could put it over on anyone, and to an inexpert eye she looked like a woman who set the tone of society and fashion. Her noble Roman profile and distinguished manners that day put on a more brilliant show than in the whole long period of the Liberal Union when García Grande was in his glory.

When she saw my brother, she embraced him so hard and made such an emotional demonstration that I thought she would faint. She recalled our good mother in pathetic phrases that made José María weep and allowed herself to observe that she was a second mother to us. Talking with Lica and Chita she was so sagacious, so delicate, so ladylike, that the ladies from Cuba were enchanted and stupefied. Lica told me later that she had never met such a refined, kindly person. During that first visit Doña Cándida also gave free rein to her affection for the children, treating them with all sorts of pamperings and flattery, and showing toward them a love bordering on idolatry. *Niña Chucha* enjoyed a brief respite from her nostalgia in the tender words of that improvised friend who managed to get chili sauce into the conversation, and to praise the excellence of Cuban cooking. She ended with a short paragraph on illnesses. Even José María fell into her astute trap, and soon after Caligula left he asked me if many persons of note attended Doña Cándida's salon. When I heard this, I laughed so loudly that the peals must have been audible to the deaf-mutes in their school in the Calle de San Mateo, around the corner.

My gadfly appeared at the house again the next day. She acted very earnest right from the start, saying: "Why, it seems as though we've known each other all our lives! I think of you as my own daughters!" Then she told them about her past, herself, and her misfortunes. She did it in a style which left me in awe of her gift for hyperbole. She had put off her trip to her properties in Zamora so that she might enjoy the company of such a splendid family, and although her interests had suffered badly thanks to her inept managers, she didn't wish to leave Madrid because her friends, the Marchioness of This and

51

the Duchess of That, were holding her back. Her physical ills were a pitiful epic; to have them properly sung, it would have been necessary to change Homer into Hippocrates. Finally, on that second day and the following ones—for the sun would sooner fail to reach the zenith than Caligula to reach the Manso house—she demonstrated such knowledge and taste in matters of fashion that she became Lica's and Chita's Council of State. No hat, no fabric, no ribbon was chosen without first counsulting Doña Cándida.

"Poor things!" she'd say to them, "don't go to the shops to buy a thing. They'll recognize immediately that you're from America, and charge you double, it's perfectly dreadful. I'll take care of buying things for you . . . No, no, my dear, no reason to thank me. It's no trouble at all; I have nothing to do. I know all the shopkeepers, and they give me a lower price because I'm such a good customer."

To forewarn my brother against the economic dangers the family was being exposed to by using Doña Cándida's services, I told him the lengthy and colorful story of her attacks on my pocket. He laughed heartily and only said: "Poor lady! If Mamma were to see her in such a condition . . . !"

A few days later I spoke to Lica about the same subject; but she cut my warnings short, in a sort of revolt against what she took for malice in me, and said in her languid voice:

"Don't exaggerate so . . . You've got something against poor Doña Cándida. Why, she's so good, the poor thing! She'd be rich if it weren't for those bad managers of hers. I imagine it's her *factor* who cheats on the accounts! And then she's so sickly, poor dear. Yesterday I had to be very stern with her to make her accept a small favor, a little advance until she gets her rent money from the plantation—well, it's not a plantation; whatever it is. She's so good-hearted, poor thing! She didn't want to accept the money, not for anything in the world. I begged her in the name of the Virgin of Charity of El Cobre to do me the favor of taking that little sum . . . I can see you're laughing; don't be so one-sided . . . The poor dear! I took offense at her resistance and I began to cry. Then she did too, and finally agreed, so as not to hurt my feelings."

Lica was a celestial creature with an angel's heart. She was unacquainted with evil; she was unaware of all the deceits and malice present in the world; and she judged others by the measure of her own innocence and goodness. I could only contemplate with equal parts of joy and amazement the pure flower of her soul, usullied by any vileness, not even aware of the contagious vice beside it. It pained me so much to ruffle the peace of that virginal spirit by injecting distrust into her, that I decided to respect her ingenuous state, better suited to life in the tropics than in great cities. So I said no more of the ferocious Caligula.

By that time Irene had taken over the intellectual, social, and moral training of the two girls and the tiny boy. They were provided, by my intervention, with a spacious room where the schoolmistress spent the whole day with her little pupils. The four of them ate together in another room nearby. I saw to it that they all went out for a stroll every afternoon, thus devoting only the hours before lunch to sedentary studies. The young teacher's discretion and sense of proportion, her reserve and her industry won Lica's heart. In this area, at any rate, she showered blessings on me for having brought such a lovely, precious jewel to her house. My brother was also very pleased, so I was able to console myself somewhat for having done evil in turning loose the calamitous Doña Cándida. Thinking of the industrious honeybee, I could forget the sucking vampire.

XI

HOW SHALL I DESCRIBE MY CONFUSION?

HOW SHALL I EXPRESS my loss of balance and the thousand annoyances which my brother's life brought into my own? Any resolve to escape from that world was useless, because my blessed relatives made me stay with them almost all day, sometimes to consult me about something and wear me down with questions, sometimes just to keep them company. It seemed that nothing got done in that house without me, and that I was the master of all knowledge, information, and news. And what shall I say of my obligatory duty to eat dinner with them every other day, or more likely, *every* day? I bade good-bye to my sweet monotony, my books, my strolls, my independent life, the freedom to set my own hours, each for its own work or purpose, or its ration of rest. But there was nothing that upset me more than the social gatherings at their house. For a long time I had been in the habit of going to bed early, and the late hours of socializing, filled with racket and stupid talk, really caused me an unutterable malaise. Besides, wearing a frock coat has always been so contrary to my tastes that I would gladly see them banished from the face of the earth. But my brother, bless him, had become so ceremonious that I couldn't get by without one of those unpleasant garments.

Eager for celebrity, José María longed to adorn his salons with all the notable folk and distinguished families who could be drawn there; but he found that difficult to achieve. Lica had not succeeded in being accepted by most of the Cuban families residing in Madrid. They surpassed her immeasurably in distinction and manners. They could not see her kind heart, but only her rustic, rural straightforwardness and her fatal mistakes in social etiquette. Some rumors and gossip had reached my ears about Lica, and they weren't very flattering. Barbed, cruel anecdotes made the rounds of the whole colony. The least offensive thing they said about her was that she had been caught with a lasso. And the innocence of the dear woman was so great that she was not upset on those occasions when she *did* cut a ridiculous figure;

most likely she didn't even realize it. She really did pay close attention to what my brother or I would tell her so that she might acquire a certain style and adapt to her new life, and soon her natural sagacity began to win out over her long-standing lack of refinement. Her very humble birth, her poor upbringing, and the fact that she had lived in a homely village in the interior of the island all worked against her turning into an upper-class European lady. Yet despite this unfavorable background, my brother's fine wife, with that delicate sensitivity of hers to round out her virtues, was little by little getting into the new ways and learning the dissimulations, the delicacies, the subtle, wily ways of good society.

José María begged me to bring people of distinction to the house, but—woe is me!—whom could I bring outside of a couple of testy professors who would bore me and bore everyone else as well. It is true that I introduced my beloved disciple, my spiritual son Manuel Peña, and he was very well received, in spite of his humble origins. But how could it have been otherwise? For in addition to having on his side the leveling tendencies of modern society, he redeemed himself personally from his lowly birth by being the most witty and pleasant, the most graceful, the most intelligent and captivating person one could imagine, so much so that he stood head and shoulders above all those of his years, without a single one of them even coming close.

My brother took a liking to him, assessing him at his true worth; but the master of the house was still not satisfied, and in spite of having joined a political party whose emblem features *democracy rampant,* he wanted above all to see in his salon people with titles—papal titles would do—and political celebrities, even though they might be among the most discredited ones. He was also pleased by famous poets and men of letters, and the former were especially favored by Lica, for nothing could match for her the sing-song of verses. It is no indiscretion to reveal that she also plucked the lyre, having written some *natales* and *décimas* back in her native land. They had all the rustic naïveté of their author's heart, and the wild harshness of the jungle as well. Right from the time of the first gatherings, there attached himself to the house, soon becoming one of its infallible attendants, one of those poets of the two-a-penny variety . . . .

XII
AH, BUT WHAT A POET!

AMONG THE GREAT NUMBERS who belong to this class, he could, by giving him the benefit of the doubt, be put in the eighth or ninth rank. Twenty-five years old, cheeky, slender of figure, with a very long name adding up to ten words; and a bulging repertoire of varied writings, scattered across all the albums of pretentious bad taste. Arrogance and sickliness made up three quarters of his person. The rest was a stiff collar, a yellowish beard, and a sour, pained voice which made one think that impious hands were strangling his gullet. That distant relative of the Muses (I do not hesitate to put it crudely) made me sick. The pompous notions he had concerning himself, his total ignorance, and the ease with which he talked about matters of art and criticism, it all made me dizzy and ill all over my body. He lived on a miserable little job that paid 1,500 pesetas a year, but he put on such airs that it made many people think that the entire burden of the administration was on him. There are men who portray themselves in a single act or a single sentence. This one portrayed himself on his calling cards:

Francisco De PAULA DE LA COSTA
Y SÁINZ DEL BARDAL
Chief of the Private Office
of His Excellency the Director General
of Public Welfare and Health

Then, his address: *Aguardiente,* 1.

And at the top of this rigmarole appeared the Cross of Charles III, not because he possessed it, but because his father had been awarded the emblem of that Order. When this fop handed out a card for any reason, one had the feeling of being given a whole library. It occurred to me that if by some demonic intervention it were ever necessary to inscribe the name of this poet in the hall of fame, it would take up an entire frieze by itself.

56

At the present time the cards have changed, but the person hasn't. He's one of those fortunate beings who compete in all the poetic contests and floral tourneys which are held everywhere, and he has often won the golden pansy or the silver violet. His odes belong under the heading of pharmacopaeia, for their narcotic and somniferous qualities; his ballads are like diachylon, a remarkable specific for curing boils. He writes *little verses*, he fabricates long poems, he shapes *Germanic whispers*, and every other thing that comes under the domain of rhyme. He pitilessly pilfers from other poets and he filches ideas. Everything that passes through his hands turns common and stupid, for he is the distillery which turns sublime thoughts into empty nonsense. He writes stanzas in everyone's albums, expressing doubts or melancholy, or perhaps emollient sonnets followed by a yard or two of his signature. He has badgered the editors of illustrated reviews to insert his poems, and they do it, since they don't have to pay him. But nobody reads them except their author, who is his own public.

This character, who still visits me and gives me a headache or gastric distress, was one of the chief adornments of my brother's salons, for if indeed José María paid him no attention, Lica and her sister held him in the highest esteem because of their fatal inclination toward poetry. I need hardly say that two days after meeting them Don Francisco de Paula de la Costa y Sáinz del Bardal—God help us!—had already composed and dedicated to them a whole clutch of elegies, laments, meditations, nocturnes which gave prominent places to cocoanut palms, mangrove swamps, hammocks, mockingbirds, ironwood trees, and the languid loveliness of the women of the Americas.

But the grand acquisition of my brother was Don Ramón María Pez. As soon as this man showed up at the gatherings, all the other figures were reduced to secondary importance; every light paled before a star of such magnitude. Even the poet suffered something of an eclipse. Pez was the oracle of all those people, and when he deigned to give his opinion of what had occurred that day in Parliament with regard to treasury reform or the use of the Royal Prerogative, there was around him a silence more respectful than Plato received in the celebrated grove of Academe. This good gentleman, a ministerial deputy and in charge of a whole ministerial department, had such a high opinion of himself that his words issued forth clothed in sibylline authority. Forced into it by the demands of society, I had no recourse but to pay attention to his hollow paragraphs, which sounded to me like an empty eggshell hitting the floor and smashing itself. Courtesy obliged me to listen to him, but in my heart I had about as much respect for him as one has for that

57

sideshow artifice called *the talking head.* He doubtless hadn't much regard for me; but man of the world that he was, he affected a certain respect for serious intellectual pursuits, which were my regular work. So, whenever the conversation turned to any weighty subject, he would say with a slightly mocking benevolence: "That's one for our friend Manso . . . "

Pez, in turn, brought Federico Cimarra to the house. Cimarra is known even to the stones of Madrid, as he was formerly known to its gambling dens. He was a majority-party deputy too, one of those who never speak but can do enough dirty work for seventy men, and affecting total independence, are eager for a piece of any shady deal. These men, rather than a class, form a cancerous growth which spreads unseen through the whole body politic, from the tiniest village up to the two houses of Parliament. A man of the most wicked political and family background, but still welcome everywhere and known by all, Cimarra was sought after because he would accommodate anybody and was considered astute. Cimarra did not behave pompously, like Pez. He was rather pleasant and agreeable. He and I used to have long conversations: he would give evidence of his skepticism, as brilliant as it was brutal, and I would comment on politcal affairs in a way which, strange to relate, was in harmony with his own. Madrid is full of people of this kind: they are her flower and her dross, for they both delight us and corrupt us at the same time. Let us take care not to seek out the company of these men except for a brief time of recreation. Let us rather study them from a distance, for these plague-ridden men have notorious powers of contagion, and it's not hard for an overly attentive spectator to become infected by their gangrenous cynicism when least expected.

And so my brother's receptions took on greater importance with each passing day, and there was even a minor daily paper which printed something about the *high level of elegance which prevailed there,* saying that we were all very distinguished. José watched with delight as titled persons came to his salons, an achievement I never considered particularly difficult. The first one we had the honor of receiving was the Count of Casa-Bojío, the son of the Marquesses of Tellería and married to a very distinguished Cuban millionairess. It was expected that the Marchioness de Tellería herself would not be long in showing up, and maybe, just maybe, the Marquess of Fúcar. But what is most worthy of note, indeed worthy of being passed on to history, is that in the Manso gatherings was born one of the most illustrious Associations formed in our times, one of those which confer the greatest dignity upon humanity. I am referring to the General Society for the Relief of Industrial Invalids, which today enjoys a robust life and renders effective services to workers who are disabled by illness or any sort of accident. I don't know who started the idea, but the fact is that it was well-received and after a few nights the Executive Committee had been formed and the Bylaws drafted. Now Don Ramón Pez was a genuine colossus in statistical, administrative, and welfare matters; he could combine these three areas into reports filled with numbers and astound us with what could be learned from those numbers. Naturally, he was chosen President of the Society. They made Cimarra Vice-President, my brother Treasurer, and Sáinz del Bardal, who seemed to have his oar in very deep, named himself Secretary. For, God have mercy, poets always appear to need to get involved in these things! As for me, though I fought nobly to remain just a private soldier in that army of philanthropists, I was unable to avoid being named to the Executive Committee. I wasn't bothered by the job or by its purposes, only by the rotten luck of having to put up with the poet and suffer at all hours from the ingestion of his incredible nonsense. Dealing with him was like absorbing, one after another, a series of unknown morbid miasmas. The confounded man just made me sick. Manuel Peña hated him so much that he had nicknamed him Typhus, and avoided him like the plague.

And now that I've mentioned Peña, I will add that he was highly thought of in those gatherings, and his merits and qualities very much valued. Once in a while—perhaps a bit more often—his butcher-block background showed through; but everyone's courtesy, the democratic air of many who were there, and above all the politeness, good manners, and gentlemanliness of Peña himself put things on a firm footing. It was strange: the one who seemed to show the greatest respect for Peña and for me was the cynical Cimarra, totally carefree, and a devotee, as he said, of people who really amount to something. He was the sort of man who mocks knowledge while admiring those who have it. But I was displeased that it should have been that very Cimarra who first hit upon the idea of calling my disciple *Young Peña,* a designation which lasted and stuck, and no matter what people say, has a certain scorn to it.

José María spent his days turning over in his mind what had been said at the previous night's gathering. He spent his time and effort only on strengthening his ideas and organizing them so that they'd be in harmony with the Party credo.

"What do you think of the Party?" he'd often ask me.

And I would answer that the Party was the best one that had come along yet. And he'd answer: "I'd like to see it organized in the English way . . . , since that's the really practical way, isn't it? It's quite a pity that no one here in Spain studies British politics, with the result that we live by an utterly sterile weaving and ripping out again."

I listened and, praising God, encouraged him to continue his commentary (and thus display to me, as something I might study, the astounding variety of human manias).

Occasionally, as he turned his attention to the concerns of his home and children, he would say to me:

"It'd be a good idea for you to look in on the children's room, don't you think? Just to see how that really remarkable governess is doing."

And I did so very gladly. I would go for a while, and without my realizing it a couple of hours would slip by, what with examining the lesson-plans and gazing like a fool at the schoolmistress, whose beauty and talent and earnestness I found extremely pleasing.

XIII
SHE WAS ALWAYS PALE

A S PALE AS SHE HAD BEEN as a child, with a good figure, quite slender, narrow-waisted, and extremely well-proportioned in all other parts, admirable in form and with an air about her . . . Without being a beauty of the first order, she was probably a delight to all who saw her; she certainly delighted me. She even charmed me a little, to put it plainly. One certainly might make critical observations regarding her separate features, but what professor of aesthetics could be so rigid as to criticize her general expression? I have reference to that tremulous surface of her soul which one saw in her every part and yet nowhere, always and never, in her eyes, in the echo of her voice, in places she was and where she wasn't, that glint of the air around her, that empty place she left when she went out. Her air was, to speak plainly, the sum of all those things in her which bespoke contentment with her lot and the serenity and firm temper of her spirit. At the very center of all her self-expression I could see her pure conscience and the rectitude of her moral principles. Everyone has a nature and a style; the former may be observed in one's character and actions, the latter not only in language, but in manners and dress as well. Irene's dress was proper, stylish, and without affectation, simple and neat enough to withstand the most searching critique.

Right from my first visits and inspections I was taken with her good common sense, her precise knack for seeing the things of this life and for putting at a respectful distance the things pertaining to another life. Her aplomb bespoke a superior and wondrously balanced nature. She seemed like a woman from the North of Europe, born and reared far from our enervating climate and this wicked moral atmosphere.

As soon as the children went to sleep, Irene would withdraw to the room Lica had set aside for her in the house, and nobody would see her until first thing the next morning. Through the mulatto girl I found out that she spent part of those nighttime hours caring for her things and mending her

61

clothes. That's how she always maintained such a constant composure and the neatness of her person. That made her stand out the way a beautiful landscape stands out against a pure and diaphanous sky. Her honest poverty forced her to this, and what better school exists, really, for teaching the way to perfection? This detail captivated me and it was, along with my daily contacts with her, the main reason for the admiration she awakened in me.

Another charming detail: she had the very finest touch with the children who, though good-hearted enough, were willful, rebellious, and full of the ugliest bad habits before she took them over. How did she manage to tame those three little beasts? With her insight she worked miracles, and with her native wisdom about the nature of childhood itself she earned the delirious affection of the little ones, never once administering corporal punishment. Persuasion, patience, sweetness, these were the natural fruits of that gifted soul.

One day when we were talking about a number of things, after lesson-time, I recalled the days when Irene used to call at my house. I was almost able to see her scribbling at my desk, making a muddle of my books and papers. Well, although I made no mention of the fatal little notes from Doña Cándida, this whole set of memories was very displeasing to the governess. I recognized it, and changed the subject immediately.

I had been so clumsy as to wound her dignity, which must still have been very sensitive as a result of the cruel injuries inflicted by her beggarly aunt, the want in which they both lived, and the poor child's hunger, her lack of decent clothing and even passable shoes.

More charms. I noticed that imagination occupied second place in Irene. Her clear judgment was capable of tossing aside trivial and tawdry things, and she didn't become ensnared in wild imaginings the way most women do. Was this natural in her, or the result of the lessons of adversity? Both, I think. I rarely perceived any facile enthusiasm in what she said. When she did demonstrate enthusiasm, it was for great, serious, and noble things. Behold, then, the woman of reason, as over against the woman of frivolousness and caprice. I was in the position of someone who has wandered along through dark, godforsaken depths, and then stumbles upon a gold mine, or a vein of silver or precious stones, and concludes that Nature has withheld that treasure for his sole enjoyment. He picks it up and secretly takes it home; first he enjoys it and appreciates it alone; then he publishes his find so that everyone may praise it, so that it may be the motive for general wonderment and happiness. And out of this situation in which I found myself there arose a whole range of thoughts that took me quite by surprise, putting me at a distance from myself, making me different from myself, in such a way that I felt a spirited impulse of my will, which kicked up its heels (that's the only expression I can find) like an untamed steed. There spread through my whole being those impulses which in another situation would be the result of a *plethora sanguinea,* and . . .

XIV
GOOD GOD,
HOW DID I CONCEIVE SUCH
A PLAN?

W AS IT BORN OF EMOTION or of reason? Even today I can't be sure, although I do try to plumb the depths of the problem, assisted by the serenity of mind which I now enjoy.

"That young woman is a treasure," I said to my brother and to Lica, who were both very pleased with the children's progress.

On fine days, Irene and the three little ones went out for a stroll. I took great care that this habit should not be broken, since it's such a healthful practice. I added myself to that good company most afternoons, sometimes because I had planned to do so, and others because I would meet them— whether by coincidence I do not know—in the street. These coincidences occurred with such infallible regularity that they ceased being coincidences. As I conversed with Irene, I noticed that she was not a woman of any pretensions to great learning, but that she did possess the culture appropriate to her sex, unquestionably superior to any which might be demonstrated by the women of our times. She had the rudiments of some sciences, and whenever she spoke of her studies she did it with such accuracy that one admired her more for what she didn't wish to know than for what she had indeed learned.

Our talks during those pleasant strolls were about general topics, likes and dislikes, tastes, and sometimes, the level of education women should be given. She agreed with me, and dissociated herself from the judgment of so many half-baked pamphleteers; *i.e.,* she rejected the idea that women should become full-fledged professionals, exercising the callings proper only to men. At the same time, however, she heaped scorn upon the ignorance, superstition, and backwardness in which most Spanish women live. All of which led both her and me to conclude that the secret is in finding a golden mean.

And the more of her precious inner life she revealed to me, the greater the harmony and kinship I found between her spirit and my own. She didn't care for bullfighting, and detested anything that had the slightest air of vulgarity. She was deeply, exaltedly religious, but not sanctimonious, and liked to spend no more than a short while in church. She adored the fine arts and regretted not having the aptitude to cultivate them. She felt an eagerness to do a fine job of decorating the place where she might live, and to fashion that agreeable, comfortable nook that the English call a *home*. She knew enough to put limits on that vapid sentimentality which takes the very heart out of things. She had the ability, rather, to judge and weigh and measure things as they really are.

Once she had become a bit more open with me, she would tell stories about Doña Cándida which had me *dying* of laughter. I realized how much the poor young woman must have suffered living with someone who represented the exact opposite of her natural rectitude and her delicate tastes. With one confidence after another, she told me bit by bit, and in a series of strolls and interesting sessions we spent together, things about her childhood; a thousand little details which permitted me to see her talent and her exquisite sensitivity as well.

About then the Christmas season was coming upon us. On the 15th of December Lica had given birth to a sickly baby boy. I stood godfather to him, and we gave him Máximo for a name. My brother, joyful over the growth of his family, so outdid himself in handing out gratuities and gifts that I was alarmed and advised him to control himself, for the excesses of his liberality were beginning to border on bad taste. But as long as he could hear the expressions of gratitude and the praises of his generosity, he didn't hesitate to empty his pockets. During those days there was a great meeting at his house of the *Society for the Relief of Industrial Invalids,* and endless committees and subcommittees were chosen, each of which named its scribe, who was to present an early and luminous report on the very grave points of theory and practice which had to be dealt with. Consider the great good fortune of the working classes, how happy they would be when that apparatus, not yet articulated, began to function, filling Spain with its admirable activity, spreading beams of benevolent light to every corner!

The afternoons of the week after Christmas, such a gay time for some people (for me it's always been a very dull stretch), were spent keeping Lica company. Doña Cándida didn't miss a single day, showing toward my sister-in-law and nephew an idolatrous tenderness whose ultimate touch was staying to supper. The tactical admiration Caligula showed for the chef was discreet, albeit entirely non-Platonic.

One afternoon the children got it into their heads to go to the theater, and since the Martín was so nearby and they were performing *The Birth of the Son of God* and *The Slaughter of the Innocents,* I reserved a box and went along with Irene and the younger members of the family. Chita, who had gotten ready to go also and came out to the stairway in such a great bulky hat that one couldn't see her face, went back in again because she felt the *catarrh* coming on. I felt light-hearted that afternoon, and the appearance of the theater, filled with children of both sexes and all ages, increased my cheerfulness, a result perhaps produced by a secret admiration for the fecundity and growth of the human race. It was rather warm inside the theater, and the cramped galleries where so many people sat looked like garlands of human heads, the younger ones being most notable. I've never seen such a hubbub: up high, one was begging to be nursed; down below, another one was bawling. In the boxes and the stalls there was enough kicking and hand-clapping and gaping around to make one confused, dizzy, nearly demented. The place was already boiling with ardent emotional appetites and a raucous, feverish impatience, and the red gaslights only heightened the similarity to infernal cauldrons or perhaps to a miniature toy Hell improvised in Limbo on an afternoon during Carnival-tide.

Pepito María, my nephew, was terrified when he saw the Devil come out as soon as the curtain had gone up. This Devil was the ugliest mess of a fellow I've ever seen in my life. The poor lad hid his face to keep from looking at him; his sisters laughed, and after everybody urged him not to be afraid, he dared just to squint through one eye until he saw the horrid horns on the actor playing the Devil. Then he shut his eyes tight again, and asked us to take him away. Fortunately an angel, armed with lance and shield, came on stage and intimidated the Devil with a few words and a half-dozen kicks. This calmed Pepito, who took courage as he heard the exclamations of satisfaction which arose from all parts of the theater.

As the action of the play proceeded, Irene and I marveled that such a serious subject, so poetic and worthy of respect, should be presented as an indecent farce. At one point the scene reveals a temple for the ceremony of the betrothal of the Blessed Virgin, and it is really quite something to see and hear. The priest, wrapped in a sheet adorned with strips of gilt paper, had the bearing of a furniture-mover right off the street. We saw St. Joseph, played by one of those low comics who do so well in farces; here he seemed all the more ridiculous for the bombastic gravity he tried to give to the colorless and untheatrical figure of Mary's betrothed. Then we saw Mary herself, an actress with a comical face, more like a vulgarian than a lady; she was trying to look innocent and sweet. Inappropriately dressed, she was unable to pose her disfigured body in such a way as to conceal the signs of impending motherhood. But the most disgusting part of that incredible farce was a crude, bestial shepherd who played suitor to Mary. In the temple scene and throughout the play he indulged in the grossest liberties of speech on the subject of St. Joseph's meekness. Irene's view, and mine as well, was that such spectacles should not be permitted; she made very sad remarks on the state of religious feelings in a nation which tolerates and applauds such caricatures.

This led me to make some general remarks on the theater as a whole, its conventionalities and the falseness characteristic of it. I spoke of this because it was the only way I could think of to get the conversation around to some other topics more in harmony with the state of my feelings. I was looking for transitional phrases and found only the most incredible clumsiness inside me. I think my mind had been reduced to a frightful stupefaction by the heat, the hubbub of the intermissions and that great, boring, sacrilegious farce. I can't imagine what fatal and unkown force led me to speak only of ordinary matters, insipid and barren, just like a lesson in my class. Irene's very grace and beauty, far from spurring me on, seemed almost to gag me, and bound my whole spirit in mysterious fetters.

I don't know how the conversation turned to the events and characteristics of her childhood. Irene spoke of her father, who had been a royal groom; she had a vague memory of his uniform with its embroidery and red jacket-front, a three-cornered hat on top of a face bending over her, so tiny, to kiss her. She remembered that at the earliest dawn of her consciousness, the very air around her breathed a profound respect for the Royal Household. An aunt on her father's side, more humane, had loved her very deeply. This lady received a pension from the Royal Family, since her husband, parents, grandparents, and ancestors far back beyond had also been royal grooms, butlers, and pantry-keepers or something like that. The enthusiasm of this aunt for the royal family amounted to idolatry. When the 1868 revolution came, Irene's aunt lost her pension and her sanity, for she went mad with grief and died soon afterwards, leaving her young niece in the clutches of Doña Cándida.

To be truthful, these things were of secondary interest to me, the more so since my own heart was in a tormented struggle to make a much-needed expression of its own feelings. In a natural reaction, my head also began to suffer, appropriating to itself my heart's state of moral anguish; I noticed a painful, aching obstruction. And I remained silent in a corner of the box, while the children watched, transfixed, the tableaux of the Annunciation, the Census-taking, and the journey to Bethlehem. Irene sensed from my silence that I had a headache, and said it might go away if I stepped into the street awhile for a bit of fresh air.

But I was unwilling to go out, and during the second intermission we spoke again. About what? Well, about the royal groom, Irene's aunt (Cándida), who had had a headache for three days, and nausea, delirium, and fainting fits as well. A bit later, as the curtain rose once more, we saw the mountainside, the cascade of *genuine water* falling from high up on the stage and running over a tiny water-course; the shepherds and their live flock, which was made up of a dozen white sheep. At that moment the theater seemed near collapse, for the flowing water and the sheep had awakened a truly wild enthusiasm. As an artist, I meditated on what times these are that we live in, when it's possible to make a musical comedy out of the New Testament. Then, while children, maids, and governesses were watching the Manger scene in wonderment, I let my thoughts rove to another area not too different from earlier ones. As I saw the most sacred events in caricature, and in a farce those things in religion called *mysteries* so as to make them more worthy of respect, I felt inside me an urge to criticize, which, in a way, was not unrelated to my nagging headache. It even seemed stimulated by it, giving to my pessimistic outlook the same sharp edge that was splitting my cranium. And the strangest thing was that my implacable hostility was directed toward the one who was most pleasing to my sight and gave the warmest hope to my spirit. No doubt the ugly Devil who had scared Pepito had gotten inside of *me,* for I couldn't stop looking at Irene, not to feast my eyes on her perfect beauty, but to look for defects and, most ominoius of all, to *find* them in great abundance. Her nose I found to be scandalously imperfect; her eyebrows were too thin and interfered with the emanations of melancholy from her eyes. Wasn't her mouth perhaps—no perhaps about it!—bigger than it should be? Next my pitiless visual tape-measure moved downwards from her neck and discovered that in one part of her dress or another there were too many folds, that her corset did not define an aesthetic profile, that she was too bent over at the waist. Likewise her dress had not been very carefully cut, her gloves had a little rip in them and her ears were too red—could it be from the heat?—and her hat was misshapen, her hair . . . But why go on? My cruel survey spared nothing and pursued defects even to her least visible parts. When I found the defects, a certain impious satisfaction calmed my spirit and relieved my headache . . .How very stupid, all that effort of mine, and how I laughed at myself later! Nothing human could stand up to such an analysis anyway! But it is a miserable thing to take such bitter pleasure in criticism and to be egged on by one's own mind to tear the petals from the very flower one is admiring. It's better to be a child and contemplate in wide-eyed wonder the imperfectness of a crude toy, or to settle permanently for a spot as an ordinary foot-soldier in the human legions. All of this leads me to suspect that the notion of an aesthetic ideal is just a convention, born of finiteness or individual inclination. I wonder if foolish people are right to laugh at us: or (to say the same thing) if fools are not really the wise ones after all.

"Poor dear Máximo!" Irene said to me unexpectedly, as the curtain was falling. "Isn't your headache any better?"

These words bit me like a cat-o'-nine-tails. I looked at her and at that moment she seemed perfect; and I felt, in equally absolute degree, clumsy, malicious, and knock-kneed, both physically and psychologically.

"It hurts a lot . . . the heat . . . the noise."

At that moment the audience was calling for the author, who was not St. Luke.

"Well let's go then," said Irene.

It was necessary to deceive the girls into thinking that the whole performance was over. But the elder, Belica, was quite aware of the program, and said dejectedly: "They haven't got to the slaughter yet . . ."

Irene convinced them that there was no more, and we left.

"I'll put some soothing compresses on your head," said the schoolmistress as we crossed the Calle de Santa Águeda.

She was going to put compresses on me! When I heard her say that she seemed not just perfect, but entirely ideal, the sister or niece of the heavenly angels who tend the ailing saints and give them their arm to help them walk, the ones who bind the wounds and care for those who were martyrs, whenever their wounds become troublesome again.

"Those sedative compresses don't do me much good. We'll just see if I can sleep for a while."

"Are you going to *your* house?"

"No; I'll stretch out on the sofa in José María's study."

69

And so I did. Quite late into the night, when I woke up and they brought me a cup of tea, and when my head had cleared, I felt a strong desire to see Irene, but I didn't dare ask after her. When I went out to the others, ready to leave for home, Doña Jesusa, in what seemed a bit of mind-reading, said to me:

"That girl, that young Irene is worth her weight in gold. She's so good! She was sewing until just a while ago. Now she's gone off to her room. But don't think she's sleeping. She's reading in bed."

As I passed her door I could see the light coming through the transom. The lights *were burning in her room! What could she be reading?*

XV
WHAT COULD SHE BE READING?

THIS QUESTION WAS the object of my profound cavilings during the time it took me to walk home. The enigma pursued me even until I went to sleep, after having read (I too!) for a while. And what did I read? I opened some especially beloved books—I can't remember which ones—and imbibed a deep draught of poetry and ideals.

As I awoke I asked myself again: "What could she have been reading?" And in class, as I went through my presentation, I could glimpse through its clauses and thoughts, like light filtered through a thick screen, the same question about what Irene was reading.

My professional duties completed, I went for lunch to my brother's house; you will notice how attractive that dwelling had become for me, even though at first I had been so repelled by it, because its inhabitants had so upset my normal routine. But I was beginning to fashion a second routine for my life, adjusting to the surroundings and atmosphere. It is a fundamental truth: we are shaped by the world, not vice-versa.

My visits to my brother's house were made easy by its proximity to my own; in 6 minutes and 560 steps I could cover the distance, following a route that seemed heavenly, as it went through the Calles del Espíritu Santo, San Pablo, San Joaquín, San Mateo, and San Lorenzo. It was a walk through the pages of *The Christian Year*. And his house looked so pretty, with its nine balcony railings lined up straight, looking like a musical staff! And how interesting I found the shop, the samples, and the show windows of the stucco-plasterer who occupied the ground floor! The great whitish stairwell welcomed me with fatherly embrace, and as I went in I was welcomed by the eternal, never-failing Amphytrion of that house: the strong smell of ink-black coffee. It was a smell associated with all the images and ideas and doings of the family; even today, whenever I live those days in memory, that smell forms a sort of sensorial background, enwrapping and perfuming my recollections.

71

The first person I came upon was Rupertico, who was turning somersaults, kissing me, and calling me *Taita*. That day he said to me, "Mistress Lica has gotten up today."

I went in to see her. Doña Cándida was there, all sugary amiability, attending to Lica, arranging the pillows in her armchair, shutting the doors to keep out drafts, and all the while devoting her whole attention to the child and the wet nurse. The rules and precepts issued constantly by Caligula with the object of the perfect health of baby and nurse would fill all the pages of the *Civil and Criminal Code*. Caligula had hired the wet nurse and chosen her uniform, which had more festoons than a catafalque; she had on red necklaces and all the rest which makes up the standard outfit of these women from the River Pas. It was Caligula who had established the schedule of feedings and regulated the voluminous food intake of the human cow, whose voracity cannot even be imagined. She had taken charge of all matters of little garments, belly-bands, and blankets for my tender godson.

"He's got your mother's face entirely," she said to me, "and I think he'll turn out to be a wise man like you. Did you ever see anything more precious than this little angel?"

I thought the child quite ugly. For a nose he had the typical Manso trumpet, and a bad-humored way about him, and a sour look, such an unpleasant smirk that I imagined he was calling down curses on Doña Cándida's tiresome compliments.

The old woman was everywhere at once, attending to everything; and when the baby took it into his head to sneeze one of those little birdlike sneezes the way babies do, my gadfly instantly put her hands on her head, closed the doors, and scolded us because she said we caused drafts as we moved about the room. When Maximín yawned, opening his toothless, outsize mouth, she would immediately shout, "Nurse, nurse, feeding time!!"

The wet nurse was chunky and untamed, with a very dark complexion and great frightening eyes that looked at people in total absorption, as if she had never seen anything but animals. She was amazed by everything she saw, and spoke in a sort of growl, half-Castilian, half-Basque, which only my gadfly understood. If her rude mask revealed anything at all, it was the savage's astuteness and distrust. When, following Doña Cándida's orders, she would take the baby to suckle him and pulled laboriously from her bodice a great dark bag, I thought the thing was going to sound forth like the bagpipes from my native Asturias. Lica was very pleased with the nurse, and out of earshot of the girl Doña Cándida would say, radiating pride:

"She's one of a kind, absolutely . . . I'm telling you, Lica, she's a real find . . . You can thank me. I sought her the way you'd seek the Holy Grail. Her milk is so rich! And she's so respectful. She's just dreadfully respectful. Quiet as a mouse."

Weak and lazier than ever, but still cheerful and happy, my sister-in-law expressed her gratitude in affectionate words, and Caligula would answer back:

"How well you are now! What good color you have! You really look very nice."

And Lica said to me, as usual:

"Máximo, tell me about something."

"What do you think this dreary man can tell you about?" buzzed my gadfly with roguish humor. "Let him start with his philosophy and we'll all go to sleep."

Despite this sarcasm, I did tell Lica about things—theaters, the latest news, what was happening in Cuba.

The hairdresser came in to do Chita's hair; during this time she obliged me to give an account of all the theatrical performances of the last two weeks. I hadn't been to a single one, so I told her whatever came into my head. Chita, just like her sister Lica, was passionately fond of dramas, and hated music and popular comedies. They couldn't enjoy any spectacle unless they saw the glitter of swords and lances, full-bearded actors dressed in green or encased in tinplate imitation armor. They hated the plainness of prose, and would go to sleep unless the actors declaimed with hiccoughing intakes of air and heavy emphasis on the rhymes. Chita bought copies of all the dramas in the modern repertoire, and the two sisters would read them with delight, while sipping coffee. Later one could see the books lying about, on the mantelpiece, on the lamp table, on the footstools or the floor. Sometimes they were still in one piece, and sometimes torn into acts and scenes and single sheets all over the place, the *catastrophe* mixed up with the *protasis,* and the *anagnorisis* with the *peripety.* On that particular day, besides the *dramatic* confusion, I observed in the sitting room the mess which no longer surprised me since it was there every day: coffee cups left around on footstools and end tables, some with just the settlings from the sugar, others half-consumed and cold as ice; on one chair, a lady's hat; on the floor, a coat; on the chimneypiece a boot; a prayer book on a plate; and coffee spoons in a porcelain bud-vase.

The sitting room had been fitted out hurriedly by a decorating contractor, who brought in expensive yet ordinary things at twice their fair price. Doña Cándida had taken charge of buying all the curtains and also several knickknacks on the mantelpiece, which she represented as the kind of bargains one rarely finds. One day when I wasn't there, an art dealer showed up—at Doña Cándida's behest, I think—and managed to palm off on Lica a half-dozen worthless paintings, which everyone in the house considered admirable for the bright, rabid colors in which the clothes were painted, admittedly with a certain flair.

There was a musical clock which let loose a toccata every hour; but after a week it quit, and there was no human agency capable of making it play, or even strike the hour again. And since the other clocks in the house ran in a frightful anarchy, one never knew what time it was; the hours had gone on strike and the minutes were in open revolt.

"Máximo, what time is it? . . . Dearie, go see what José María is doing. He's been in the study the whole blessed morning with Sáinz del Bardal. I know this is the day the mail arrives from Cuba, but it must be lunchtime by now."

In the study I found José María, very busy with the mail from Cuba. Sáinz del Bardal was helping him, and between them they had already written enough letters to fill the packet-boat.

"You realize, don't you," said my brother, "that I am quite sure of being elected to one of the vacant seats for Cuba. The Minister has insisted on my candidacy. He really twisted my arm. How can I refuse? And then, the people in Cuba write in support, too. Just look at all these letters from Sagua . . . Just imagine . . . they say that I'm the only one who inspires their trust . . . I'm really very obliged to those gentlemen . . . My dear Sáinz, take a rest; we can go have lunch. Hey, chums, let's all go eat!"

And so we ate. José María was so eager for his election, and about political life in general, that even at table he didn't let up, and leaning a newspaper against a goblet, he read in nibbles and sips, as it were, the report of the previous day's parliamentary session.

"That Cimarra," he said coming up for air, "is really a remarkable man. They say that he leads an immoral life . . . But look here: I refuse to stick my nose into a man's private life, don't you agree? Cimarra is really energetic and able, and a loyal friend. We were together last night in the Minister's office till 2 o'clock . . . And now that I think of it, we spoke of you, brother. It's about time you moved up to a University chair, and it might even be that after a while you'd get as high as Director of Public Instruction. Hey, hey!

No modest protests! You're really a disaster. With that kind of an attitude, you'll never get anywhere."

And when my brother had engulfed himself again in the newspaper—one of the Party's papers—the poet took me in charge to tell me, without missing a swallow, of the progress of the philanthropic society of which he was secretary. One of the committees had already made a report. The debates on it would be very hard-fought. It had to be voted on by each individual, and opinion on the Executive Committee was very divided.

It had to do with a very important problem, a failure to resolve which would leave the society without a solid base to rest upon: the point at issue was the degree of success that could be achieved by a philanthropic campaign without any change in the current relationship between capital and labor, and without legislative action which once and for all . . .

The damned fellow wanted to give me a summary of the report, but I cut him off; I was afraid my meal might not be properly digested. We all went back to the study. Sáinz del Bardal, who had offered his services as secretary to his patron, continued writing letters and José María, as he smoked, gave me a clearer idea of the vanity and ambition which had taken hold of him. For although he made a great show of being simple and retiring, it was perfectly obvious that he was yearning for political celebrity. Good old José! I imagined him in the front bench, at the head of his party, faction, or little group. They would be called the *Mansists*. When I said this he laughed heartily, revealing through his joviality how pleased he was by my brief fantasy.

"They've done it all *for* me," he said, "I haven't raised a finger, or asked for anything . . . But they insist . . . It's a real honor for me, and I'm truly grateful . . . Last night I received the most respectful note from the Minister . . . He just won't leave me alone . . . I don't seek out anyone; they come looking for me. I prefer just to be a stay-at-home, and they won't let me."

This show of modesty was a new symptom of the political infection from which José was beginning to suffer; it is very much in character for ambitious persons to act as if they seek nothing, ask for nothing, and want only to stay within their own four walls. As an excuse for their intrigues they always give the explanation that they are wooed and forced against their will into being great men. Alongside this symptom I also noticed in my brother the no less obvious one of constantly using certain little tag lines and speech patterns characteristic of politicians. The ease with which he assimilated these commonplaces was proof that his was a genuine calling. He'd say: *We are at the brink of realizing; the gentlemen seated on the opposite benches; matters have reached the point of no return; first we must build a nation; there's more than meets the eye; the minority party is out for blood*; etc. He would refer to a speaker's oratorical failures as *gorings,* and use the word *corralled* to describe a Minister who was threatened with a serious interpellation. (Our Parliament, so accomplished in high-flown oratory, also has its low-life side.) Nor did my neophyte statesman fail to pick up any of the profound apothegms which are the only evidence of intellectual activity in many notable men; for example: *Things will fall to the side toward which they are leaning.*

In his habits as well one could perceive his rapid conversion to a new style of life and thought. Poor Lica had already begun to complain of her husband's long absences; for whenever he hadn't any guests of his own, he would eat out, and come home at two in the morning. When he *was* at home he had started to act just the tiniest bit sharp-tongued and gruff, very hard to please in all matters relating to social details and the management of the household. The slightest slip by one of the servants brought down harsh scoldings upon Lica; and I shall omit the details of the painful episodes the poor woman had to endure in her efforts to reform her rusticity and forget all her Cuban vocabulary, and think and speak only in a European way. Docile and studious, she paid such close attention to her husband's harsh reprimands that she did learn to reform her manners and speech, and stopped calling frocks *dresses* and petticoats *slips* and bustles *back-pads.* About the same time Castilian diction also began to take over in the names used for people, so that Lica was now called Manuela, her sister became Mercedes, and the elder daughter who had been named Isabel after my mother, lost her nickname Belica. Only *Niña Chucha* resisted these new designations, for as she said, to lose her way of speaking would be like tossing into the streets of Madrid the last thing left to her from her beloved homeland.

And that very same morning I observed there in José María's study other signs of dementia which made me very sad indeed, for they left no doubt in my mind that his disease was malignant and that soon he would be beyond hope of saving. On the table there were samples of heraldic devices made up in different colors. This and some rumors that had reached my ears (and those of a newspaper columnist who put the rumors into print) confirmed my suspicion. No longer able to contain my curiosity, I asked:

"But is it really true that you're going to acquire a title?"

"Oh, I don't know . . . To tell you the truth . . . All this business is a great bother . . . ," he answered, somewhat disturbed. "It's at *their* insistence; I'm resisting the idea. And then, the Party members have taken it up as a matter of their own . . . It's really just foolishness, but how can I refuse to do it for them? It would be quite ridiculous . . . At any rate, old chum, do me a favor and don't waste my time! We're really swamped with this mail from Cuba."

I left him with his letters and his secretary-poet. Soon I would be the brother of the Marquess of Casa-Manso or some such thing. Actually, the question was entirely immaterial to me, and I shouldn't have been concerned about such a thing. But I gave it some thought because it offered confirmation of the diagnosis I had made of my brother's growing madness. The detail of a noble title was an utterly telling phenomenon in his psychological process, in the mental evolution of his vanity. José was reproducing in his personal development the series of general phenomena which characterize these eclectic oligarchies, themselves the product of a state of intellectual and political crisis linking a world now destroyed and a world just now being formed. It's a curious thing to study the philosophy of history in one individual, one corpuscle, one cell. Just as in the natural sciences, one must use a microscope.

There is no doubt about it: everything seems to call for, or even presage, a change or transformation that will be the greatest in history. Everything points to it: these transitional monarchies, hanging by a legalistic hair; this system of responsibilities and powers, resting on a loose rope held by rhetorical maneuverings; this society which tears the old aristocracy to bits and creates a new one out of men who've spent their youth behind a shop-counter; these Latin nations which fill their lungs with the air of equality, carrying that principle not only to their laws but to the formation of the most formidable armies the world has ever seen; these times we see and live in, both as victims of the aftertaste of tyranny and also as the masters of something new, as we become part of a sovereignty which slowly informs our existence. My brother, who had washed dishes and rolled cigarettes and whipped blacks, sold hats and shoes, been sutler to the army and trafficked in manure, was about to enter the select front ranks of national leaders, the image of established political power, and, as it were, the guarantee of its solidity and permanence. We must say, as someone already has, that "either the Universe is becoming unhinged, or the Son of God is perishing."

As these thoughts ran through my head I went to Irene's room, but I forgot it all as soon as I saw her. Without even hearing her reply to my initial greeting, I asked her:

XVI
"WHAT WERE YOU READING LAST NIGHT?"

AND LIKE A PERSON whose cherished secret is all at once revealed, she gave a start and was unable to answer. She made two or three evasive remarks, and then asked me something or other in her turn. I interpreted her confusion in a way favorable to me personally, and I said to myself: "Perhaps she was reading something of mine." But instantly realizing that I hadn't written any work of a diverting character, she would have had to be reading my *Notes on Psychogenesis and Neurosis* or my *Commentary on DuBois-Reymond* or my translation of Wundt or maybe my articles refuting *transformism* and the crazy ideas of Haeckel. It was precisely the aridity of these subject matters which provided a subtle explanation for the blushings and the displeasure I noticed on my friend's face, for "doubtless"—I reasoned—"she is unwilling to admit having read such things in order not to seem like a pedantic bluestocking."

The two little girls ran toward me. They were as charming as could be; they said they were my sweethearts and fought for my kisses. Pepito also came jumping and running to greet me. He was only three, and wasn't studying anything; they had him there so that he'd be under control and not make a disturbance elsewhere in the house. He was an amusing little creature who thought of nothing but food, and engaged furiously in the struggle for survival. When I asked him what he wanted to be when he grew up he said a *candy-man*. Isabelita and Jesusita were very judicious; they did their studying devotedly and wrote in their copybooks with that childish kind of effort which gives lots of exercise to the muscles of the mouth and the eyes.

The schoolroom was the only orderly place in the house, and also the room with the worst light; one had to light the lamps at three in the afternoon. What a lovely tint of poetical, statuesque serenity you took on, pale schoolmistress, in the discreet glow of the flame and the dying brightness of the day! Because of you my soul went a-straying from its normal course, bounding off in childish wanderings and flights, totally unsuited to a well-

79

bred person. The schoolroom had once served as a dining room and was papered in a design made to imitate woodgrain with nailed-on moldings. On a low platform stood the desk where the girls worked; a short distance away there was a big table, a large gutta-percha settee, and some black chairs. On the wall hung some new maps and two very old ones—Oceania and the Holy Land—which I recalled having seen at Doña Cándida's house. I can only surmise that my gadfly had palmed off those two maps on Lica, charging her the same kind of price she got for the other bargains she regularly brought to the house.

"Now then, Isabel," Irene was saying, "let's check our irregular verbs."

The occasion and the place made it necessary for me to be totally serious; thus, in order to come close to Irene in spirit, I would have to assist her in her scholastic task, helping with conjugations and declensions or sharing with her the descriptions of the world in the geography lesson. Sacred history took a large part of our time, and the life of Joseph and his brothers, as I told it, held a very lively charm for the girls, and even for their schoolmistress. Then there were French lessons, and I helped them a bit with their compositions, and also with Spanish syntax and analogy, departments of learning in which their teacher herself, one may say impartially, was, like good old Homer, subject to nodding *aliquando.*

While the girls were writing, there was a little more free time. Isabel and Jesusa would smudge their fingers with ink as they wrote. To keep him still, Pepito had to be given a pencil and paper on which he drew lines and hieroglyphics, off in his corner, coming back every few moments to show me his achievements, which he called horses, donkeys, and houses. Irene was taking a break, and picked up her tatting, making knots with the shuttle. I watched her fingers; they were lovely. By doing that handwork she aided herself, increasing her miserably small income. Blessed industriousness, the crowning glory, the final touch on her multiplicity of winning ways! As I inspected the girls' penmanship sheets, I would say constantly: "Narrow strokes, dears; now wider; press down now . . ."

All of a sudden, an inner urge made me turn to Irene and ask:

"Are you contented with this life?"

And she shrugged her shoulders, looked at me, smiled . . . and why not say so, if I wish the purest truth to shine forth in my story? Yes, I seemed to perceive weariness and boredom in her. But her words, full of deep significance, revealed to me how rapidly her strong will had triumphed over faint-heartedness.

"One must take life as it comes. I'm contented, Maximo: what more can I desire for the moment?"

"You are called to a grand destiny, Irene . . . Jesusita, for Heaven's sake, don't *paint,* don't *paint;* make a free stroke of the pen and let it come out as it will. If it's not right, try again and so on again . . . the superior qualities which shine forth in you . . . But Isabel, what're you doing with your elbow? Reaching for the ceiling? Goodness! It looks as though you wanted to hug the whole table! . . . Not so much ink in your pen, my child. It's dripping . . . Elbow! Elbow! Quite so, your superior qualities . . ."

And I stopped there, for in a way similar to what had happened in the theater the day before, I felt my mind obstructed. It was as if certain special ideas refused to let themselves be expressed and were hiding in shame, fleeing the words that were trying to pull them out by force. Common flattery was repugnant to my sensibilities; I don't know why, but my taste in literature had taken a cruel role in all of this. And since at the same time I was unable to find a select and graceful formula for my thoughts, one with a really exquisite and original design, some expression that would put an unbridgeable distance between my sensitivity and that of striplings and college boys, I was reduced to striking a grandiose posture of silence, adding to it a mere brushstroke of praise from time to time.

"Irene, you rank among the greatest perfections I know of."

She kept making knots and more knots, answering my praises only with other equally hyperbolic ones of me, so much so that I found them offensive. To hear her tell it, I was the perfected man, the man without blemish, the unique man. Not to mention all the praises she had heard from everyone who had had dealings with me! . . . . No, it just wasn't possible for such perfection to exist in a human person, and anyone who knew me really well would just *have* to find some slight defect. Answering her back, I think I was apt, and even somewhat sparkling, having decided to toss out some leading remarks which I think she understood perfectly. And then more praise of me from her, especially of those things she considered very special qualities of mind. "You are really *something,*" she said, and after this sentence we both fell into a long silence.

It was a beautiful afternoon, and we went out for a stroll. I can't remember whether it was that afternoon or another one that I returned home with

81

the idea and intention not to rush into the execution of my plan until time and a long relationship might show me clearly the nature of the ground I was treading.

"No, it won't be advantageous to go too fast," I thought. "Facts, just facts will guide me and the chain of observed phenomena will trace a secure path for me. Let us go forward in this most important matter using that same methodical rigor we use even in trivial things. In that way I'll be certain not to make any mistakes. I'll put some brakes on my feelings, for they could let me be carried away impetuously. It's better to continue my observations. Do I really know her well? No, each day I sense something in her that remains hidden from my view. What I see most clearly is her prodigious tact, for she says only what suits her best, concealing the rest. Let's give time a chance to work. For just as steady contact will uncover those inner regions still hidden in the mist, so a continuing acquaintance, and the frequent conversation implied thereby, will spontaneously bring her to a realization of my intentions and bring me to a perception of her acquiescence, all of it without recourse to all that pretentious verbiage which is so repugnant to my own intellectual and aesthetic standards."

And as I purposed, I did. On many mornings I attended the lessons and went walking many afternoons, affecting indifference and even curtness. I came to like her dignified reserve more and more. One day we were caught in a rain shower in the Retiro Park. I hailed a carriage and the five of us were thus packed into it, heading off for home. We were dripping wet, and our clothing was soaked. I was very upset; I was fearful that she and the children might catch cold.

"Don't worry about me," Irene said. "I've never had a sick day. I'm so healthy, it's really . . . *something.*"

Blessed Providence, to add good health to all this creature's other eminent gifts, enabling her to respond more fully to the human purposes of family life! Whoever is lucky enough to be husband to that elect among the elect will never be obliged to entrust the upbringing of his children to a surrogate or mercenary mother; he will never see enthroned in his home that monster called the wet nurse, curse of motherhood and of the present age.

"Take care of yourself, Irene, take care of yourself," I said with eager foresightedness, "so that your splendid health may never be upset."

For two days in succession I failed to go to my brother's house. Was it coincidence or astute planning? The reader may believe what he wishes. My methodical affection still had its tactical features, and some knowledge of the amorous ambush. When I did go there, after an absence that seemed so long to me, I discovered an expression of very lively joy on Irene's face.

"It seems to me," I put in, "as if we've not seen each other for two centuries . . . I've thought of you so much! . . . We spoke yesterday . . . We didn't *see* each other, but I said this and that and the other thing to you."

"You are . . . really *something.*"

"I shouldn't like to make a mistake, but I think I perceive a note of sadness in you. Has something unpleasant happened?"

"No, not a thing," she answered quickly, giving a little start.

"Well, it just seemed . . . No, you can't be satisfied with this kind of life, this routine so unsuited to a superior being."

"Well, it's obvious that I'm not," she said vehemently.

"Speak openly with me, let all your thoughts come out; don't conceal a thing from me . . . This life of yours . . ."

"Is really *something.*"

"You deserve something else, and what you deserve you shall have. It can't be any other way."

"How could I possibly spend all my youth teaching children to scrawl?"

"And acting as nanny?"

"And teaching about things I don't understand?"

And she cast such a scornful look toward the books on the nearby table, that they seemed to me to be grieved and confounded under the weight of a major excommunication.

"You are wearying of this, aren't you? You're too intelligent, too beautiful, to live on a daily wage."

In a sweet glance she expressed her gratitude for my having interpreted her feelings so well.

"This will come to an end, Irene. I assure . . . "

"If it weren't for you, Máximo," she said in accents of generous friendship, "I should have left this place."

"But what is it? . . . don't you like the family?"

"No . . . I mean yes, but no . . . no," she said, contradicting herself with almost every word.

"There must be something . . . "

"No, no; I tell you there isn't anything."

"We've known each other a long time. Can it be that you don't trust me as I deserve?"

"Yes, I do, I will," she replied, taking courage. "You are my only friend, my protector . . . You . . ."

What a lovely spontaneity spread over her face! Truth was stirring in her mouth.

"I'm so concerned for you, for your happiness and your future that . . ."

"I realize that, and so I'll have to discuss some things with you, oh it's really *something!*"

"Something!"

I attached no great importance to the word, since Irene used it in every circumstance.

"I swear to you," she added, crossing her hands and looking so beautiful, so astonishing in her emotion, candor and piety. "I swear to do nothing except what you order me to do."

"Well . . ."

My heart was leaping out of me in that *well*. I don't know how far I might have gone if Lica hadn't opened the door at that moment.

"Máximo," she said without stepping in, "come here, dearie . . ."

She wanted me to compose the invitations for that evening. Poor Lica, how angry she made me with her bad timing! I didn't see Irene again that afternoon, but I was just as happy as if I were in front of her, listening endlessly to her conversation. The little speech, whose first word was all I had spoken, echoed in me as if I had delivered it a hundred times and received from her a hundred times in turn the beautiful approbation I was hoping for.

XVII
I CARRIED HER WITH ME

IT WAS AS IF her nature had been miraculously engrafted into my own. I could feel her within me, spirit next to spirit, and I felt a joy which became even livelier that evening when I went to the Thursday gathering. This radiant joy poured forth from me like something inspired and sparkling. It burst from my lips, my eyes, and even from my pores, I think. I was suddenly filled with optimism akin to the delirium of a feverish person, and everything seemed beautiful and pleasing to me, like a projection of myself. I conversed with everyone and everyone was transfigured in my eyes, which, like Don Quixote's, made castles out of country inns. My brother seemed another Bismarck to me; Cimarra far outpaced Cato; the poet eclipsed Homer; Pez was a Malthus in statistics and a J. S. Mill in political ideas; and my sister-in-law Manuela was the most aristocratic, refined, elegant, distinguished woman ever to tread upon a carpet. To give a clear idea of the extent of the diseased aberrations into which my wild optimism led me, I need only say that even the poet heard benevolent words from my lips, and that I almost promised to devote some attention to his poems in a forthcoming book of literary criticism. This rendered him widly ecstatic, and as the conversation turned from one celebrity to another, he affirmed that I left Kant and Schelling and all the fathers of philosophy far behind me. His unmerited flattery opened my eyes and acted as a corrective to my optimistic debility. I believe there was some physical disorder inside me, some unknown softening of those organs most closely related to one's strength of character. Sáinz del Bardal gave me an interminable *solo* regarding the enormous progress being made by the Society for Industrial Invalids, and this also was very useful in restoring me to my normal state. In the service of said Society the poet was performing at a feverish, demented level of activity. He was in several places at the same time, trying to organize the work, increase the number of members, and obtain official government recognition. He had managed to recruit three ex-ministers and another well-known Madrid personage, a tireless propagandist who gave six speeches per week to different organizations.

It was all going ahead admirably, and would go even more admirably when the plans of the charitable founders were fully developed. For the time being it had been agreed to earmark the considerable funds already raised for the purpose of publishing the very remarkable speeches which had been delivered at the turbulent meetings. (What a great pity if such admirable pieces of eloquence should be lost! Spain is, above all else, the classic land of oratory.) The regular voting members and the majority of the Committee had not succeeded in reaching agreement on this delicate point, but to settle the matter a Joint Committee had been appointed, made up of people from Publicity and Action, to write up a new report. This august body had met and decided that the first step would be to set up a poetry contest for the best *Ode to Labor*. The first-prize poem would be awarded a golden cauliflower and a free printing of five hundred copies; the runner-up would win a silver sunflower and two hundred copies. I could see the dark clouds coming as soon as I heard of these baneful plans, and sure enough, I was named president of the panel of judges. They were also considering a giant raffle, to be organized by the ladies, and also a splendid, resounding *evening* or perhaps *matinée,* at which—after Sáinz del Bardal had read the record of the Society's achievements—there would be music, speeches, and poetry readings, the very salt and savor of these philanthropic festivities.

As best I could, I shooed away the horse-fly who was perplexing me, and I took a turn through the various rooms. Suddenly I felt a little clap on the shoulder and a pleasant voice saying:

"Hello, maestro . . . I saw you with Typhus and didn't want to approach."

"Oh, Peña! What an attack he gave me; I think it'll take me all night to recover . . . Let's sit down; I feel weak."

"That's the *febris carnis* . . . I don't even give Sáinz del Bardal an opening. When he zooms in on me, I just turn my back. If he still speaks to me I throw carbolic acid at him—that's to say I call him an idiot."

"But what've you been up to?"

"This and that, maestro . . . Let's get out of here. Let's *huddle* in this sitting room alongside."

"What've you got to tell me?"

"Nothing special."

"Is it true you're no longer courting Amalia Vendesol?"

86

"Ugh, maestro! That was over and done with a thousand years ago. She's unbearable. So demanding and touchy all the time! For example: if I didn't visit her every single day, Holy Mary, what a fit she'd throw! If my attention wandered in the Retiro and I looked at somebody . . . ! In short, she's got a worse temper than her Aunt Rosaura, who put out her husband's eye in a jealous rage. I've seen Amalia bite into a fan and make fifty pieces of it . . . Would you believe why? Because one night I couldn't get odd-numbered seats at the Comedia Theater and we had to sit in the even numbers. And what an education, Manso my friend! She writes an awful scrawl, she says *perdominance*, and puts in h's all over the place!"

"Like all women . . . well, like most of them. And so it's true you've turned your attentions to one of the Pez girls?"

"There they are, the two of them. Did you see? I have a good time with them, especially with the younger one, who's quite amusing. They're well brought-up, I mean they have a certain veneer . . ."

"You're right, just a veneer. They are ignorant of everything one can be ignorant of; but something of what they've heard people say has stuck, and they seem like real women. Actually all they are is dolls, the kind who say *papa* and *mamma*."

"Ah, but they don't say *papa* and *mamma*; they say *hubby, hubby*. The older one, especially, doesn't miss a trick. The things she knows about! Last night I was terrified to hear her talk. I really can't decide whether they're cute and charming, or a couple of crashing bores. They have in them something like iridescent particles or the shine of lusterware. They can bore you silly or dazzle you, by turns; they're tiresome yet captivating. They inspire both amusement and affection. The older one, Adela, is inconceivably vain. If a prince were to propose to her, even that might not be good enough."

"Just wait and see; she'll end up marrying a very distinguished . . . lieutenant."

"Right. She's so stuck-up! And some of it has rubbed off on the younger sister, too. There you have 'em! With that stiff old mamma of theirs; why, she looks like a figure pulled out of a medieval painting . . ."

"And their puffed-up papa, the epitome of bombast and pretension . . ."

"But doesn't their luxurious life sort of catch your eye?"

"Nothing having to do with human stupidity catches my eye any more."

"It's a mysterious, unaccountable luxury. What's behind it all? Señor de Pez's 12,000 peseta salary, and nothing else?"

"Madrid is a chasm of unanswered questions."

"I think the girls' pretensions leave mamma and papa far behind. The law of inherited characteristics has been fulfilled to excess. I don't know who's going to have to put up with those two little numbers. The poor fellow who marries either one of 'em might as well count on marrying the dressmakers and upholsterers, and theater-owners, and Binder the coach-maker, and Worth with his dresses, and every destroyer of humanity. Those girls have become so accustomed to luxury that they'll never find anybody with enough hard cash to keep them. Maestro, this whole situation is beyond redeeming; there's going to be a tremendous collapse. People talk about young men and how corrupted *they* are, and how alienated *they* are from their families; they say that we have antidomestic tendencies because we've been students and frequented cafés and casinos. But, what about the girls? The maidens of our Latin countries are so frivolous and spoiled and enamored of false refinement that they can hardly be counted on to shape the families of the future. What's going to come of it? The destruction of the family, a society based on atomistic individualism, a wild pluralism without harmony or unity, the power of the nation in the hands of women . . .?"

"Ah, the eternal female," I said gravely, "has laws which must be fulfilled. Don't be a pessimist, and don't generalize on the basis of facts which, though numerous, are still isolated."

"Isolated!!"

"You know little of the world. You're a child. Up till now innocence consisted in being unacquainted with evil; now that the age of paradoxes is fully upon us, the condition of innocence is usually accompanied by knowledge of all the vices and ignorance of virtue; and virtue herself fails to shine forth, but rather hides, like everyone who is in a minority. Believe this, do believe it, for it comes from the heart."

And taking hold of the buttonhole in his lapel—how well I remember that!—I continued my remarks to him as follows:

". . . There are great treasures, great blessings, much good fortune that you can't yet see, for your eyes are blinded by innocence, and the resplendency of evil keeps you from seeing anything else. There are exceptional beings, gifted creatures, blessed with all of the perfections Nature can create, and all the exquisite refinements education can offer. The holy and solid principle of universal harmony would be shaken to its foundations if things

88

were otherwise. And without harmony we might as well say good-bye to variety and the higher unity . . ."

"I can't argue with that . . ."

And distractedly, though still attentive to my words, he stuck his hand in his coat-tail pocket and pulled out a slim tobacco-case.

"Oh! I'd forgotten you don't smoke. I'm just dying for a smoke myself. With your permission, maestro, I'm going back in there to light up a cigarette. Coming along?"

I didn't follow him because my curiosity had been drawn to a group that had gathered around my brother. I thought I heard words of congratulation, and Señor de Pez had taken on such a protective air that I wonder the whole human race didn't prostrate themselves in contrition and gratitude at his feet.

The cause of all the congratulating and the boisterous disturbance was the receipt of a cable from Cuba declaring José María's election assured.

XVIII
"REALLY AND TRULY, GENTLEMEN . . ."

SAID MY BROTHER; and obstructed in his exordium by that mental blockage he always suffered at critical moments, he repeated after a few moments:

"Really and truly . . ."

He was at length able to formulate a flowery speech of sorts, whose clauses came out in spurts like water from a fountain whose spout is clogged with a pebble. I drew closer and caught odd snatches like these: "I don't wish to leave my own four walls . . ., it is also possible to serve the nation from a corner of one's home . . . But these gentlemen insist . . . I'm indebted to the good will of these gentlemen . . . In short, it's a real sacrifice for me, but I'm really and truly prepared to defend the sacred interests . . ."

From that moment the evening took on a political tone and gave it an extraordinary brilliance. Present were three ex-ministers and many deputies and journalists, all talking nonstop. The card room looked like a corner of the great Lecture Hall. The most racket of all was being made by the members of *Rampant Democracy,* a party as young as it was restless. José had joined it because of his preference for anything that might result in a *deal.*

José's spirit of reconciliation reaches delirium: he has dreams of joining and pairing the most disparate things. This, he says, is *the real English way.* He never ceases talking of *the successive series of deals:* it is his political *Our Father,* and with it he makes universal compromises, never failing to find ways of applying his bridge-building ideals. There exists no historic or fatal rivalry to which he hesitates to apply the remedy of a Vergara embrace.* That's the answer: embraces between separatism and nationalism, insurrection and the military, the monarchy and the republic, the Church and freethinkers, aris-

---

*A facile and superficial solution. The reference is to the Peace of Vergara (1839), which brought an end to the First Carlist War, but settled nothing.

tocracy and egalitarians. Any pure idea is for him *unquestionably excessive,* and he cuts off discussions by saying: *That's quite enough exclusivism.* He thinks it's not proper that there should be exclusivity in art or religion or philosophy. Every idea, every theory of art or morals should surrender part of its sovereign territory to the opposite idea or theory. Beauty cannot exist if it doesn't mix with the commonplace in a Vergara embrace. Jesus and the Popes are out of line, exclusivists: they haven't made a deal with heresy.

The foolishness of those people was so tiresome for me that I left the salon and went to the inner part of the house. Fed up with poets, journalists, and politicians, I longed for the solace of a chat with Doña Jesusa. In the remote room where she lived I found her that night, motionless in her armchair, wrapped in her shawl and accompanied by Rupertito, to whom she was telling tales.

"I don't want to go to bed," she said, "because the hullaballoos in the big room and all the noise from the servants going back and forth would keep me awake. On Thursday nights this house is like a sugar mill going full-tilt. Lord, it's a regular earthquake! You don't like it either; I know you don't. And the food these folks eat! The tea and sweets and cold meat and pastries and ices they've had already would feed an army. Poor Lica can't stand up to all this; if it goes on she'll get sick . . . Let me tell you about last night, if you'll promise to keep it to yourself . . . Well, she and José María had a tiff; Lord, what a set-to it was! All because she didn't know how to 'do the honors.' I know perfectly well she's been babied too much. But José really threw a fit. They brought it all out in the open. That he only thinks of unimportant things. That he spends the night at the Casino, and maybe even worse places . . . Apparently he's been caught at something . . ."

She drew her chair up to mine and almost speaking into my ear she said:

"Woman stuff, d'you see? José María's like all the rest. Oh, this Madrid! A playboy in the family. Think of it, a man who's going to be in Parliament and a Minister . . . Too many temptations in Madrid! Oh, what awful women they have here in Spain! They could even pervert St. John's lamb. If *I* saw them I'd say: 'You great shameless hussies, why are you playing games with a family man, a simple, plain, good man? . . .' Because José María has always been good, up till now; but, my dear boy, he's not been like his old self for some time now."

I defended my brother as best I could, and soothed his mother-in-law by trying to convince her that our looseness in manners is more in the form than

91

in the substance, and that she oughtn't to take as evidence of sin things that were just ordinary easygoing ways . . . That was all I could think of.

Lowering her voice, she said, "I don't mix in at all. It's their business; they'll have to deal with it. I'm not leaving this chair; my health isn't up to anything at all. This evening, while they were all laughing and carousing in there, Irene and I prayed the Rosary and spoke of things gone by . . . Where is that angel of God, anyway?"

She looked all around the room.

"But surely she's retired by now," I said. "Staying up this late is *not* a habit of hers."

"Quiet, my boy, she's probably still up and about. Sometimes she goes down the corridor to see the big room for a bit."

I had already started off to look for her when she came in. Her face seemed happy and she was less pale. She seemed flustered, her eyes glowing and her cheeks reddened as if she had just run a long race.

"Irene, how are you? Did you see . . .?"

"Just a bit . . . , from the corridor . . . What luxury, what clothes! It's just dazzling!"

"I'd thought that by this time—it *is* one o'clock—you'd have re-tired."

"Well, I stayed here a while to keep Doña Jesusa company . . . And then, well, one has to see things, Manso my friend, some of the things one doesn't come in contact with."

"Oh, quite right!" I said, thinking how Irene would shine if she entered the circles of elegant society, and how her great beauty would be further enhanced by opulent clothing. "But it's a question of one's nature; neither you nor I get much pleasure out of all that. Luckily we are contented with what we have so that we don't miss those blatant, brilliant pleasures. We prefer the quiet joys of home life, our modest daily bread with its natural mixture of sorrow and joy, always keeping within the unchangeable limits of good order."

"Lord in Heaven! What a gift the man has, and how fine he says things!" exclaimed Doña Jesusa.

Irene laughed at *Niña Chucha's* enthusiasm, and indicated approval of her praises with vigorous nods of her head.

"Máximo," said Doña Jesusa abruptly, "Why don't you get married? What are you waiting so long for, my boy?"

"Oh I still have time, ma'am. We'll look into the matter . . ."

"You'll spend your whole life 'looking into the matter'!"

And looking over at Irene, who was watching intently, I said, just for something to say:

"And how are the girls?"

"They stayed awake quite late. You can understand . . . with all this racket . . . They wanted to see a bit of it too. Then they were playing and joking and celebrating, jumping from bed to bed and throwing pillows at each other . . . But now they're asleep."

"And you . . . you're not sleepy?"

"Not a bit."

"But it's so late."

"Well, yes, I *am* off to my room now."

"Are you going to read?" I asked as I followed, carrying the lamp for her.

"Oh, it's very late . . . I'll see if I can't drop right off to sleep. Tomorrow . . ."

"Tomorrow, what?"

"I was saying that tomorrow's another day, and then we'll talk about things . . ."

"We'll talk about things," I repeated while my mind felt the stimulus of what novelists call *a whole world of thoughts,* and my lips the temptation of impatient words.

"Bring me what you promised."

"What, my child?" I asked, suspecting that in an anxious moment I had promised her my very life.

"What a bad memory you have! Ahn's *English Grammar,* of course . . ."

"Oh, of course . . . All right . . . "

"And the two Eberhard Faber pencils, number two and number three."

"All right, all right, that's enough; why not ask for the sun and the moon?"

"Oh, but you're really *something* . . . G'bye."

"Don't tire your mind by reading late . . ."

"I'm falling asleep right now."

"That's it, a good rest . . . good night."

"What, you still there, Manso my friend?"

"I thought you were asleep, ma'am."

"Why no, just saying my prayers . . . Good-bye."

And I withdrew. Something stuck in my head about Irene's lighthearted joking; it seemed a bit at odds with the seriousness and control I had always observed in her. But as I thought further, I decided that such a contingent phenomenon did not alter reality in itself, or, more precisely, that a passing and circumstantial dissonance in no way destroyed the admirable harmony of her character.

By then it was time for me to leave the gathering; but Cimarra and my brother detained me, giving my modesty a frontal assault by trying to get me to turn politician and set off with them down the only path that leads to prosperity. I fought back, alleging that I had neither the character, the fitness, nor the ideas of a politician. Cimarra assured me that it would be possible to ease my entry into Parliament by arranging my election from one of the vacant constituencies. José had already said a few words to the Minister, who had replied: "Oh, yes; really and truly . . ." My brother would lend himself with great good will to smooth out the differences between my ideas and the oligarchic system now in place; he heatedly urged me to be a truly practical man, to leave behind me once and for all my utopias and absolute ideas, searching in the vast dominions of my wisdom for the formula for a deal, a way to reconcile theory and practice, thought and action.

The same opinion was expressed by the Marquess of Tellería, who happened to be present. He was a sworn enemy of all utopias, an essentially practical man, so much so that he managed to live at his fellows' expense; a great worthy who used the word *logomachy* to designate anything he didn't understand. This gentleman later performed *solo* for me, flattering me beyond all measure and telling me finally that men like myself should devote themselves to defending the interests of the productive classes against the menace of the proletariat, the enshrined beliefs of our forebears against the inroads of the barbarous freethinkers, and good practical government against the madness of theoretical ideas. I concealed with courteous phrases the scorn which this person merited at my hands. I had known him by reputation for some years, from the stories León Roch (his son-in-law and my friend) had told me. As he let me go, he said:

"I'm going to send you a small pamphlet in which I've reprinted all the speeches and all the incidents which gave rise to the draft of a bill I've presented to the Senate on the issue of vagrancy. Please do me the favor of reading it and giving me your impartial opinion."

Manuela, who had found out that they were trying to strap me into a parliamentary seat, couldn't conceal her joy. But she couldn't imagine why I refused to enter political life and, scolding me for my withdrawn personality and my love for a life of obscurity, she said:

"Oh, don't be such a stick-in-the-mud, old dear."

XIX
THE DINING-ROOM CLOCK
STRUCK EIGHT

AND PERFORMING the computations necessary, given the disordered state of the clocks in the house, I concluded that eight strokes meant three. Terribly late! For me to be going home at that hour seemed absurd, a joke, as if my time had been cruelly kidnapped from me. I saw myself as a figure in a nightmare, or as if I were another man I was dreaming of from the placid calm of my bed. I left the room. Drowsiness was giving me the symptoms of drunkenness. When I went to the dining room for a glass of water I was astounded to see that there was still light in Irene's room. The rectangle of brightness above the door drew my glance and for a brief time I was brought to a halt half-way down the corridor. "But didn't you tell me two hours ago that you were very sleepy and you were going to bed at once?" I didn't say this out loud. I asked the question from spirit to spirit, for it seemed unsuitable to cry aloud at such an hour. Was she praying? What *was* she doing? Reading novels? Devouring my philosophical works?

As I drank the water I calmed down. For really I was an intruder demanding an impossible regularity in Irene's behavior. What was so remarkable about her putting out the light two hours later than she said she would? It might be that she was mending her clothes, or preparing the next day's lessons . . . Three-thirty! How many hours' sleep did the child get, rising as she did at seven?! Quite a deplorable habit, working your brain at late night hours! Oh! In *my* family I would have all rules of hygiene most strictly observed.

At the street door young Peña joined me. Capes over our faces, we advanced against the street's icy cold.

"On your way home, maestro?"

"Where do you think I'm going, you brute? And you, where are you off to?"

"Not to bed yet! It's still early."

"You call it early, when four o'clock is about to strike?"

Walking briskly along, I gave him a tirade on his disorderly habits, especially the unhealthful one of making night into day, which causes so much illness and lack of vigor in the younger generation. He laughed.

"Out of respect for you, maestro," he said, "I'll walk you home. Then I'm going to the *Pharmacy*."

"And your mother's there at home, waiting up for you, scared to death! Manuel, what've you turned into? I can't believe you're my disciple!"

"You're a fine one to talk, maestro! You're up just as late as I am! Unforgivable in a metaphysician! Why, you've turned into a real dandy! You'll end up going to class before you go to bed. You'll appear before your pupils dressed in evening clothes! A bad example is certainly contagious!"

His little gibes threw me a bit off balance but I wouldn't give in.

"Look, you rake," I said, taking him by the arm. "Like it or not, I'm taking you home. You're *not* going to the *Pharmacy*. I command it and you must obey your teacher."

"We'll make a deal . . . Let's try to conciliate everything, as your brother says. I won't go to the *Pharmacy;* but I can't go to bed without putting something in my mouth."

"But surely you had supper at José's, you great loafer?"

"Yes . . . How can I make it clear? It's not because I'm hungry, exactly. I just want to go somewhere."

"And where do you want to go?"

"I'll forgo the *Pharmacy* provided you come along and have crullers with me."

"Where, you libertine?"

"Right here, in the fry-shop in the Calle de San Joaquín. It's a cold night, and a glass of brandy would sit well."

"Are you mad? Do you think I . . . ?"

"Come now, *magister,* be kind. You must admit that to please you I've given up going out with my friends. It'll only take ten minutes. Then we'll go home to our nice warm house like the most orderly people in the world."

And he pulled so hard on my cape to get me into that ignoble establishment that I couldn't fight back, nor did I consider it appropriate to argue any further over an action which was in truth insignificant.

"Willful!"

"Let's sit down, maestro!"

XX
I COULDN'T BELIEVE IT

I, SITTING ON A BENCH in a fry-shop at four in the morning, with a plate of fritters and a glass of brandy in front of me! Why, it was enough to make me burst out laughing, and I did. Can one ever claim to be in control of one's life, can one ever boast of subjecting life to an idea or method, without being contradicted—when one least expects it—by the despotic will of life itself and by the thousand fatal events which jump out at us from our relations in society, or sequester us like skulking bandits? Society, that rogue, with a bland and innocent gesture, had defrauded me of my philosophical serenity, and the time was coming—unless God should save me—when I would find in myself none of those traits which went to make up my strong character in happier days.

These reflections were going through my mind as I watched two couples who were seated at the tables across from us. I was amazed to find myself in such company. They were four *artistes* of the Flamenco variety, two males and two females, and they had just come in from the corner café-theater where they sang every night. The women were divertingly insolent; one a bit stout and the other more slender and "spiritual"; both wore taupe shawls and head scarves carelessly tied on and forming hoods over their foreheads. Their hands were pretty and their feet shod to perfection. The men were dressed in capes, broad-brimmed Andalusian hats, and shaggy jackets; they made the most disagreeable sight in all Creation. The four hoarse voices were carrying on a sharp, buzzing dialogue full of interjections; all one could understand were the expletives and the barbarisms. It was the first time I had been so close to types like that, and I couldn't take my eyes off them.

"The fat one is really a knockout!" Manuel said to me. "I can see you've got your eye on her!"

"I?"

"You're practically devouring her with your eyes."

"Don't be silly."

"And she's not taking it amiss, maestro. She's giving you the eye, too. What's called *flirtation* in other latitudes is known down here as *sizing up*."

"Have you finished drinking your brandy, you reprobate?" I asked him, eager to get out of there.

"Aren't you drinking?"

"I? Take away that disgusting stuff, it's poison . . ."

"You know, maestro, tonight I have a kind of nervous excitement, a burning in my blood, as if an electric current were flowing through my whole body . . . I have an appetite for action, for violence; I don't know what's happening inside me . . ."

I was watching him closely and reflecting upon the state my disciple was in, so completely new for him and so displeasing to me, who cared for him so much.

"For yes indeed, sir," he went on, "there are times when one has to do the wildest things, just to compensate for the stupid, routine dullness that makes up so much of our life; something violent, something dramatic. If you take the dramatic element out of life, you've kissed your youth good-bye. What do you say to having some fun now by my starting a row with those people?"

"Them? For God's sake, Manuel, you're not yourself. You've gone mad, or else you've drunk too much."

"After all, what would really happen? Nothing. They're cowards. We'd all go off to the city jail and tomorrow—today, I mean—you'd miss class and maybe the Rector and the Dean would have to go and get you out of the clutches of the police."

"If I had a ferule and a whip with me, I'd deal with you the same way a schoolmaster does with his most unruly boy. You've changed so much since you left my tutelage that sometimes I hardly recognize you. You think and speak so meanly; it pains me to think that everything I taught you was fruitless."

"Not at all!" Peña exclaimed, vehemently striking his heart with a fist and his forehead with the palm of his other hand. "Some of it remains. There's a lot in these two parts of me, and it will stay for good, maestro. This light will never be snuffed out, and as long as space exists, and time . . ."

The four Flamenco artists got up to leave. As they observed Manuel's enthusiasm, the two men exchanged astonished glances, and the women stifled a laugh. They appeared to me like the two now-famous girls who were at the gate of the inn when Don Quixote arrived and pronounced those resounding phrases so out of tune with the place and the occasion. Heaven seemed to open to me when the singers left, for then Manuel had no one for that brawl he so much wanted to start.

The fry-shop was painted red, in the style of a Madrid tavern. The dirty walls were papered in a design which repeated rustic cottages, each with shepherds; the general appearance was of an overdecorated and greasy surface. The furnishings consisted of a counter covered with sheet brass, several rickety chairs, a clock, and a wall calendar whose purpose I could not imagine. A heavy haze from the fried oil made the air thick.

"Let's get out of here, Manuel, this is scandalous."

"Just a few more minutes . . ."

"I'm collapsing from weariness."

"Well, I'm so wide awake, it seems like I'll never sleep again."

"There's something wrong with you."

"I've already told you; I've got an urge for action running through me, maybe in my body, maybe in my soul; it's all ticklish and prickly. I want to *do* something, *magister;* I need action. This life of still sociability and dull, passive routine is wearing me down, it's boring me to death. I am at my dramatic age (and now *I'll* be pedantic), at the moment of my history that I forthrightly call *Florentine,* because its byproducts are art and passion and violence. The Medici family has got into my body and taken it over the way little demons do with a bedeviled man."

I couldn't help laughing.

"Come now, what have you been reading, how've you been spending your time?"

"I'm reading Machiavelli. His *History of Florence* and the *Mandragola,* his commentaries on Livy, and *The Prince,* are the most amazing books ever wrought by the hand of man."

"An evil and perverse lot of books to read if one is not first appropriately prepared for them. As I keep saying, my dear Manuel: if you won't pay attention to me, your mind will be corrupted. Devote yourself to studying general principles . . ."

"Oh maestro, please don't go on like that! Philosophy makes me sick and I can't get metaphysics into my head. It's all just playing with words. Ontology! For the love of Heaven, let that emetic cup pass from me! When I take a potion of substance, cause, and effect—I'm sick for three days. I prefer facts, life, concrete things. Don't tell me about theories, tell me about events; not systems, but people. Machiavelli gives me the rich, accurate panorama of human nature, and I'll take him in trade for all philosophers past, present, and future."

"We're acting like fools, Peña, we're discussing in the middle of a fry-shop *the* profound and eternal theme. Let's not debase our intelligence; let's go off and get some sleep . . . We'll speak of this another time. You've changed a lot, and grown into a vigorous and exuberant young man, though a bit crooked. I need to straighten you out. There's something in you I don't like, something that doesn't come from my lessons. Perhaps it's some passing fire in your spirit, the sort of thing that marks the flood tide of your youth . . . At any rate, whatever it is, let's be on our way."

And I finally succeeded in getting him to rise from the tavern banquet-table.

"I'm going to let you in on a secret," he said as we passed by the market, in whose bays and stalls a noise or a sad little light here and there announced the first stirrings of the day's tasks. "Since I've been feeling this way . . ."

"What way?"

"This way, nervous, excited, with these muscle-impulses that call for violence, arbitrary actions, drama . . . Well, since I've been feeling this way, my dislikes are so dreadful, that instead of merely not liking somebody, I detest him with all my soul. Do you know who I find the most unbearable person in the whole world?"

"Who?"

"Your brother, our host this evening, Señor Don José María Manso, and marquess-presumptive, according to what people say."

Wounded by his cruel antipathy, I defended my brother warmly, telling Peña that if indeed José María had certain manias and ridiculous traits, he was still a good, loyal man. But my defense exasperated the young man even more, and he asserted that all of José's goodness and loyalty weren't worth two pins. I suspected that in the little conversational groups of my brother's salon Manuel had heard some biting commentary or allusion to his own low birth, and that, mortified by it, he had mingled the gossips and the host in one and the same abhorrence. I told him this and he admitted that in fact he had heard some bits and pieces which wounded his dignity most painfully; but that in the manner of insults, the culprit was Leopoldo Tellería, Marquess of

Casa-Bojío, and thus my friend was just waiting for the appropriate moment to break open the man's skull.

"So it's little duels we're into?" I said, unwilling that my disciple, in whom I had inculcated the strictest notions of morality, should come back to me talking about settling his affairs of honor by the barbarous and ineffective procedure of challenges and savagery and ignorance.

"You don't live in the real world," he replied. "Your shadow moves about Manso's salon; but you yourself remain in the grandiose never-never land of pure thought, where everything is ontological, where man is an incorporeal being, without nerves or blood, more a child of ideas than of history and nature; a being without age or country or parents or sweetheart. You can say what you like; but I think that if I didn't get the chance to lay a hand on the head of the Marquess of Casa-Bojío, and throw him to the ground and walk all over his body, I'd come to think that the universe was out of balance and the order of nature had been destroyed . . . And will you believe one more thing? There's another individual who irks me even more than darling Leopoldo, and that's my teacher's own worthy brother."

"And will you challenge him to a duel as well? Have you gone mad? Come, come . . . you've declared war on the human race . . . Manuel, Manuel, my boy, soften those impulses or we'll have to put you in a straitjacket. You've become a prating coxcomb, a monster made of sugar-icing, a baby playboy like those who are the fashion now, who in fact are only shameless dolls playing Don Juan but dressed in a clown's rags and speaking with a clown's voice."

As we were mounting the stair, Señora de Peña opened the door. She never went to bed until her son came home at night. That night, the great Doña Javiera, sleepy and ill-tempered because of her darling's extreme lateness, gave us both quite a dressing-down:

"Well! I must say this is a fine hour to be coming home, a fine hour indeed! But surely, Manso my friend, you've not got into these bad habits too? You're so quiet, so home-loving, such an early riser, and here you are wandering home at 4:30 A.M.?! Some teacher! Some wise old owl! I must say!"

"This rascal, madam, this rascal is the one who's leading me astray."

"Oh, my dear boy, you're so pale . . . What's wrong! Has something bad happened?"

"Nothing, mamma; not a thing."

103

"But aren't you coming in to go to bed?"

"I'm going upstairs for a moment with our friend Manso. I want him to lend me some books I need."

"Books? You?" I said, as we went into my flat. "What do you want books for?"

"To prepare my speech."

"What speech? Have you taken up speech-making?"

"You really are out of touch. Didn't I tell you that I intend to give a speech at the big charity benefit evening?"

"What big evening?"

"The one being organized by the Society for the Relief of Industrial Invalids."

"Oh, that's right. What are you going to deal with in your speech? Take all the books you want . . ."

I was dropping from fatigue. I left him in the study and went to my bedroom, which was the adjoining chamber. From my bed I could see him rummaging through the shelves, picking up and putting down one book or another.

Before I went off to sleep, I said to him:

"Tomorrow you'll have to tell me why you've taken such a strong dislike to my poor brother."

"I can't tell you; it's a secret . . . Is it all right if I borrow Spencer?"

"Good grief, take anybody you like, and let me rest."

And just falling into my first sleep, I heard him say:

"He's a bastard, a bastard."

And deep in sleep, the only thing from real life left in my brain were those words, twinkling on the dark, trembling surface of my sleep, like the glow of stars reflected on the sea.

XXI
THE NEXT DAY . . .

B UT FIRST I WISH to share a confidence. What I'm going to relate puts me in a bad light and may perhaps make me look like a very ordinary man, insensitive to the delicate preferences of our reformist society; but I place my duty as recorder of history above all else, and so if I'm frank on this point I will earn credit for being candid at other places in my narration. Let's have at it. The excellent food and elegant dishes of my brother's table were beginning to make me feel stuffed, and since whole weeks would go by without my being able to avoid eating there, I finally started to miss my habitually humble fare, and my favorite dish, chick-peas, for which in my view there is, as I have said, no possible substitute. My appetite for that legume grew and grew, and became irrepressible. I had become like the habitual smoker who is deprived of tobacco over a long stretch of time. Whenever I went through the Corredera de San Pablo and past the place where we shop, a store called *The Food Custom-House,* my eyes were drawn to the great sack of chick-peas placed right at the door. Their raw state made them no less delicious-looking to me. Unable any longer to restrain my appetite, I declined one day to eat with Lica, and notified Petra to prepare a regular, proper *cocido.* I have nothing else to say except that I took barbarous revenge upon the privation I had suffered. And now, on with my story.

The next day I found my brother in the children's schoolroom. He wished to inform himself personally of the children's progress. Jocular with their governess, and affecting toward the pupils a bombastic severity which seemed to me inappropriate, the marquess-to-be made it impossible for me to say to Irene several little things I had thought up. To me she seemed inhibited and almost stunned by the presence, the questions, and the amiability of the master of the house. She couldn't get anything right in the lessons, and the pupils had to correct the teacher. To make things even worse, my brother also deprived me of my afternoon walk, by making me go with him, willy-nilly,

105

to see the Director of Public Instruction on a matter in which I had no interest at all.

At length I became convinced that José María was not a model husband. Lica had dropped remarks several times about this subject, but I had taken them to be exaggerations or whims. One afternoon, alas!, my sister-in-law arranged for Irene, the children, and the wet nurse to go out in the carriage. Mercedes had gone out with some lady-friends. I stayed in the house, for although my preference would have been to go to the Retiro Park with Irene, I had no choice but to remain and keep Manuela company. She gave eager signs of wishing to speak alone with me, and I told myself: "Get ready, Máximo my friend; you've got a big job coming your way. Clear out your brains and refresh your knowledge of interior decoration and epicurean gastronomy."

But Lica gave little time to such matters, and seemed to have taken an aversion to the soirées and elaborate menus, to judge by the scornful way she spoke of them. Her wifely afflictions left her no room for attending to matters of foolish vanity, and no sooner had she touched upon the delicate point at which she felt wounded than she began to cry. I listened to her woes and was unsuccessful in giving her any real consolation. Poor Lica! Her exotic words, her truncated clauses, were given persuasive eloquence by the truth and the sorrow they contained. I haven't forgotten her American hyperboles and I never shall. She was very angry: her heart was scorched and her whole life made sick by Pepe María's behavior. It was no longer of any use to her to complain and weep, for he paid not the slightest heed to her complaining and crying. He had turned very *beastly*, very bad, and he always found the words to slip out from under and prove that he hadn't so much as broken a teacup. He had left his wife in oblivion, along with his children; he spent the whole blessed day out of the house, and he went out at night after the gatherings, not to be seen again until lunchtime the next day. Husband and wife exchanged only a few words concerning invitations, teas, dinners, and that was all . . .

All of this might have been overlooked if there hadn't been other things, worse things, really serious faults. José María was a ruined man; his companionship and dealings with Cimarra had poisoned him; he had gone rotten like a piece of good fruit next to a spoiled one . . . The poor woman was no longer in any doubt regarding her husband's dreadful infidelity. She felt so ashamed that just thinking about it brought the color to her cheeks, and she was unable to find words to discuss it . . . But to me she could tell the

106

whole story. Yes! One morning as she was going through José María's pockets she had found a letter from *one of those women* . . . A letter asking him for money! It was driving her mad to think that her children's wealth was ending up in the hands of a . . .

But the suffering wife was not really concerned for the money, but for the *brazenness* of it all. Oh!! She was raging. Even though she was a decent person, if she got her hands on the so-and-so who was stealing her husband, she'd give her a good drubbing and a couple of well-placed slaps. Oh this Madrid, this awful Madrid! It's better to walk through the forest in a shift, live in a hut, eat legumes, wild hare, and sour oranges than to do your hair up in style and wear a train on your dress and talk fancy and have dinner with Cabinet Ministers . . . She'd be better off in her blessed homeland than in Madrid. There she was queen and mistress of the town; here the only people who paid her any mind were the ones who came to eat her out of house and home, and then laugh behind her back. And then there's this life, good Lord, this life where everything comes down to *making* one's self do things, putting up a front and tormenting oneself to do everything the Spanish way, and having to forget Cuban words and learn new ones, and learn proper greetings and welcomes and all kinds of silly nonsense . . . No, no; this was just not for her. If José wouldn't mend his ways, she'd head straight off for Cuba, and take her children with her.

I comforted her by telling her what she had told me so many times; that is, not to exaggerate so much. Her imagination, formed by tropical colors and dimensions, made things bigger than they really were. Couldn't it be that the letter she'd found did *not* have the sinful import that she sought to give it? . . . She answered this query with certain clarifying details which left me no doubt concerning my brother's wicked behavior. His friendship with Cimarra, by then very intimate, foretold countless disasters and perhaps a rapid depletion of Lica's husband's fortune. She didn't limit her confidences to what I've written down here, but proceeded to bring to light other examples of the great vileness of our marquess-to-be; I was left stunned. In his own house, the wretch had had the effrontery to . . . to do certain things which tarnished the good name of the whole family, and especially of his fine wife . . . For had he not indeed had the impudence to pay court to Irene?

"To Irene!?"

"Yes; why he's just . . . !" Poor Lica was beside herself when she touched on this matter. She could express her fury only in half-articulated words . . . In her own house, right in front of her! For there was no particular

107

dissimulation about his pursuit . . . Lately he'd been proceeding with great boldness! During the mornings he slipped into the schoolroom and stayed there for hours on end . . . One night he went into Irene's room as she was retiring. Well, why speak any more about such an unpleasant thing? The previous afternoon there had been a bitter clash between husband and wife, right at the door . . . how poor Lica choked on her words! . . . at the very door of the governess's room. It was perfectly clear that Irene had not encouraged in the slightest degree this indecorous courtship by the master of the house. Quite the opposite: Irene made no secret of her own vexation. She was a decent girl, utterly above reproach, and couldn't possibly be held accountable for the bold advances of such a . . . At any rate, that very morning Irene had signified to her mistress that she wished to leave the house. They had both wept . . . She was such a fine girl!

And the end of it was that I, Máximo Manso, the man of rectitude, the faultless man, the brains of the family, the philosopher and wise man, was summoned to set everything right, by making José see the meanness and the dreadful consequences of his iniquitous conduct; I was to point out to him . . . I forget all the things Lica said I should point out to him. The poor woman would bear her husband no grudge if he mended his ways. She had made up her mind to forgive him, yes, forgive him from the bottom of her heart if he'd return to the straight and narrow, because she loved her husband very much and she was all heart and feeling and affection and fawning and sweetness . . . And that's all she told me; it was all she needed to tell me, for I had learned quite enough that afternoon and had ample material to put my advisory functions to work.

XXII
THINGS ARE MOVING

"THINGS ARE GETTING STICKY," I thought as I departed. We are right in the middle of the complete unfolding of events; we are present at their natural development. To us is assigned the fatal duty of taking part in them, whether it be as mere witnesses, which isn't always so pleasant, or as victims, which is even less so. We are now faced with a situation in which moral energy—call it character if you will—acting within the small compass of a family circle or a group of acquaintances, has completed what we might call in the language of drama its *protasis;* and now that the said energy has matured and grown, its opposing elements begin to jostle and compete for space, starting with *brushings,* and then *bumps,* and later perhaps leading to furious *frontal assaults.* Let us remain calm and keep a sharp eye on things. Let us hold on to the serenity of spirit which is so useful in the midst of a battle. And if fate, or the suggestions of others, or our own self-interest should propel us into the role of commanding general, let us attempt to carry into the field all the tactics we have learned through study, and all the discernment we have acquired in observing the comparative topography of the human heart.

I couldn't sleep that night thinking about what was going on and speculating upon what *might* go on. The next day I hurried to my brother's house and said to Lica:

"You keep an eye on Doña Cándida, and I'll do the same with Irene."

Lica was surprised at my distrust of Caligula, and told me that she harbored no evil suspicions of such an affectionate and obliging friend.

"Do be careful with that woman," I replied, feeling that I was on firm ground. "Despite her being a protégée of this household, my gadfly's character has not been altered and she dreams up new necessities for herself every day. Nothing is enough for her: the more she has the more she wants. Her hunger has been satisfied and now she longs for certain comforts she didn't have before. Give her those comforts and she'll want luxuries next. Give her luxury, and she'll be after opulence. She's insatiable. With the passing years her appetites have taken on a certain ferocity."

"But, old dear, what's that got to do . . . ?"

"Just keep an eye on her, that's all; watch her and say nothing."

"And you'll watch Irene?"

"Yes. I consider her to be good, even exceptional among the young women of the present day. She is far above all I've seen, a real wonder, but . . ."

"You always end with a *but* . . ."

"Ah, Manuela! You don't realize the temptations that beset virtue these days. Just consider it. There are examples of innocent, angelic creatures who in a moment of weakness have given in to a vain temptation, and fallen from the heights of an almost superhuman virtue into the abyss of sin. The serpent has bitten them, infecting their pure blood with the virus of a wild desire. What desire? Luxury! Luxury is the same thing that we used to call the Devil, the serpent, the fallen angel, because luxury also was an angel—it was art and generosity and nobility. But now it is a mesocratic curse, within easy reach of the bourgeoisie, because industry and machines have placed it in a fair way to corrupt the entire human race, without distinctions of class."

"Stop right there, Máximo; to tell the truth, I don't understand what you're talking about. But it must be true since you have said it . . . All right, keep a sharp eye on the governess . . ."

And that phrase was branded on my brain: "A sharp eye on the governess," so much so that the mere idea of being a spy sharpened my suspicions.

For some terrible distrust had welled up inside me, why deny it? My faith in Irene had been damaged a bit, without any rational cause. It's just that the procedure of skepticism (which I've cultivated in my studies as a means of support as I seek to discover the truth) keeps alive in my heart this leaven of malice, the groundwork on which all problems must be posed. And in that particular case, the greater my mortification from doubt, the more I *wished* to doubt, secure in the effectiveness of that way of thinking. In the same way that human thought has made great strides by treading the pathway of doubt, I expected the moral triumph of Irene, and that following upon my scanty faith would come the proof of her virtue. And that after the rigorous tests my spirit of hypothesis was going to put her through, the perfection of her precious soul would be demonstrated by rational means. Besides, the restlessness

I had felt ever since learning of José's advances had made me see the deep concern, the *love,* let's say it once and for all, that Irene had awakened in me, sentiments which until then I could have mistaken in good conscience for any whimsical aberration of my feelings or my senses. I was suffering from a burning jealousy; thus my love for the person who caused it was equally ardent.

I resolved first of all to conceal my feelings from Irene, until such time as the schoolmistress should show as clear as daylight her resistance to the clumsy snares of my brother. I went in to see her. And a great confusion overcame me when I found her in a state of melancholy meditation, paler than ever, as if her soul had fallen prey to gloomy, contradictory thoughts. What could be wrong with her? All my deftness and captious chatter were of no avail in getting her to open the sanctuary of her soul, or in discovering within one single sentence of hers the mystery which lay enclosed therein. Not once on that ill-fated day did I see her smile. She contradicted, completely, the idea I had held concerning her equanimity and the reposeful, serene balance of her character. All I could elicit from her was monosyllables. Her eyes glued to her needlework, she kept tying knots and more knots, and it occurred to me that each one was an *ergo* in the tangled dialectic going on in her head, for she was undoubtedly thinking and reasoning and *ergotizing* in a marvelous sophistry.

Very badly affected, I withdrew to my house. I was so upset and so hounded by suspicion and curiosity that the next morning, as soon as the children's lessons were over, I broached the subject and said to her:

"I already know everything that's troubling you. Manuela has told me the wild things José María has done."

She listened calmly and just smiled a bit. And *I* had expected her to be overcome by confusion.

"Your dear brother," she answered, "is very peculiar. How unlike you he is, Manso my friend. The two of you are like day and night."

I continued the conversation, speaking of my brother, and his vain and flighty character; I offered some slight excuse for him; I praised Lica to the skies, and . . .

Irene interrupted me, saying:

"Although Don José has not come in here nor spoken to me since that episode, I believe that I can no longer stay on in this house."

I made only a slight movement of surprise, for I didn't dare contradict her. I realized she was right. I asked her whether the cause of the sadness I

111

had observed in her the preceding day could be the unpleasant gallantries of the master of the house, and she answered:

"Yes and no . . . It would take a very long answer, so . . . yes and no."

"Yes and no!" What a perfect recipe for achieving the maximum of confusion, or even madness!

"But do be frank with me. You told me that you would seek my counsel on some grave matter or other, and I even think you said: 'I swear to do what you command.'"

Then she fixed a firm gaze on me. Her eyes penetrated my soul like a luminous sword. She had never looked prettier to me, nor had I ever seen so strong in her that intelligent beauty which the greatest artists have succeeded in copying in their allegorical paintings of Theology or Astronomy. I felt inferior to her, so inferior that I nearly trembled when I heard her say:

"You've not kept your faith in me . . . Therefore you're not worthy of being consulted about any affair of mine."

It was true, it was true. My captious questions and my inquisitorial interrogations of the preceding day had clearly not been to her liking. Her resentment seemed beautiful to me, and gave me such great pleasure that I was unable to conceal from her how much joy I took in her noble tenacity. I made protestations of firm friendship, never overstepping the bounds or letting on to any other feelings; for the time wasn't right, nor had I marshaled the evidence I was seeking, even though I could feel it coming.

We went out for a stroll. She acted calm and cordial; but as we talked and engaged in verbal prancing and playing she made it clear that there was something she was not ready to reveal to me, and that very *something* hit me squarely between the eyes, causing me great mortification.

"We'll see. For the present . . ."

"What?"

"For the present, please don't pepper me with questions. The more you ask, the less you'll learn. Be more patient and trust my impulses. I'm really *something* when it comes to spontaneous impulses. I mean that when people don't ask anything I feel like telling things. As for earnest little consultations, they lose all their spice if they don't happen at the right time; I mean they should just happen spontaneously."

This made me laugh, and as we were saying good-bye at Lica's house, I laughed even harder at the following sally by Irene:

"To earn a few more points, you will please do me another favor . . . I'd

112

be so grateful if you'd make a short little notation, a résumé, I mean just on a bit of paper like this—of the history of Spain! Can you believe that I get the eleven King Alfonsos all muddled up and I can't tell them apart? They seem all to have done the same things. And then I get a kind of mixed salad in my head, with Castile and León, and I don't know what I'm doing. Will you make a little outline for me?"

"But, my child, the history of Spain on a slip of paper?!"

"Just the eleven Alfonsos. From King Pedro the Cruel onwards I can handle it. How awfully boring! Those wars against the Moors, always the same, and royal marriages between this one and that one, kingdoms uniting and splitting up and Alfonsos all over the place . . . It's really *something,* to be frank with you. If I were the Government, I'd ban the whole thing."

"History?"

"Yes, just what I've said. Don't get angry over my heresies! G'bye."

XXIII

HISTORY ON A SLIP OF PAPER!

WHO EVER HEARD of such a wild idea? Just too many whims lately, it seems to me. First she wants the *Grammar* of the Royal Academy, a book she scarcely understands; then it's pencils and drawings she doesn't use; one day she wants poems in Asturian dialect and then a new song by Tosti. And now the history of the Alfonsos on a slip of paper. Who ever heard of such a thing? I really must say that reason is not completely in charge of her actions, and that the determination of spirit I thought I saw is not there; nor do I find that scorn for frivolity and whimsy that so pleased me when I *did* find it. But the strange thing is that in spite of her having lost, in my view, some of the unusual qualities I supposed her to be gifted with, my strong attraction to her has not diminished in the slightest; quite the contrary . . . It appears that the less perfect she is, the more womanly she becomes; and the further she falls short of the ideal of my dreams, the more I love her, and . . .

That's what I was thinking that night. Deep in abstract thought, I was staying away from the group. And the next day I was fully engrossed in an academic matter which had me running for hours from pillar to post, from the Rector's office to the Division of Public Instruction. I attended a luncheon given by my students for three professors, and before going home I made a stop at my brother's house, where I learned a stunning piece of news, which Lica related to me in full detail. Manuel Peña and the Marquess of Casa-Bojío had exchanged very bitter words the previous night. It was a question concerning good manners which soon brought in the matter of class distinctions and then personal remarks; the three things became one, and it was now necessary for the two young men to crack each other's skulls with swords or guns on what is called *the field of honor*. Peña's sharp, provocative phrases in that ill-fated argument, and his refusal to clarify them, made a duel unavoidable.

José María had tried to fix things up, racking his brains for some formula for a *deal,* which he was so good at; but on that occasion a Vergara embrace was not forthcoming, as it was in 1839,* until after blood should have been drawn. Everything was set up for very early the next morning. Cimarra and some other two-bit gentlemen were Manuel's seconds. Lica was extremely displeased, and I deplored with my whole heart that a young man of bright talents and sound ideas, educated by me to abhor human barbarism, should have sunk to the stupid, weak expedient of a duel. This is not the place to repeat all that I said on this subject that evening. I was very nearly eloquent, and Lica wholeheartedly approved my ideas. She wondered that such a sound criterion as mine did not triumph in society, doing away with error and its consequent worries.

I was at great pains that evening not to talk back in the worst possible taste to the insufferable and ever-more-boring poet, who was the Secretary of the Society for Invalids. But rejected though he was by my turning aside, he only returned to the charge with more determination, and shot me a barrage of inhuman blandishments. He wanted, no more and no less, for me to take part in the great *evening* that was being organized, for me also to give a little speech, thus rivaling the other orators who had already been signed up, among whom were several of the first rank. I resisted at all costs, offering as a reason my scanty oratorical powers, but not even that availed me, for my brother and Pez and another pair of grave gentlemen (one of them an ex-minister) who were present, attacked me on my flank, arguing that what was needed was not brilliant speeches, but solid, well-reasoned ones. They told me that my words would give the solemn celebration an authority not conferred by warblings and flowery talk. Finally they said that the Society, were I to insult it by withholding my *valuable support,* would be faced, in my absence, with an empty spot impossible to fill with any other speech or with poetry or music.

This flattery made no dent in my resistant character and I refused obstinately to participate. My dear brother told me I was a calamity; Lica said I was silly, and the *talking head* favored me with a rather harsh declaration regarding the scanty practical sense of philosophers and the small assistance they lend to the progress of civilization. The harangue I got from this gentleman, a sort of shower-bath of wisdom, and not unlike aromatic vinegar, was like a newspaper article of the "by-the-people-and-for-the-people"

*See note on p. 90.

115

variety, one of the articles which are the daily diet and training-school of ordinary minds. I paid no heed and left for home.

I wanted to find out whether Manuel Peña was in the building, and whether Doña Javiera had had word of her boy's chivalresque carryings-on. I was preparing a fine sermon for my disciple, although to be strictly truthful there was no way to stop things from moving ahead. The savage question of honor, a wart on the face of modern culture and the shame of philosphy, would be respected and carried through inevitably. The idolatry of the "point of honor" seems today as absurd as if my contemporaries were suddenly to take it into their heads to reestablish human sacrifice and immolate their fellows on the altar of a clay doll representing some savage deity or other. But so great is the power of our social milieu that I, for all the rigor and intolerant puritanism of my ideas, wouldn't have dared try to pull Peña back from that barbarous terrain nor suggest that he not show up for the appointment. And do you know something else? Even being who I am, I think that I would be unable, physically or mentally, to fail to show up on the *field of honor,* if exceptional circumstances were to impel me there. Let us never forget the *great* examples of human weakness—or rather, compromises of conscience—determined by the environment: Socates sacrificed a cockerel to Aesculapius and St. Peter denied Christ.

Doña Javiera knew nothing of it. Manuel had had the presence of mind to deceive her with the story that he was going to Toledo with some friends and would spend the night there.

And this had left the poor woman perfectly calm. I was not, for although these days most duels end up being nothing but farces, and the people who participate in them as seconds or arbiters also go into the thing with a farcical attitude, it could still happen that natural forces (with their profoundly serious and antihumorous fatalism) might provide us with a tragedy.

At a very early hour the next day, I went out to find out what had happened, but I couldn't learn a thing. At 10 A.M. Peña still hadn't come home, and I was worried. but Doña Javiera, who of course suspected nothing amiss, said:

"He'll come on the evening train. Just you imagine, in one day you can't see everything. Why they say there's enough just in the Cathedral for a *week's* visit."

I ran to José's house, where Lica, dreadfully upset, gave me the awful news that Peña had killed the Marquess of Casa-Bojío. I was so grieved and terrified that I was unable even to make a comment on such a regrettable incident, which was proof positive of the injustice and barbarity of duels. That young man, endowed with such a noble heart and such a bright and engaging mind, so very notable and likeable in mien, manner, and all the qualities of his soul, had taken away the life of a wretched but innocent fellow whose only crime—if such it were—was stupidity! . . . And all for what? For a few hollow words, common and idle ones, a mere accident of the voice and the product of witlessness. Words not worth enough to allow Nature, on their account, to kill a fly or change the order of the world in the slightest way!

But, dammit! The news had been brought by Sáinz del Bardal. Might not the character of the messenger be sufficient grounds for doubt . . . ?

"Oh yes," Lica said to me. "Go and find out at Cimarra's house. José María went out very early. I haven't seen him today. He said he wouldn't be back till tonight."

I call down all the devils together, if indeed devils exist, or all evil spirits, if such exist outside the human soul, to carry off Sáinz del Bardal and punch him and cut him up and slice him and prick him full of holes, and tear his flesh and break his neck, and strangle him, and grind him up and pulverize him and smash him until he's in such tiny pieces that he can't be put back together again, until it is no longer possible for poets of his brand ever to exist in the world again!! What a fright the damn fellow gave us! Where in the deuce, you infernal creature, did you get the story that the finest among the fine, Manuel Peña, had ended the precious life of poor young Leopoldo, whose immortality is in any case guaranteed by his armor of idiocy (like a tortoise's by his shell) and his absolute uselessness to everybody? From what spring did you drink, you miasma-ridden poet, scourge of Parnassus and plague of the Muses? Who deceived you, who gave you that story, you nozzle of nincompoopery?

For nothing at all had happened, only that the edge of Peña's sword had barely grazed the ear of that mirror of morons and cut it ever so slightly, causing about 14 drops of Tellería blood to come forth!

And since the duel was only "to draw blood," this ended the conflict and both knights were stuffed to bursting with honor, and shook hands, and the fellow who was playing doctor took out a piece of court plaster and stuck it on young Leopoldo's ear, leaving it as good as new, and thus everything was settled to the rejoicing of Humanity and the discredit of those accursed medieval ideas which are still alive . . .

Cimarra himself told me the whole story, praising to the skies Manuel Peña's serenity and generous bravura. I couldn't wait to tell Lica, who had already drunk five cups of coffee to get over her fright. Doña Jesusa thanked God out loud. Mercedes sang for joy, and even the wet nurse and Rupertico and the mulatto girl were happy that nothing had happened.

After lunch Manuela and I went into the schoolroom to see the girls' writing. Irene received us with lively joy. Why was she—far from pale— almost rosy-cheeked? I could see she was restless, with who knows what sort of childish liveliness in her lovely eyes, voluble and in a more jocular, quick-witted, loquacious mood than usual.

"Please forgive me," I said to her, "I've been very busy and haven't been able to bring you *History on a slip of paper.*"

"Oh, that was foolish! Don't trouble yourself . . . It's not worth the bother . . . Really, I can't see how you put up with me. I'm just the most impertinent thing! I suppose it's just that you're so good and I'm so ignorant that I allow myself to bother you with questions once in a while. But don't pay any attention to me. It's true, isn't it, Madam, he shouldn't pay any attention to me?"

"Oh, no! He should work and help you, my dear. That's not asking much. Otherwise, what good is it for him to be so smart?"

"But so insipid too, how *very* insipid," said Irene, looking at me with a laugh; she was shooting fire at me from her eyes and making me shiver with a nervous chill. "See how he refuses to take part in the charity evening? It's as I always say: he is really *something*!!"

"I'll say he is!"

"Well, you must give a speech, yes, sir. Order him to do it, Madam; he pays no attention to anybody."

XXIV
"YOU MUST GIVE A SPEECH!"

A ND SO I WILL, there's no escaping it. In her words there's a certain undefinably imperious and irresistible quality, which blocks my retreat into modesty, leaving me defenseless before the organizers of the charity benefit. I shall succumb at last. I must give a speech. About what?

These were my thoughts as I walked home that evening after a stroll with Manuela, Irene, and the children. As I came closer to my house I considered what order of ideas I might select to put together a pretty speech. No sooner did I walk into my study and see my bookshelves, than my mind became illumined and produced a splendid inspiration. The knowledge stored up in my library seemed to be coming at me in beams of light, the way some painters show celestial voices in their pictures. I felt within me those varied, learned voices and tones and echoes, each of which uttered its own idea or sentence. What an admirable speech I would give! An immense panorama, a grandiose synthesis, a rich fabric of detail! It occurred to me that I could explain the Christian concept of charity, one of the loveliest fortresses constructed by human thought.

I would analyze the dogmatic definition of that theological, supernatural virtue which allows us to love God for Himself and our neighbors as ourselves through God's love. Then I'd get into the Church Fathers . . . But, oh! My memory was not reliable at this point; I could only remember the gradations of St. Francis de Sales, who says: "Man is the perfection of the universe, the spirit is the perfection of man, love the perfection of the spirit, and charity the perfection of love . . . " After doing a thorough job on Catholic charity, I would go on to the philosophical area, using by way of transition Newton's beautiful phrase: "Without charity, virtue is an empty name." I would establish the principle of brotherhood, and by small steps move into the terrain of economics and politics, where the theories on public

119

assistance and mutual aid would provide me with abundant material . . . Then on to sociology . . . In short, I had more than enough to talk about; I had enough ideas for seven speeches at seven different benefits. The hard part would be to condense it all. Nothing is harder than to say a few words on a big subject. Only truly great minds possess the secret of enclosing immeasurable spaces in the compass of a few terse words. And thus I was somewhat confused. I didn't know what to select from among all those ideas, all that varied wealth. After reflecting upon it for a long time, I came to a clear vision and realized that it would be the height of pedantry to trot out Christian dogmatics, the Church Fathers, philosophy, social science, brotherhood, and political economy. The erudite fever I had felt upon seeing my books now seemed ridiculous to me, and I considered the wild exaggerations to which one is led by the piling up of books. Erudition is a wine which almost always leads to drunkenness. Let's liberate ourselves from it, especially on certain occasions, and learn instead the art of bringing to each time and place the things that are appropriate to it and fit into it with admirable preciseness. I turned my back on my library and said to myself: "Careful, Manso my friend, about the way you act. If you show up at this well-publicized event looking like a mosaic of dreary book-learning or bearing a catafalque of transcendental philosophy, the audience will laugh at you. Remember that you're addressing a Senate of ladies; and that these ladies and the young dandies and all the other unsubstantial people who attend events of this kind will be wanting you to finish quickly so that they can listen to a violin solo or a poetry reading. Prepare a brief, discreet little speech, with its touch of sentimentality and a nod of gallantry toward the ladies; to put it another way, whenever you let loose a bit of philosophy, follow it with a puff of rice-powder. Say simple things, if possible, and make them pretty and pretty-sounding. Throw in a couple of metaphors; for that all you need to do is leaf through any good poet. Be very brief; offer extravagant praises of the ladies who outdo themselves organizing charity functions. Speak of easily understood generalities, and remember that if you exceed in the slightest the limitations of the well-dressed vulgarians who are listening to you, you'll come off badly, and the papers won't call you inspired or eloquent."

This is what I told myself, and having done so I fell silent and began to eat, since by the rarest luck I was also able that day to eschew my brother's official luncheon and devote myself in delicious tranquility to my homely victuals.

The upcoming charity benefit and my agreement to take part in it had me worried. I have never been fond of these ceremonies where, on the pretext of a charitable purpose, a great number of publicity-seekers put themselves on view. If at some earlier time I had been told: "You'll give a speech at a charity benefit," I'd have thought it as absurd as somebody telling me: "You shall fly." Yet nonetheless (Dear God!), I flew.

But this concern over my speech was by no means my most serious one during that time. One afternoon I went to José María's house firmly intent upon seeing Irene and speaking to her in more explicit terms. For my own reserve was beginning to annoy me, and I was wearying of the role of mere observer into which I had placed myself. The strength of my feelings had grown so greatly as the days went by that my reason was somewhat shaken, like an authority-figure who loses power in the face of widespread popular insolence. I consider this figure of speech a good one, because my feelings were expanding inside of me, like a plebeian movement for freedom, life, reform. My feelings were revealing their own awareness of their just cause and their signs of strength, while icy, humdrum reason was making weak concessions, evoking the past at every step and refusing to relinquish the codex of its time-honored pragmatics. I was thus in the throes of a revolution brought about by the fatal law of my own inner process, by my own tyranny and that special sort of absolutism or philosophical Inquisition by which I had governed my life since childhood.

So on that particular day, the vigor of the *plebs* was terrifying, and the *masses had risen,* as one says in speaking of revolutions: the Bastille of my plans had been taken amid riot and clamor. And as I remembered Peña and his ideas on the need for drama at certain points in life, I decided he was right. One must be young *once* and allow to the heart some of that inevitable process of reform and education which History calls revolution.

"Enough of wisdom," I said to myself. "No more character studies, no more dissections of words. All *that* does is get me into more and more torments of suspicion and hesitation. Let's get down to facts and cases, at last! Once I pose the question and make known my desires, all my own clarity will be duplicated in her, and I'll see and judge her more clearly. I can't live this way any more. Woe to the man who tries to get to know women studying them the way a botanist studies a flower! Idiot! Inhale her perfume, contemplate her colors; but don't count pistils or measure petals or analyze calyxes. If you do that, the more facts you learn the less you'll really know. And what you do end up knowing will be the things least worth knowing of all those that Nature keeps in her great workshop."

These were my thoughts, and with them I headed straight to Irene's room. Disappointed! Irene wasn't in. Nor were the girls. Lica came out to meet me and explained why the governess wasn't there. She had gone to her aunt's house to get her things in order. They were moving to a new house, it seemed. Doña Cándida had taken a sweet little apartment and was going from one clearance sale to another for furniture to make the place presentable. Irene was at my gadfly's old apartment putting her belongings in order for the movers, and helping her aunt.

I tried to start off for Doña Cándida's but Lica detained me. She had to give me an account of the horrid time she was having with the wet nurse, whose bestial greed and evil temper and fierce demands could no longer be borne. She started a row with the mulatto girl every day and got so angry that her milk went bad, and my dear godson was slowly being poisoned. She wanted for herself everything she saw, and since Manuela always gave in to her, there came a time when neither velvet skirts nor jewelry (real or fake) would keep her contented. When they told her *no,* she'd put on an awful pouting face and you had to coax and cajole her to get a word out of her. She didn't show any affection for her breast-son, and talked of going home with her *man and young'uns.* Several valuable article which had disappeared were discovered by searching through the beast's trunk. Lica was afraid of her, and trembled in her presence; she didn't dare stand up to her or cross her in the slightest way.

"Let her take everything," she said to me whimpering, while we two were alone, "as long as she nurses my dear baby. She's the mistress, and I'm the servant: I don't dare take a breath in front of her for fear she'll do something awful and kill my baby."

"Doña Cándida has really brought you a beauty! You see: nothing good can come from my gadfly."

"How is Doña Cándida to blame? The poor thing! Don't exaggerate. But if only I could find another wet nurse without this one doing anything awful, and then just throw her out! Oh! Máximo, you're so good, *you* help me! I can't count on José María for a thing. Why . . . it's as if he weren't there at all. He never comes around here. So Máximo, it's you, old dear."

"But Lica . . . what does Doña Cándida have to say?"

"Why she hardly ever comes to the house . . . since she's sold her land in Zamora and has some cash . . . "

"Cash? Doña Cándida?" I exclaimed more surprised than if I'd been told Manzanedo* was begging on the streets. "Caligula's got cash?"

"Yes, she's rich; you ought to see her, my boy . . . , she's putting on such airs . . ."

"Oh, Lica, Lica! I warned you to keep an eye on my gadfly. Have you done it?"

"Oh come, don't exaggerate so!"

I didn't know what to think. My need to see Irene, together with a mysterious feeling of suspicion which impelled me to watch Doña Cándida up close, drove me to her house. As I arrived, my heart was apprehensive with fear and distrust. I pulled again and again on the grubby cord of the hoarse doorbell, but nobody answered. The concierge shouted down that madam and the young lady were in their new house already. But where was that house? Neither the concierge nor the neighbors knew.

I returned to Lica's side. Irene came in very late; tired, paler than ever, and with circles under her eyes. Her aunt's new apartment was in the brand-new neighborhood of Santa Bárbara, with a view of the Salesas Convent and the Saladero Prison. Both aunt and niece had worked hard that afternoon.

"I've gotten so dusty!" Irene said to me. "I'm worn out with fatigue and I'm so sleepy. Until tomorrow, Manso my friend."

Until tomorrow! And that tomorrow came, and with it Irene disappeared. A driving curiosity impelled me to her new house, rented and furnished with the money from that land in Zamora which never existed anywhere except in the wild Caligula's always inventive numen.

I went out and walked up and down the newly laid-out streets of the Santa Bárbara quarter; but I couldn't find the house. According to what Irene had told me, the building hadn't even been given a number yet, nor the street a name; I asked in several porters' lodges, and went up to several flats, but nowhere could I get any information. It seemed as if I were traveling through a made-up city, like Doña Cándida's land, and the thought even crossed my mind that the *sweet little apartment* might be on one of the vacant lots where no

*A well-known millionaire.

123

building had been put up yet. I went back to the center of town. In the Calle de San Mateo, and as night was beginning to fall, I came upon Manuel Peña, who told me: "García Grande and her niece are just now walking down the Calle de Fuencarral."

We parted after talking for a moment about his speech and mine. I went home, and returned once again to the streets. It was night . . .

XXV
MY THOUGHTS WERE TORMENTING ME

THEY TORMENTED ME the whole night, inside my house and outside of it. I can't say how that image reached my eyes. I found her; I saw her walking alone, hurriedly, ahead of me on the opposite sidewalk, the one that runs in front of the Government Accounting Office. I was behind one of the acacia trees that adorn the gate of the Hospice, and she didn't see me. I followed her . . . She was in a hurry, and fearful, it seemed . . . Now and again she would stop to look at the shop windows. As she stopped by one that was especially well lit, I took a good look at her, to be certain it was indeed she. Yes, it *was;* she had on her navy blue dress and a dark hat that looked like a great stuffed cow casting a shadow over her face. Her elegant, slightly foreign air set her apart from the other women passing by in the street.

She walked past the mat shop next to the tobacconist's, stopped for a moment to look at the yard goods in the *Comercio del Catalán.* Then later she had to stop short, for a tramcar had been derailed, and a cab had run up onto the sidewalk. There was a great commotion. Irene took a look at things and crossed over to the opposite sidewalk, hiking her skirts a bit, for there was a lot of mud. It had rained that afternoon. She walked along the even-numbered side past the dosimetric pharmacy, and continued on in some haste, like a person who doesn't wish to keep another waiting. She passed by the chapel of the Arco de Santa María, and crossed herself as she looked inside. So she's sanctimonious, too!! She continued ahead. Cruel suspicions were gnawing at my heart. The better to observe her, I followed along the opposite sidewalk. She passed one corner, then another. She stopped to identify a house. On its outside corner one can see the set-in column of a water meter, and above it a green iron plate which reads Reservoir Route, Meter number 6B, Reservoir number 18B. She read the sign and so did I. It was the inscription over the gate of Hell. She took a few steps and slipped into the dark doorway . . . I was struck dumb, seized by the most awful terror, and I

125

felt myself in the throes of death. Nailed to that sidewalk, I was looking across at the somber, narrow, unattractive doorway, when a carriage pulled up and stopped. The door opened, and out stepped a man . . . It was my brother!!

I shall conclude this feverish episode by stating with all the candor of a writer of short stories who has just unloaded upon his reader a most improbable sequence of events: "Then I woke up. It had all been a dream."

But this dreadful dream of mine, which tormented me as I awoke, was born of my hypothesis of the preceding evening, and had a certain element of terrifying probability. It made such a strong impression on me that I could recall the imaginary walk in the Calle de Fuencarral; its details seemed as clear to me as reality itself. The world of dreams is not entirely arbitrary and meaningless, and if one patiently analyzes the cerebral phenomena which give it shape, one may perhaps find a hidden logic. And once awake I set about scrutinizing the relation which might exist between reality and the series of impressions I had received. If dreams are the intermittent repose of thought and of the sensory organs, how *did* I think and see? But, that's nonsense! There I was in bed, interpreting dreams like Pharaoh, and it was nine A.M., and I had to go to class and then prepare my speeh for the great charity affair which was to take place that evening . . . My cavilings of the preceding two days had not allowed me to take up that matter, and I still had no plan nor any clear ideas about what I would say. I've always been abominable as an improviser. So there was no recourse left but to string together somehow a little speech in words of facile clarity and simplicity, which had seemed to me most appropriate.

I put so much work into to it that by nightfall it was all satisfactorily completed. I had written out my whole speech and read it aloud three or four times to fix in my mind, if not every single sentence, certainly its principal parts and its harmonic structure. This done, I could get through the thing all right, for I was sure that if I had my ideas firmly in hand, my actual language would not refuse to cooperate.

When the time came I got dressed—and I hauled myself off to the theater! I put it this way because I forced myself, as if I were a criminal trying to escape. I was acting as bailiff to myself and had to exercise all the strength of my dignity to keep myself from escaping halfway there and going back home; but my Authority-self had such a stranglehold on my Timidity-self that the latter couldn't even move.

As I approached the theater it became obvious that there was to be a gala there that night. It was still early, and people were already thronging the doorways. Even though care had been taken to prevent profiteering by resale of tickets, there were ten or twelve scalpers in gold-braided caps blocking the way and importuning everyone. Carriages were arriving in rapid succession, their doors clacking shut with a sound like firearms, and when it struck me that I was part of the spectacle attracting all those people, a sort of tickling sensation went up and down my spine. My speech suddenly disappeared from my mind, only to reappear and then be eclipsed again, like those gaslight signs over theater doorways which the wind intermittently blows down without completely snuffing out.

Scarcely had I taken two steps into the lobby when I collided with a hard and dreadfully active object. It was Sáinz del Bardal, who that night (as never before) was in several places at once, so incessant was his movement. In a quarter-hour's time I saw him in diverse parts of the theater, and came to believe that the reproductive forces of the Universe had that evening created a dozen Bardals, just to drive the human race into agony and desperation. He showed up on the stage arranging decorations and lecterns and the piano; then in the lobby, setting out the potted plants which at the last minute hadn't been properly placed; then in the boxes, greeting who knows how many family groups; then inside, outside, upstairs and down. I even think I saw him hanging from the chandelier and coming out of the holes in a string bass. At one of the many moments he flitted past me, he said:

"Up there in the second proscenium box are Manuela, Mercedes, and . . . g'bye, g'bye."

I climbed up there. It surprised me to see Lica in such a high place—in a box next to the topmost gallery. The audience would no doubt be bemused not to see the wife of Manso in one of the lower proscenium boxes. It seemed like a desertion, utterly shocking in the lady at whose house the gala had been planned. When I entered, Irene was hanging up coats in the tiny entryway. She greeted me in a hushed voice, ever so sweet, sort of like an intimate friend sharing a secret or confidence.

"I was concerned," she said, "for fear you might have . . ."

"What?"

"Played a trick on us, and refused to speak at the last minute."

"But, I gave my word, didn't I?"

127

XXVI

SHE PUT ONE FINGER TO HER MOUTH
AS A SIGN FOR ME TO
STOP TALKING

H ER SENSE OF DISCRETION charmed me. She seemed to be saying: "Later we'll talk about that and a host of other pleasant things."

"Did you know," Lica asked me, "that José Maria has gotten into an awful temper because I wouldn't sit in the lower proscenium box? He says I'm acting like a silly goose . . . So much the better, let him get as angry as he likes. I don't feel like putting myself on view. We're just fine right here. Take a look, my lamb, we've come dressed in our wrappers. And don't make any smart remarks! Here we can see, but nobody can see us . . . Lord, you should hear my husband carry on! He says I'm only fit to live in a stable . . . Can you imagine? Oh, well, let him blow off a little steam."

Mercedes was looking down at the stalls, and the birds'-eye view of the animated panorama made her a bit sad to be so far from all that glitter and beauty. Doña Jesusa was there, too, an unheard of event for a person of such sedentary habits.

"I've come only to hear you, m'dear," she said with the greatest kindness. "Because if it wasn't for the fact that you're going to outshine them all, all the Powers in Heaven wouldn't get me out of my armchair."

The good lady was horrendously attired in dress-up clothes, with heavy, glittering jewelry, and, at the center of her bodice, a medallion containing a photograph of her deceased husband, the whole thing about the size of a salad plate. Until that evening I had had no idea of what Lica's father looked like: he was a handsomely bearded gent, in the uniform of the Cuban Volunteer Corps.

"It seems there's to be a solo by a harpist," said Mercedes, all agog with the mysteries of the program.

128

"Yes, I think so. And also . . ."

"Oh, Sáinz del Bardal's poems are so lovely!" said Manuela. "He read them to me this afternoon. They mention Socrates, and a fellow called . . . I don't know just what."

"And who else is reciting?"

"Oh, the main actors, I suppose. I'll go have Sáinz del Bardal send you up a printed program."

Irene didn't open her mouth. Seated just as far from the railing as she was from the vestibule, she kept at a decorous distance from Lica, showing her inferior status, but without giving the slightest hint of servility. Modest and dignified, she would have captivated me if that had been my first sight of her. As I left the box, I saw in the red half-light an object, something black, a face . . . I burst out laughing as I recognized Rupertico, who was watching me and pinching his nose to keep back his peals of laughter. He was sitting stiffly on a bench, circumspectly drawn up and moving neither arms nor legs, all respectful. The only signs of life in him were the impulses to laughter; to quell them he would press his hands tightly over his mouth.

"There was nothing for it but to bring him," said *Niña Chucha.* "Oh my, what a dear he is! Crying all afternoon because he wanted to come hear your speech."

"I think he'd have had an attack if we hadn't brought him," added Lica. "He was driving us crazy. 'I want to hear my master Máximo, I want to hear my master Máximo . . .' And crying on and on."

Giving him a little tug on one ear, I saw a package in the corner, wrapped in a red handkerchief. The little black boy, noticing my glance, quickly put his hands on it and tightened the handkerchief so as to hide it even more. He was convulsed with laughter, and Mercedes and Lica were laughing too . . .

"You fresh thing, fancy-pants, get out of here, nobody needs you here," Lica said. After you speak you can come back and see us."

On stage it was impossible to take a single step. Sáinz del Bardal and the people who had helped him organize the affair were incapable of keeping out anyone who wanted to get in, and the whole place was crowded and disorderly.

Newspapermen looking for details to put in their columns, speakers, the speaker's friends, musicians and all their friends, actors who were going to recite poems, and the poets whose works they were going to recite, members of the Society and a multitude of people whom nobody knew: all these

129

filled the stage. Sáinz del Bardal, red as a beet, and another philanthropic gent, whose specialty is giving speeches at affairs of this kind, were making great efforts to create some order out of the chaos and were gallantly getting the intruders out.

In the midst of all this the orchestral overture ended, and the curtain parted. The members of the Executive Committee were seated in a row of chairs beside the pompous table, behind which appeared the gravest image among all imaginable images, *i.e.,* Don Manuel María Pez. This gentleman was to utter some brief words to explain the purpose of the occasion and to thank those eminent and distinguished persons who had been so kind as to *lend their brilliance for the good of Humanity and of the poor.* This gentleman's oratory was of a fine finish, a model of the bombastic style, empty and hollow, full of pleonasms and amplifiers, decorated with adornments and glittering with bits of tinsel. It was that sort of oratory which allows nonentities to play a small role in Parliament, to tire the stenographers and solidify that immense paper pyramid called the *Parliamentary Proceedings.* If one wished to uncover one of Señor Pez's ideas, one had to demolish with a pickaxe a solid wall of words, and even then, one could not be sure of finding any profitable thing. He said something like this:

"It is surely laudable, it is highly edifying, it is in the utmost degree praiseworthy for our age, our times, our generation, for so many eminent persons, so many illustrious gentlemen, so many of the nation's glories in one and another branch of knowledge, to come forward to offer themselves, to lend their . . . " All of the pieces of his speech were perfectly timed, with bombastic pauses and pompous rhythms, in pretentious and ringing cadences about as tiresome as the hammers of a fulling mill. I stopped paying attention, for I had quickly to apprise myself of the order of events in the celebration, so that I might find out when my turn came, and when I would—oh dear God!—have to go out behind the footlights.

The program was vast, immense, varied, full, like no other I'd ever seen. One could tell right away that Sáinz del Bardal and his unscrewed head had taken part in its concoction. Speeches by a famous orator, by Manuel Peña, and by me; a string quartet by four stars from the Conservatory; readings from the works of celebrated poets by three of the most famous actors. The only poet who would recite his own works would be Sáinz del Bardal, who, owing to the special nature of his character, would not entrust to another's mouth the confections of his genius. Also, there was to be a piano number, performed by a young lady of twelve years, a prodigy at the

130

keyboard; there would be a grand performance on the harp, executed by a famous Italian soloist who had come to Madrid just a few days earlier. Finally, a tenor from the Royal Opera House was going to sing Mozart's famous aria "Al mio tesoro intanto," and then the tenor and a baritone would knock off the *I marinari* duet. I don't know if there was anything else. I don't think so.

Sáinz del Bardal informed me that my place on the program was right after the harpist's solo. This disconcerted me a bit, and more so when I saw him, for he looked like a bird of ill omen. He was far backstage, preparing his instrument and surrounded by a cloud of musicians and Italian people from the Opera House. As I watched him, it occurred to me, as a sort of superstition, that in the company of that damned musician nothing good could happen. He was frankly obese, with the face of a fat woman. He had his hair combed into two charming little horn-shaped curls, and a tiny moustache curled with spittle. It looked like little horns too. And he had two spots on his cheeks: they looked like rouge.

I was walking about by myself, waiting for my turn. A columnist came up and asked, "What are you going to talk about? Would you give me some quotes from your speech?"

"Just a few general remarks . . . ; you'll hear it when the time comes."

"Señor Pez certainly wasn't very felicitous."

Another one came up and said, "Well, the *Dies Irae* is over. That Pez is a talking bassoon. Oh, just get a look at that harp fellow. What a picture, Manso my friend! If that really should make any sound . . . !"

"It seems incredible," added a third newsman, a bit of a dandy and an old student of mine to boot, a good fellow who belonged to the Ateneo. "What a disgrace, the scalpers have been at it! This could only happen in Spain. The governor has had one of them arrested. I'd be interested to know who gave them the tickets that weren't sold, since they're all complimentaries anyway."

Gradually some acquaintances came along and formed a lively circle around me.

"Señor de Manso, when are you on?"

"After the harp. Too bad *my* speech has so few harpeggios."

"If I'd been in your place, I'd have asked for a spot earlier in the program."

"What's the difference? Soon or late, I'll do rather badly."

131

"Oh, come now, man, don't be such a rascal. Badly, you say?!"

"Bosh!"

"You know only too well . . ."

"Nonsense. The man doesn't know his own value."

"Come now, Señor de Manso, wouldn't it be a good idea for you to give me your speech for the *Review*? We'll publish it in Number 15, and then if you wish, we can print up a few copies separately as a pamphlet."

"Nonsense, it's too short."

"Oh, well, so much the better. Anyway, it'll do me for the *Review*."

"What's it about?"

"Nothing, gentlemen, nothing. How can one speak of serious things in front of these people, between a harp solo and a tirade in verse? Just a few general remarks . . ."

"That actor's going on now to read poem number 30. It's splendid. The author read it to me yesterday evening. It's astounding."

"Yes, but just listen to how badly it's being recited."

"That man's an epileptic. He's turning green."

"It'll be a wonder if he doesn't burst a blood vessel."

"But how about that description of the shipwreck, eh?"

"Top-drawer."

"And now, when the cabin burns down . . . bravissimo!"

"The poem's a knockout!"

"Gad, what beautiful poetry!"

"But the recitation itself . . . Oh, if only we had actors like the Italians."

"He's putting on an old woman's voice for the transitional passages."

"Good job, good job!"

We all applauded at the end, wearing out the palms of our hands. From the audience there came a sound of applause which seemed like a tempest. Suddenly, in the friendly circle which had gathered about me, Manuel Peña appeared, his hands in his pockets and his hat tilted back. He looked like a libertine leaving the roulette table.

"Hello there, wastrel!"

"Maestro, lucky you: you're calm."

"And you're afraid?"

"Afraid? I'm like the condemned man in the death house."

132

"What are you going to talk about?"

"The first thing that comes to mind."

"You haven't prepared anything?"

"That's the greatest part," put in a friend. "Would you believe Manso, that this morning he didn't even have any ideas about the speech he's going to give?"

"I don't now, either . . . We'll see what comes out. That's sort of how I do it. This afternoon I read some verses by Victor Hugo and picked up a dozen images."

"Monkey-see-monkey-do?"

"Each image loftier than you can imagine. And that's enough for me . . . I'll talk about the ladies, the influence of women in history, Christianity . . ."

"The Christian woman, eh?"

"Yes, and charity. Come now, gentlemen, who was it that said that thing about *charity running to need the way water runs to the sea?*"

"Chateaubriand."

"No, no, I think it's from Father Gratry."

"No, no, Manso, do you know?"

"Well, I can't remember."

"Well then I'll offer it as my own."

"Oh yes! It's a phrase out of Victor Cousin."

"Well, whoever it was . . . , maestro, you're on soon."

"After the harp. That's where you speak."

The Italian and his Italianesque retinue passed by us. My worthy predecessor was doing gymnastics with his fingers, as if he wished to pluck at the air.

There came an expectant silence which impressed itself on me, for it made me think that soon there would open up before me the mute and fearful cavity of a similar silence. Then one heard *pizzicatos*. They seemed to pinch the very air which ticklishly answered with peals of childish laughter. Then we heard a sonorous, steady strumming like a cloth being ripped. Then, the falling of some light droplets, a shower of hard, steely, little sounds; finally an immense flagellant musical flood, full of mysterious harmonies.

"God, the man plays well!"

"Indeed he does!"

"This is really something! What melodiousness! But what's it from?"

133

"It's a fantasia on *The Star of the North*."

"Oh, those fingers!"

"They're like spider's feet running along the strings."

"And just see how breathless he gets! Look, Manso, how his little horns of hair are shaking."

"And have you seen the number of decorations the man's wearing on his chest?"

"What *man*? It's the bearded lady, the one from the circus!"

"Shh! Gentlemen, please don't laugh."

When he finished his solo and the applause broke forth, my heart seemed to go all wrinkly and my eyes seemed to cloud over. My hour had come. I took a few mechanical steps.

"Not yet. He's doing an encore."

"What joy! Five more minutes of life."

In order to take courage I feigned a happiness, nonchalance, and valor which I was far from possessing. The effect of such artificial stimuli is usually of very short duration . . . And finally, the fatal moment arrived. The Italian came off stage, went back to applause and at last withdrew for good. I saw him wiping the sweat off his purplish face—it looked like a shiny tomato— and I heard the congratulations of the musicians who surrounded him. I broke through their group to go on stage; my legs were shaking.

And there I was facing the dragon, like someone about to be swallowed up, for the footlights were a set of fiery teeth; the rows of seats were furrows of an undulating tongue; and the concave red space of the theater, warm and breath-laden, was a horrendous mouth. But the very sight of danger seemed to restore my valor and strengthen me. "Really," I thought, "it's foolish to be afraid of these good folk. And I won't do so badly as to be ridiculous . . ."

I lifted my gaze, and way up there, against the badly painted clouds on the ceiling, I could make out clearly the outline of a group of heads.

XXVII
IRENE'S HEAD DOMINATED
THE OTHER THREE

O R AT LEAST, hers was the one I saw most clearly. When I began to speak, in a rather insecure voice, the pseudo-Moorish decorations of the box seats seemed to be making grimaces right into my eyes. People adjusting their opera glasses, plus the movement of so many ladies' fans—it all distracted me. In one of the lower proscenium boxes there was an accursed woman whose extra-large fan kept opening and closing constantly with an impertinent scraping sound. I imagined that she was either emphasizing certain of my sentences or mocking me with cloth peals of laughter. Damn the commentary! As I would be finishing a sentence, bringing it round to a full and well-wrought ending, I heard that *scritch* and it turned my nerves into taut wires. But there was nothing for it but to be patient and go on, because I couldn't say to the fan-lady, as I would to a pupil in my class, "Please have the courtesy not to butt in!"

And I went on, and on. One phrase after another, sentence upon sentence, the speech kept coming out clean, clear, proper, with that easy flow which had cost me so much hard work. It kept coming out, yes it did, and I was not displeased. And as I kept speaking my critical judgment was saying, "Not bad, no sir. I like it; keep it up . . ."

What shall I say about my talk? To copy it here would be out of order. One of the many periodicals we have, all of them distinguished by their eager efforts to gain regular subscribers, published it verbatim, and any curious person may read it there. It offered no great novelty and contained no idea of the first rank. It was a short, simple dissertation for what is called an *audience,* that's to say a gathering of *many people* whose total sum is really *nobody.* The whole thing came down to a few observations on indigence, its causes, its relationship to the law, our common life and our habits of work. There followed a review of our beneficent institutions, during which I gave special emphasis to the ones which attempt to protect the young. In this section of

135

my talk I managed to put in a sentimental touch which brought forth admiring murmurs. But the rest was unadorned, proper, cool, and precise. Everything I said, I knew, and I knew it well. None of this stuff you pick up the night before and stick in with saliva. It was all solid; logical order controlled the several parts of my talk, and there wasn't a single superfluous phrase or word. It was characterized by precision and balance, and had absolutely no padding or cheap effects.

I praise myself in this way without the slightest hesitation. I am entitled to do so by virtue of my frankness in declaring that there was in my speech not the smallest spark of oratorical brilliance. I might just as well have been reading a brainy and learned report on something, or a treasury regulation. And I could clearly notice the effect on the audience of this shortcoming of mine. Yes, through the warp and woof of my talk, as through the openings in a piece of cloth, I could see the thousand-headed little dragon, and I noticed that in many boxes the ladies and gentlemen were chatting away, oblivious of me and paying as much heed to me as they would to the clouds of yesteryear. On the other hand, I noticed in the first row of the stalls a couple of professors whose glasses reflected the light into my eyes like arrows: they were nodding their approval of my ideas. And the *scritch* of that accursed fan was still scratching the limpid surface of my language, the way a sharp diamond marks the surface of a window pane.

The end was not far. My conclusions were to the effect that official charitable institutions solve the problem of pauperism only to an insignificant degree; that individual initiative, those societies formed from the warmth of Christian ideals . . . ; in short, my conclusions offered hardly anything new and the reader knows them as well as I do. Sufficient to say now that I did finish, something which I desired ardently to do, and part of the audience desired it as well. I was dismissed with a mechanical, routine, unenthusiastic round of applause, albeit with a good measure of respect and agreement, too. It had come off well, as I had hoped and wished. Discretion and truth from me; good will and courtesy from the audience. I gave a satisfied sign of acknowledgment, and was already leaving the stage when . . .

What was that thing flying down from the ceiling, trailing ribbons behind it? It was a multicolored object, a collection of small green branches, red trimmings . . . A *crown* or *wreath,* oh vengeful Heavens!! It had been so badly aimed that it fell onto the footlights.

I don't know who picked it up; I don't know who handed me that outsize piece of artificial leaves with acorns like livery buttons. It had more ribbons than the insignia of a bull in the ring, carnations the size of sunflowers, gilt letters, I don't know what else . . . I accepted that extemporaneous tribute, but I don't know how I did it. I was so upset that I didn't know *what* I was doing, and almost put the crown on Señor Pez's bald head. As I passed, he said, "You had it coming to you, yes indeed."

The murmurs coming from the audience made one aware that the dragon, like myself, had considered that offering absolutely improper, inopportune, and ridiculous. And then it had been so badly tossed . . . I had an urge to throw it into the middle of the stalls.

"It's a gift from your family," I heard someone say.

I was left in confusion, and then I got so angry . . . ! At last I realized what it was that the rascally black boy was hiding under that cloth! I could just see it! It must have been *Niña Chucha's* idea.

I went offstage with my sickening burden of foliage and cloth. To tell the truth, the best way to handle it was as a joke, and that's what I did. Very soon, as the program continued with the piano peice, a circle of friends gathered around me, and I listened to the felicitations of some, and the sincere or malicious remarks of others.

"Very good, Manso my friend. One could expect no less from you."

"I liked it a lot, really a lot. No, none of your modest protestations. You must be very satisfied."

"Orator laureate, no less!"

"Pity you didn't speak a bit louder! From row eleven one could scarcely hear a thing."

"Well done, well done . . . Heartfelt congratulations. A bit more warmth wouldn't have been out of place."

"But so well expressed! What clarity!"

"And all the time you said it was just a light little thing . . ."

"Right to the point, Manso my friend; right to the point."

"Bravissimo, Sir Manso."

"Well, old man, you could have put a bit of strength in your voice and have given the thing some power, yes, some power . . ."

"Look, next time move your arms with more jauntiness . . . But people liked your speech a lot. The ladies didn't understand it; but they liked it."

"And even a crown for you . . . !"

The harpist also came over to congratulate me, taking the liberty of introducing himself so as to have *l'onore de stringere la mano d'un egregio professore.*

The flattery obliged me, against my inclinations, to dedicate a few sentences to a panegyric of the harp, its lovely effects, its difficulty, exalting its cultivators far above all other ranks of musicians and performers.

As I was speaking with the Italian and other musicians and some of my friends, my attention was diverted from the subsequent portions of the program. But there began to reach us, like the errant emanations of an impending incense-attack, some rhetorical effluvia of the verses Sáinz del Bardal was reading. His puffed-up declamation was letting loose into the air those soap bubbles so much admired by women and fools. The bubbles would burst, resounding in different ways, sometimes gravely, sometimes plaintively, or like a homily. And amid the chatter buzzing about me, we could all hear: "Believe and hope, sublime immensity, mystical transports, . . . hail holy faith." From several isolated words and phrases caught on the fly we concluded that Señor del Bardal was nestling *neath the coverlet of religion;* that he was *adrift on the sea of life;* that his soul was *forcefully ripping through the veil of mystery,* and that the rascal was going to sever the chains which bound him to *human impurity.* We also heard a great deal about *beacons of hope,* and *havens of refuge* and *raging winds* and the *gulf of doubt,* which latter signified not that Bardal had set up a launch operation, but that he was in a mood to get onto a ship (his own inspiration) with no fixed destination, and that everything was being reduced to shipwrecks and storms—rhetorical ones, that is.

"Will the man *ever* stop?!"

"Let him row along . . . Too bad we can't send people to the galleys any more!"

"And just listen to that applause!"

"Sure. As long as the female sex exists, the Magpie Muses will have their weapons kept sharp. The public gives more praises to this ordinary stuff than to the really fine verses of thirty good poets. That's the way the world is."

"And art is, too. Let's leave, here he comes."

"Bardal's coming! Who could *endure* him now?"

"I'm afraid I'll be sick. My stomach is no good anyway, and that emetic poet also makes me throw up . . . Let's clear out."

"Every man for himself!"

I departed also, fearful of being accosted by Bardal. I left the stage area, and in the lower corridor I met a lot of people who had come out to smoke, taking the poet's recitation as a convenient intermission. Some people congratulated me coldly, others directed looks of curiosity toward me. While I was there I learned that the famous orator who was to take part in the occasion had begged off at the last minute, having been stricken by an attack of colic. There were only a few numbers left on the program, and there was no doubt that part of the audience was supremely bored, thinking that the organizers of the affair should take a leaf from their own book, and *charitably* bring the celebration to a close as soon as possible.

I met my brother on the stairway. He was visiting from box to box, and had a boutonnière in his lapel. He was smoothing out with his hands a copy of *La Correspondencia.*

"You were geniunely philosophical," he told me with false bonhomie, "but there was too much metaphysics and we poor mortals don't understand that. Too bad you didn't use the statistics on mortality Pez gave you at the last minute, and the percentages of poor people recorded in the principal European capitals. I've studied the matter, and it so happens that our primary schools register four hundred fourteen and three-quarters children for each . . ."

"Were you up there, in the family box?" I asked him so as to cut off his deadly thread of statistics.

"No, and I have no intention of going. A fine show indeed! Can you imagine? Stuck up there in that wretched box! How unsuitable and foolish and stupid! My wife makes me look ridiculous a hundred times every day. But you're in the same boat, eh? What have you to say about that wreath they tossed down?"

My brother's burst of laughter brought to my mind the image of the ill-fated gift I had received, and I couldn't hide the displeasure it had caused me.

"They're such foolish people! I'll bet it was one of *Niña Chucha*'s ideas. As far as Manuela is concerned, she's stubbornness on two feet. All I have to do is want *one* thing, and she . . ."

I made excuses for Lica: he got angry and told me that all my wise man's nonsense was simply encouraging his wife's stubbornness and finicky ways.

"But José . . . "

"You're a disaster, too, just one more disaster, do you hear? You'll never amount to a thing . . . because you're never really *into* things. Just take a look at the speech you gave tonight: practical and philosophical and whatever you like. All right, but nobody *liked* it. And they won't be enthusiastic about anything you write either. And you won't make your way in the world or ever be anything but a miserable professor, and you won't become famous . . . And it's you who's sounding off in my house all the time about ridiculous modesty and philosophical gobbledygook and stupid methodicalness."

"Oh, come now, José!"

"I said it and I meant it, chum."

We were in the midst of this when we were interrrupted by an outburst coming from inside the hall itself. At first we were frightened. But, tut, tut! It was applause, wild applause, a demonstration of the liveliest enthusiasm.

"But what's going on?"

The corridors had been left empty. Everyone was going back to their seats to discover the cause of such an attack of madness.

XXVIII
"IT'S YOUNG PEÑA SPEAKING"

THAT'S WHAT THEY were all saying, and I, wishing to hear my disciple, left my brother and climbed to the upper box where the family was. I went in. So enraptured were the four ladies in their contemplation and audition of the speaker that not one turned her head to see who was coming in. Only the black boy looked at me and, stroking my hand, came close beside me. I moved in closer and without making a sound I looked down into the theater over the tops of the four heads. Never have I seen a more attentive crowd nor a greater degree of interest, all directed toward a single point. To tell the truth, I have seldom witnessed a greater or more brilliant display of human eloquence.

The audience was fascinated and quite overcome. A young man of captivating utterance, he had a semidivine gift which brought together elegance of idea, boldness of image, and the physical charm of a robust and flexible voice—this young man had caught, ensnared as in a net of empathy, the heterogeneous mass of diverse folk, and in one and the same outpouring of delight there were united the fool and the wise man, men and women, the frivolous and the sober. With celestial vibrations of the strings of his noble spirit, the speaker awakened the cardinal sentiments of the human soul; and not a single spectator failed to respond to his admirable invocation. Doña Jesusa turned toward me, and I could see by her face that she was nearly stupefied. Even the portrait of her deceased husband, occupying its prominent place on her breast, seemed to have come alive in its ivory or porcelain setting. Mercedes looked at me too, making a face that said: "This is really good." Lica and Irene weren't moving a muscle: emotion had turned them to statues.

For myself, I must say that I had a lump in my throat as I stood there in admiration of Manuel, filled with joy as I witnessed the great triumph of one who had been a disciple of mine. Yes; I could claim for myself a part, be it

141

never so small, in the glory that the divine boy was so abundantly garnering that night. For if indeed he had received from Nature his remarkable power with words, I had cut the facets of his gemlike genius, I had given to his native gifts the adornments of art, without which his speech would have seemed careless and crude; I had taught him who the great models were and how they had been formed, and from me he had got many of the basic technical devices which he used to such astounding effect. So, actually, when he would come to the end of a paragraph and the audience would burst into wild applause, I also clapped my hands sore and wanted to be next to the speaker so as to clasp him in my arms.

What was the subject of his talk? I can't say exactly. Everything and nothing. He wasn't very specific, and his eloquent digressions were a kind of flight of the spirit and ramble through the regions of fantasy. And yet one could perceive his powerful efforts to enclose his fancy within a logical design. I could see that he was firmly reining in that spirited, winged steed who was rearing up to the heights, feeling neither rein nor crop. Fascinated though I was (along with the rest), I never lost sight of the fact that the brilliant speech, once subjected to a careful reading, would offer some vulnerable points and as many contradictions as it had paragraphs. My enthusiasm did not stifle my gift for analysis, and quaking with delight, I proceeded to a dissection right down to the logical skeleton, clothed though it might be with such an opulent array of verbal flesh.

But what was the use of all that analysis if his main purpose was to stir people, and he had succeeded utterly in doing that? What admirable sentence structure, what sparkling enumerations, what a splendid way of presenting ideas, what a variety of tones and cadences, what an inimitable secret technique of making the voice suit the mood and, by combining the two, getting the most surprising effects; what varied shadings, and finally what sober, elegant gestures, what energetic yet gentle diction, never getting out of hand, never becoming bombastic, never making a phrase sing-songy! Image followed upon image, and if they weren't all strictly original—indeed a few were rather hackneyed, like a flower too much handled—the audience, and I as well, found them admirable, fresh, lovely. Some were charmingly new.

But what was he talking *about*? He himself had announced it earlier. Christianity, the redemption and exaltation of women, liberty, a bit about the grand ideals of the nineteenth century. Queen Isabella came in for a mention, pawning her jewels, Columbus *rounding out civilization,* and Stephenson, who with his locomotive, *has joined the world into one family.* Then I heard something about the catacombs and Lincoln, the *black man's Christ,* the Sisters of Charity, the Andalusian sky, Newton, the Pyramids, and the Caprichos of Goya, all of it woven and linked together so artfully that the listener followed Manuel from one surprise to the next, astounded and bewitched, weary from the bedazzlement of such a range of tones and such graceful transitions.

When he finished, you might say that the theater toppled over, that its very framework creaked and came unstuck, so vibrant was the applause. Those who were near enough leaned over toward the stage, as if they wished to embrace the speaker. The ladies raised their handkerchiefs to their eyes to dry a tear, for it is well known that any deep feeling, even enthusiasm, will make them weep. Manuel left the stage, and the applause called him back, three, four, I can't say how many times. Señor de Pez, unwilling to be denied a conspicuous role on such a solemn occasion, led the young man back by the hand and presented him to the audience with fatherly solicitude. Someone said: "He's just a boy!" Others: "A prodigy!" And I shouted to the people in the neighboring box:

"He's my student, ladies and gentlemen; he's my student."

Lica turned to me and said, "A pity his dear mother didn't come to hear him."

And Doña Jesusa, imagining I was feeling rebuffed, looked benevolently at me and said:

"You did well, too . . ." And at that moment I hadn't even remembered my own speech, or the fatal wreath!

"Too bad we didn't bring *two* garlands!"

"As for that, Manuela, you could hardly have done anything more inappropriate!"

"You be quiet, ducky; you deserve better."

"The fact is that Máximo"—Doña Jesusa was pushing good will to the limit because she imagined me to be sad at another's good fortune—"Máximo did very well too . . . Everyone, everyone did very well."

And Irene remained silent. When the clapping stopped she went back to her seat. I looked at her; her cheeks were red. She'd been weeping too.

"How fine, how fine!" Lica kept exclaiming endlessly. "That boy is a marvel. What did you think, Irene?"

Irene looked at me, and came up with a heavenly remark.

"He does honor to his teacher."

"That boy," I affirmed, "will be a great orator. He already is. It seems as if Nature has chosen to make of him the model man of the present era. He

143

is patterned and molded for his age, and fits into it like the key piece in a machine."

"A gentleman there in the next box over was saying that Manuel will be a Cabinet Minister before ten years go by."

"I believe that's true; he'll be whatever he chooses to be; he is Destiny's fair-haired boy. All the good fairies must have been present at his birth . . ."

"I think we should leave now. I'm quite tired. How about you, Mamma?"

"Yes, do let's go."

"And miss hearing the tenor?" said the disconsolate Mercedes.

"My child, we'll hear him at the Opera House."

They got up. Irene stood in the antechamber handing out cloaks. Once everyone was wrapped up she put on her own cloak. I assisted Doña Jesusa first, then Lica, then Mercedes; then Irene, who was holding her hatpin in her mouth as she unfolded her head scarf in preparation for putting it on. Irene thanked me. I don't know what gave me the idea that she was still crying. A deception of my own treacherous eyes! We went out. The black boy hung on my arm, forcing me to bend over to the right. His idea was to reach my ear with his pursed lips and say in timid secrecy:

"Nobody was as good as you, old daddy. Master Máximo is better than all the rest, and anybody who says he isn't . . ."

"Quiet, silly."

" 'Cause they don't understand him."

The necessity of accompanying the family kept me from going backstage to embrace my beloved disciple. But I would see him soon enough at his house, and there we could talk at length of that evening's colossal success . . .

And to think that my wreath had been left on the stage! *In mente* I made a gift of it to the harpist. Lica was obviously not in agreement, and said as she was getting into the carriage:

"Irene is right to call you dreary: why didn't you bring your crown? Don't you think you deserve it? Well you surely do. It was my idea. What do you think of it?"

"No, it was *my* idea," *Niña Chucha* quickly interposed.

"No quarreling, ladies; let's just say it was *both* your ideas, something which doesn't change the fact that it's a *revolting* idea."

"Ingrate!"

144

"Stuck-up!"

"We had so little time; it was the best we could do. Lica chose the flowers."

"And I picked out the green leaves."

"And I the red ribbons."

"Well, all of you showed dismal taste."

"Well, all right for you! No more presents for you!"

"What a conceited man!"

Irene said nothing. She was beside me in the forward seat, and the jogging of the carriage caused our elbows to rub slightly. If I were more given to tricky metaphors, I'd say that the rubbing struck sparks, and the sparks went straight to my brain and produced a combustion of thoughts or explosive illusions . . . The rocking of the carriage put Doña Jesusa to sleep. Lica burst out laughing, and said:

"Mamma's in dreamland already. Have you gone to sleep, too, Irene?"

"No, madam," the governess replied, a bit curtly.

"Well you've been so quiet . . . And what's the matter with you, Máximo? You haven't said a word."

I realized then that in fact I hadn't opened my mouth for a good space of time. I'm not sure I said anything in reponse to Lica. At last, we reached their house. Nothing happened that's worth telling. Boredom all around, everyone heading off to their own rooms. I was determined to say something to Irene; I could sense her behind me when I was taking my leave of Doña Jesusa in the passage; I turned around, took a few steps, but she was already gone. I asked the mulatto girl . . . Miss Irene had withdrawn to her room . . . ! Oh, my goodness, how hasty! . . . All right, all right, I'll withdraw too.

The black boy hung onto my arm to make me bend over and listen. He always spoke to me in secret, in an affectionate whisper that entered my spirit like the purest distillation of human innocence. His words were few, and showed a candorous pride:

"I carried the wreath from the shop."

"Fine, my lad, good for you. Good-bye."

Before going up to my house, I decided to stop and congratulate Doña Javiera. The poor lady was beside herself. She *had* gone to the theater after all, and had witnessed her beloved son's magnificent triumph from the topmost gallery. Manuel had reserved her a box; but she had been reluctant to sit there, and gave it to some friends; she was afraid lest her mother-love should induce her to exaggerated demonstrations which might make her look ridiculous. Alone with her maid up in the gallery, she had wept to her heart's content, and when she heard the applause and saw the audience's wild enthusiasm, she felt transported to Heaven. At the end, the good woman had passed out, and they almost had to take her to the First Aid Station. She embraced me with ardent joy, saying that I had the greater part in Manuel's triumph, since I was teacher to that marvel of Nature.

"Up where I was," she went on, "all you could hear was: 'That boy will have a great career . . . Any day now they'll make him a member of Parliament or a Cabinet Minister. Quite some young man indeed . . . ' Just imagine, Manso my friend, how set up I was. I was fairly drooling and weeping like a fool. I wanted to stand up and shout from the railing: 'He's my son! I gave him birth, I nursed him at my breast . . .' Just as well that I fainted . . . I was just wild, that's all. My heart was in my mouth . . . And I *did* see you in an upper box with those ladies. I kept looking at you to catch your eye and make a sign to say: 'We're *all* here.' But you didn't look over . . . Oh! Now that I think of it, you did very nicely, too. Up there, next to me, there was a very disagreeable fellow who said some stupid things about you . . . I almost came to blows with him, and when they threw down the wreath from the box, he shouted: 'Yes, that's what he deserves!' To tell you the truth, from up there we couldn't hear anything you said, you talk in such a low voice. Actually, I heard so little that I just about went off to sleep. I woke up with a fright when they were tossing the wreath at you, and then I clapped like mad . . . Then the poetry. And so lovely, too! I just loved it! . . . Hearing pretty poems is just like being tickled. You laugh and cry . . . , I'm not sure I'm getting my meaning across."

And she kept on chattering in this vein. I was worn out and wanted to leave. It was very late and Manuel hadn't come home. I wanted to see him that very night to congratulate him with a sincere outpouring of affection; but he just *didn't* come in, so I went up to my third-floor flat and retired, eager for silence, tranquility, peace.

XXIX
O DARKEST SADNESS!

HEAVY FUNEREAL VEIL, who cast you upon me? O thoughts of death, why did you rise, slow and fearsome within my soul, like vapors rising from the face of a torrid lake? And you, long night hours, what harm have I done you to make you punish me, each in your turn, implacable, piercing my brain with the rhythm of your sharp-pointed minutes? And you, Sleep, why did you stare at me with pained owlish eyes tickling my own eyes, and yet refusing to snuff out with a holy puff the flame of wakefulness in my mind? But O you tenuous arguments in a hairsplitting sophistical train of thought, you are the most to blame . . .

You, Imagination, were the cause of my agony during that ill-fated night. You it was who plotted all night and turned a single idea every which way; you it was, ill-mannered, capricious intruder, who overheated my brains and stretched my nerves as taut as the harpstrings I had heard plucked at the theater. And when I thought to have you forever under control, you snapped your fetters, and conspiring with Distrust and Self-love, two rascals just like you, you tossed me as on a blanket into the air. And so as dawn broke, my poor, battered, wounded spirit offered anything of value it had left in exchange for a bit of sleep.

The fact is that my sleeplessness and sadness had no rational explanation. A famous astronomer discovered the planet Neptune without having seen it, by calculation alone, just on the strength of some irregularities in the orbit of Uranus which pointed to the existence of a heavenly body as yet unseen by human eyes. And he, by mathematical effort, succeeded in establishing the existence of that distant, mysterious traveler in space. In just the same way I divine that across my personal firmament there travels an unknown body; I have not seen it, nor has anyone told me of it. But since by my calculations I know it exists, I shall now put all of my mathematics into practice in order to discover it. And discover it I will; the irregular orbit of Uranus, the beloved planet, foretells it. Such an irregularity can be produced only by physical attraction. This deep sorrow I feel is really the influence upon me of that distant, unknown body. My reason affirms its existence. Now my senses must confirm it, and so they shall; if not, I shall consider myself mad.

I said all this, and went off to class, where several pupils congratulated me. I was so dejected, that I did not lecture that day. I asked them questions, but I don't know whether they answered poorly or well. Restless till I might go to my brother's house, I left class before the beadle called the hour. My wish realized, the first person I met was Manuela, who said mysteriously:

"Something's up. Can you imagine Doña Cándida and José María locked up in his study? It's business . . ."

"Poor José; this time she'll clean him out and he'll be off to the poorhouse."

"Be still, you ninny. why she's so rich now! She's sold some parcels of land."

"Land! Maybe the dirt on the soles of her shoes. Lica, Lica, there's something rotten here . . . I'd better try to protect José. Caligula is terrifying; she's probably mounted an attack based on all sorts of lies, and he's so generous that . . ."

"No, let them be . . . But shh! Here comes Doña Cándida now."

It was she indeed: she came into the sitting room a bit fearfully, settling something into the deep pocket of her dress. Oh! she was doubtless caressing her prey, the fat harvest of her most recent depradations. Her greenish gaze revealed completely that her ferocious covetousness had been soothed, her rapacious appetite newly placated! She looked at us with counterfeit sweetness, sat down majestically and feeling her pocket once more, deigned to remark:

"Well, I've finally negotiated those bills of exchange . . . José is such a good fellow! Hi! Is that you there, Mr. Inanity? I've heard tell that you were only fair last night. Seems people went to sleep in droves. So I've been told. Apparently the standout was young Peña, the son of that butcher-woman who's your neighbor. Well, to change the subject, my dear Manuela—do you realize I'm being forced to do something very disagreeable to you?"

"To me? What?" exclaimed my poor sister-in-law, all in a fright.

"My dear, I think I shall have to take Irene away. Just consider . . . I'm so alone and feeling a bit poorly . . . And then my status has undergone such a change that really, it's not proper for Irene . . . or so it seems to me . . . , to be a governess on salary, now that her aunt is . . ."

"Rich."

"Well, rich, no, but I do have enough now to live comfortably. Don't you agree? Don't you agree that I should take her with me to be my companion, to care for me?"

"But of course!"

"She's all the family I have, I've reared her, she'll inherit what I have . . . , because I'm not well, Manuela, not well at all, believe me . . ."

She shed a tiny tear which dissolved into a wrinkle and was not heard from again.

"This doesn't mean," she went on, "that I'm pulling Irene out of here in any great rush; that would be perfectly dreadful. She may stay on for some days yet, and finish out her lessons . . . , or if you wish she could stay until you find a new governess. That's up to you and her. She is so grateful to you that she will surely shed a few tears at having to leave. She *adores* the girls."

I thought Manuela seemed bemused.

"Well, how's it going with the wet nurse?" asked my gadfly, evincing a lively interest. "Still as capricious and willful as ever?"

"Oh, don't even mention her, Doña Cándida . . . Unbearable, unbearable. She's a demon."

I left as they were discussing the wet nurse, and ran to the place where my burning curiosity was pulling me. Irene was giving her grammar lesson, and I came in on her as she was saying sweetly: "You might have, you would have, you could have *loved*."

My anxiety had robbed me of breath, and I scarcely had enough to ask her:

XXX
"SO YOU'RE LEAVING US, THEN?"

Y ES, SHE SAID in a resolute tone, looking me square in the face as
if to empty (as it seemed to me) the entire luminous contents of her
eyes upon me.

"You don't say! When?"

"This very day. What must be . . ."

"You're a rascally girl! But do you have any reason to be unhappy with
this house?"

"Don't be silly. I, unhappy with this house? You might rather say,
very grateful."

"Then . . ."

"But I must leave, Manso my friend. I can't spend my whole life like
this. And if I must leave this house, wouldn't it be better to get it over with?
Each passing day would be more difficult. So there it is, I pull myself
together, make the effort . . ."

"You're *something!*" I exclaimed like a fool, repeating her favorite
expression.

"Yes, sir. I'm going into retirement . . . from school-teaching!" she
replied in a burst of laughter.

Wasn't there a mad joy in her face? If there wasn't, I'm the world's
greatest dullard at reading your signs, O human soul. Her joy made me ill at
ease, because we had reached a point where everything made one ill at ease,
and all I said was:

"Do you have plans?"

"Yes, sir, I have my little plans . . . and they're good ones, too! Did you
think only wise men had plans?"

The two little girls, Isabel and Merceditas, were looking at us en-
tranced, their books open in their hands but lying unheeded in their laps.
They were perhaps savoring that break in the lesson, and would surely have
thanked us if we'd kept on chatting all day.

150

"No, not at all. I'm glad to know you have some plans and are leaving this life behind . . . There's much to be said on that subject . . . But do go on with the lesson. Later we can . . ."

"Talk? Yes, sir, I'd like to talk with you, too; it's just that there's so much to say . . ."

"Later then, here," I said, and in the moment I said it I thought of the solemn way actors on a stage pronounce that phrase.

I was turning melodramatic in the most natural way there was. I think I turned pale and began to speak with a tremor.

"No, not here . . ." she said, answering my confusion with confusions of her own, looking back toward the children and the grammar book, as if recalled by an awareness of her pedagogical duties.

And that "not here" did not pass her lips tinged with any sweet tone of amorous caution. It was said out of a fine instinct for prudence, which already in a woman's first exercise of feminine mischief appears as fully developed as if it had had the benefit of many years' practice.

"You're right; not here," I repeated.

I no longer held the initiative. She had it entirely, and said:

"At my house, my new house. You'll visit us of course?"

"Tomorrow at the latest."

"Not so fast, please. I'll tell you when."

"But soon, surely?"

"I surely think so. But on no account should you visit before I've said you may."

And she wrote down her new address for me on a slip of paper.

I could hear a buzz of voices at the door, and all four of us began to conjugate the verbs with exemplary fervor . . . !

Lica came in, in a very bad mood. We could hear José María's voice as he went off, and I could tell that there had been a spat between husband and wife . . . But my brother was gone; he was having lunch out, thus suspending hostilities. As Manuela and I were having lunch she said, very upset:

"Well, Doña Cándida's gone. I must say! I never saw her in such a hurry to leave. She was coming apart. Just the fact that she declined to stay for lunch. I can't understand it; it's the end of the world. I don't know what I'm feeling, Máximo. Doña Cándida has really set me thinking today. She was in such a rush . . . When I asked about her new home, she answered by changing the subject and talking about other matters. Really you know, unless you're right and she turns out to be simply a vain, conceited woman . . ."

I held my tongue. Well, I didn't actually, but all I said was:

"We'll soon find out."

And she, taciturn, kept eating, sighing all the while. I was deep in thought and hardly ate a mouthful. José María came back after a while. The tasks he had to do in his study seemed like a pretext for being in the house at certain hours. He behaved agreeably toward me and Manuela; but one could see through his feigned pleasantness from a mile away. He told us the weather was splendid, and pulling out some complimentary tickets to some charity affair or other at the Retiro Gardens, he encouraged us to go along. Manuela said no, and so did I.

"Why don't *you* go?" she asked her husband.

"I really can't. I have things to do here."

He obviously had plenty to do. In the front hall and the drawing room there was a full ration of favor-seekers, some of them dismissed civil servants and others just plain hopefuls. Ever since my brother had begun to be a power, the thunderclouds of passion for the civil service were dropping a daily drenching of office-seekers on his house. Auditors, foresters, octroi officers, innumerable characters who had been, or were, or wanted to be something, they all came in an endless line seeking a recommendation. This one had a card from a friend, that one a letter, the other one just introduced himself, José María, whose selfishness could avoid any kind of annoyance (excepting always those cases which might be of some benefit to him), always got out from under the pesky swarm of office seekers, and almost always in great style; he would go out simply leaving them waiting in the entry or telling them to come back. But that day my benevolent brother was at great pains to give evidence of his concern for the disinherited classes, and received his besiegers one by one, giving hope to all, even encouraging them in their need or their aspirations.

"Fine; give me a note . . . I've passed your note along to the Minister . . . Here's the answer from the Director: he wants a note from me . . . Why, you forgot to give me the note yesterday! . . . I think we made an error in writing that note; that's what the Office has . . . I think you'd best send another note . . . I *have* made a note of it, my good fellow, I *have* made a note . . ."

And so, giving and making notes, offering them and sending them, the rascal spent the whole afternoon.

Meanwhile, Irene was getting her things together. She was shut up in her room for over two hours. Only the little girls were with her, helping her pack and tie up different bundles. A bit later I saw her large trunk in the passage, all tied up with rope. When she said good-bye to Manuela, tears moistened her face, and her nose and cheeks were red. The two little girls, fearful of their own grief, had taken refuge in the schoolroom, where they were crying their eyes out.

"Don't be so silly!"Irene said to them, rushing in to give them a good-bye kiss. "I'll be coming by every day."

The good-byes were very touching; but Manuela was rather bewildered, and hadn't let herself be overcome with weeping. Serenely, she said good-bye to the woman who had been her girls' governess, and saw her to the door.

At that moment José María came out of his office. All of his busyness and *notes* disappeared as if by magic.

"Oh, were you leaving right now?" he said joyfully. "I have to go out now, too. I'll take you in my carriage."

"No, thank you sir; no need at all," Irene answered, starting to run down the stairs. "Ruperto is going with me."

José María went down after her. Manuela and I went to the sitting-room windows to see . . .

Indeed, Irene had not been able to escape my brother's gallantry, and got into the carriage, followed by José; and thereupon we saw the berline dash off toward the Calle de San Mateo.

"Did you see that, did you see that?" Lica burst out, fixing her angry eyes upon me, and running to throw herself into a rocking chair.

"What? Don't make hasty judgments . . . It's still . . ."

"Still what? This is awful . . . The cheek of the man! Taking her in his own carriage . . . That's why he's been here all afternoon . . . waiting . . . Máximo, how insulting! Good Lord, the infamy of it! . . . If I hadn't seen it myself . . . Don't make light . . . I see it now . . . I'm furious, I'm wild . . ."

Rocking in the chair, she expressed her grief in a sort of indolent paroxysm, as another woman might have done in an outburst of violence.

"I'm dying, I can't live like this," she cried, breaking into tears. "Máximo, what do you think of that? Right in front of me, before my very eyes! This high-class behavior . . . It's shameless, that's what it is, and shamelessness is something I can't forgive."

"But, my dear, if you've only this one thing to go on, do calm down. We'll see what happens later . . ."

153

"You're a fool; I can guess what's going on. My jealousy has a thousand eyes," she said to me, rocking so hard that I thought the rocker would tip over. "I don't know anything for certain, but even so there's something to it, something . . . I told you Irene seemed like a very good girl . . . What a joke! She was hoodwinking us all in the most . . . I'm telling you, I've discovered things in her . . . Oh! I may be stupid, but I can tell when a woman has something up her sleeve, no matter how much she pretends. Irene is tricking us all. She's a hypocrite!"

XXXI
"SHE'S A HYPOCRITE!"

THIS FELL ON MY HEART like a hammer on an anvil, and it set my whole spirit shaking.

"But Lica, calm down, just reason it out clearly . . ."

"I don't reason, you fool, I feel, I sense things, I'm a woman."

"Just what have you observed?"

"Well, Irene has been doing a very bad job with the lessons lately. She's been moving backwards, the way crabs do. Teaching everything backside to. One afternoon . . . I'm beginning to see how important these things are. I caught her reading a letter. When I went in, she put it away quickly. Her eyes were all red. And then this eagerness to move in with her aunt. the cheek of the girl! I'm beginning to see that Auntie is quite some number,too . . ."

"So she was reading a letter. Why does it have to have been a letter from you husband?"

"I don't know . . . I saw it from a distance, just for a moment . . . It was like a bolt from the blue . . . I couldn't see the writing letter by letter; but you know, I thought I could see those special p's and h's José María writes . . . That girl, she's a . . . No, Máximo, something's wrong here, really wrong. Tonight I'll have some straight talk with my husband. I'm going back to Cuba. If he wants to keep mistresses, and go to rack and ruin, and throw away my children's bread, I'm still their mother and I'm going to my own country. I'm choking here in Spain. I don't want people laughing at me when my money's being spent by trollops on their own whims. Mamma, Mamma!"

And just as the heavy, panting Doña Jesusa walked in, good, peaceful Manuela threw such a fit of violent anger and jealousy that we had all we could do to bring her back to her senses. After weeping copiously in her mother's arms—the old lady was uttering heart-rendering moans herself—Manuela lost control and had such a violent nervous attack, complete with convulsions and arm-thrashings and leg-pullings, that we couldn't quell her.

155

Only the wet nurse, with her brute strength, was able to subdue the poor wife's uncontrolled muscular spasms. Finally she did calm down, and we gave her, as a kind of last remedy, a cup of linden-flower tea.

"We *will* go, my darling child." Doña Jesusa kept saying to her. "We'll go back home, where there are no *hullaballoos* like here."

I had to spend all evening and part of the night there at her side. When I left, José María had still not come home. But the next morning, when I went back after class to see whether any fresh disaster might have occurred, I found Manuela quite calm. Her husband had come home late and, when he saw how upset she was, had given her an explanation which must have been very satisfactory, because the poor woman was quite relieved and almost cheerful. She was the most impressionable creature in the world, and gave in so eagerly to her most recent sensations that she could become furious over nothing, and lose her fury for less than nothing. In her moods, fury and delight changed places at the impulse of a single word, like tiny flames blown out by a puff of breath. Credulity was always stronger in her than wariness, and so it's hard for me to see how my dullard brother wasn't able to keep her constantly happy. That day he managed it, for at the critical moments of his life the marquess-to-be always pulled out some clever trick, or rather some bit of cajolery. He was in a light-hearted mood too, and when we spoke of the grave matter of Irene, he said to me: "You all seem to be fools in this house. Just because I made a couple of casual remarks to Irene and gave her a lift in my carriage yesterday, everybody thinks . . . You are really, all of you, a disaster, and you, wise man, profound man, analyst of the human heart, do you really think that if there were anything wicked in all of this I would have acted so openly?"

"No, I have no opinions about it. The truth of the matter will come out at last, for nowadays, no evil thing escapes the corrective of public exposure, a gentle corrective, certainly, and illusory for some, but of value nonetheless, when no others are available . . . And now that we're on the subject, perhaps you could cast some light on a matter which has filled us with confusion. Could you perhaps tell me where Doña Cándida got that little fortune which has allowed her to set up housekeeping and to put on such airs . . . ?"

"My dear fellow, how should I know? She brought me some bills of exchange for discounting . . . I gave her the money. Not much; a pittance. She just makes a big show over everything, you know, and counts pesetas as if they were duros. Of course, later on she spends them like céntimos. If you want me to tell you where the bills of exchange came from, I really don't know. Land she sold, or mortgages . . . ; I just don't know or care. I imagine her new home is some attic flat furnished with a few pieces of junk . . . Poor lady! Well, what did you think of yesterday's session? You should have been there! The Minister walked out with his hands on his head, and the center-left was fused with the right wing . . . Did you hear what Cimarra had to say? We . . ."

"I haven't heard a thing about it."

"Day after tomorrow's mail should bring my certificate of election. If you weren't such a disaster, you could accept the offers the Minister has made me."

"Do please spare me all that . . . To get back to Doña Cándida . . ."

"Do please spare me Doña Cándida."

I realized that that wasn't an agreeable subject for him, and I *made a note* about it.

"Oh! Here are a couple of newspapers that mention the charity benefit . . . Look, here they call you *conscientious;* that's the adjective they usually use for mediocre actors. This other one praises you to the skies. You come out just even. As for Peña, opinions are divided; everyone agrees that he speaks marvellously well, but some say that if you squeeze hard on what he said you won't get one drop of substance. Know what I think? I think that fellow Peña is all show. They set such great store here by brilliant oratory and that fine Spanish faculty for saying pretty things that really mean nothing in practical terms! They're already talking about putting Peña up for Parliament and waiving the age requirement . . . As if we didn't already have serious men in our country, men along in years . . . To tell you the plain truth . . . ; that kid and his speech-making annoy the devil out of me. If he were a preacher, he'd be a champion at making old women weep . . . ; but in Parliament . . . My dear fellow, for the love of God! It's really a shame that reputations can be made in this way. After all, what *did* he say? The Crusades, Christopher Columbus, the Sisters of Charity and their white head-dresses . . . For the love of God, my dear fellow! I think we shall end up talking in verse, and then go on to music, and finally our legislative sessions will be genuine operas . . . Just go to the U.S. Congress, listen and observe how things are dealt with there. There may be an orator who seems like a drunk trying to do sums. But never mind, just take a look at the practical results . . . Really astounding. No, really, I must say, these speakers of ours, these beardless eminences, these parliamentary *trovatori,* they give me an attack of nerves. And that young Peña just annoys the blazes out of me. I'd put him to work with a pickaxe on the public highways, so he'd learn to be a practical man. And anybody who starts talking about human ideals, evolution, palingenesis, him I'd send to unload sacks on the Havana docks or dig for minerals in Ríotinto, to give him a couple of ideas on plain hard work. For the love of God, my dear fellow, don't tell me I'm wrong. Suppose they set me up as autocrat, beginning tomorrow, with arbitrary powers to do and undo as I wish. Well, my first order would be for the establishment of a prison for baby orators, philosophers, poets, novelists, and all other hopeless cases. By doing so, I'd leave society clean and prosperous."

"José," I cried in a humorous outburst, even enthusiastically, "you're the biggest fool I know."

"And you're Balaam's ass." He seemed a bit piqued . . . Well, so was I.

"All, all of them to jail; you'd see then how well off we'd be."

"Yes, the nation would be a feeding trough."

"That's . . . as it may be. I'd have something to say."

"And what you'd say would be *moo*."

"Oh, these learned types are unbearable. They're so vain, so sure of themselves, so brassy. They don't *do* a thing, they're good for nothing, just a pack of idiots . . ."

And he was getting even more peeved.

"But the vanity of the ignorant man," said I, "is not only unbearable, it's a disaster as well, for it sets up and confirms mediocrity as a norm."

"But look at the state we're in, governed by so many learned men."

"You look at the state we're in, governed by so many fools."

"No, sir!"

He went pale.

"Oh yes, sir!"

"You are the most . . ."

"And you are the . . ."

Quaking with rage, he went out, slamming the door so hard that the whole house shook. And when we saw each other later, he avoided speaking, acting very stern toward me. For myself, all that I retained from that childish quarrel was the unease of recalling it, plus a bit of remorse. What a pity that a few rash stupidities should have upset the harmony and communication which always ought to exist between brothers! If I had detected in him the slightest inclination to forget the argument, I should have hastened to conclude a cordial and lasting peace. But José was grim, scowling, and didn't even deign to look at me when he passed.

XXXII

A CLOUD WAS HOVERING BETWEEN
MY BROTHER AND ME

WOULD IT PRODUCE a bolt of lightning? I was resolved to avoid that at all cost. I spoke about it to Lica, who in the short space of one day had fallen back into her worries and her sorrows. The reconciliation between wife and husband had been of such slight effect that the specter of discord was quick to destroy it, usurping dethroned Hymenaeus' place on love's altar. Throughout the whole day following my trivial argument with José, I stayed with my sister-in-law, listening patiently to her interminable complaining. Yes; he wasn't going to deceive *her* any more. *She* was catching on to his vileness. No longer would he bamboozle *her* with a few sweet words and a caress or two . . . She was convinced there was something in her husband's life that was driving her mad. José was no longer his old self.

In jeremiads like these we whiled away the hours of the afternoon and the evening, desolate hours because Lica had canceled the usual gathering and was receiving no one. José María appeared in the house only for a few brief moments because he had recived his certificate of election. He had presented it in Parliament, taken his oath, and been elected chairman of the Molasses Committee. The worthy representative of his nation, dedicated body and soul to the sacred duties of parliamentary and political paternity, had no time for anything. Four days went by in this fashion, dreary and annoying ones for me because Irene had not sent the promised bidding to visit her, and I, scrupulous creature that I am, didn't wish to infringe at all upon the terms of a message that seemed a command. So I spent most of each day with the forgotten but worthy wife of José María. In among the monotonous chants of a wronged wife, she made use of my prolonged presence there to try to interest me in marrying her sister, thus becoming doubly her relative. A kind intention, but an impossible one as well! I was second to none in my apprecia-

160

tion of Mercedes' fine qualities, but I felt not the slightest amorous inclination toward her; besides, I had a feeling that I was far from being her idea of a husband, much less a suitor.

Our monotonous conversations were interrupted—very unpleasantly, to be sure—by the wretched episodes the wet nurse put us through. She had a kind of animal greed and fierceness, and Maximín was in constant danger of going hungry. I cursed all wet nurses, and would have given anything to be able to punish that one, even more of an animal than the others of her mountain breed, for the sins of the whole lot. Lica and I feared some disaster, and sure enough, the blow fell when we were least prepared to receive it.

I was preparing to go off to class one morning when in walked Ruperto all out of breath.

"Miss Lica says you go there right now. The wet nurse walked out a while ago. The baby has nobody to nurse him."

"Didn't I say something like this would happen? A fine mess indeed! And what's your master José María doing about it?"

"My master didn't come home last night . . . The footman has gone out to find him . . . my mistress says you come quick . . . and find her another nurse."

"I? Where shall I find one? But let's go over there! What's Miss Manuela doing?"

"Crying. They're giving the baby milk out of a bottle. But all he does is bawl."

"All right, all right. Now I've got to find a nurse."

I was going down the stairway when a girl coming up handed me a letter. How Nature works! It was from Irene. I ripped, opened, unfolded, read it, shaking like a stalk of sugar cane under the fury of a hurricane:

> Come today without fail, Manso, my friend. If you don't, you will never
> have the forgiveness of
>
> > Your friend,
> > Irene

The writing was indecisive, as if done in haste by a hand moved by fear and peril . . .

Merciful Heavens! So many things for a poor mortal to do all at once! Find a wet nurse, go to the relief of Irene . . . Because, no doubt of it, I had to rescue her . . . From whom? There was some danger . . . Of what?

161

"What's wrong, Manso m' dear?" said Doña Javiera, on her way back from mass.

"Well not much! Just imagine, madam . . . Finding a nurse, rushing to rescue . . ."

"Is there a fire?"

"No, madam, it's just that the wet nurse . . ."

"The one who was nursing your brother's baby boy? Oh, those women are worse than the plague. In my case, just imagine, I was ever so weak, but I refused to stop nursing my Manolo. And the doctors were dead set against it. And my husband scolded me. Well, my son is the picture of health, and me, well just look at me."

"You wouldn't know of any . . . ?"

"We'll just have a look around; I'll go out right now . . . By the way, Manso my friend, did you see Manuel last night?"

"How should I have seen him, madam?"

"Well he's *still* not come home yet. I think they had a late supper at Fornos. These boys nowadays! Oh, but you're really pressed! Poor Don Máximo! What did *you* ever do to bring this down on you? Well, you can learn something for when you're a father yourself."

"Madam, if you would just be kind enough to find me somewhere one of those wild beasts they call wet nurses . . ."

"Yes, I'm getting around to that . . . Wait a minute, my neighbor said she knows . . . Yes, now I remember . . . It's a first-timer, a servant-girl who got in trouble. She was working at the home of a councilman who keeps the records of all the babies born . . . , a widower; by the look of it, he was interested in having the population grow. I'll go over there . . . I think she has wonderful milk; a great big brunette, a cheeky buxom girl . . . ; bit of a thief, too. Oh, then I know of another one, very delicate type, a regular *traviata* who used to dance at Capellanes, she's married but not living with her husband. Knows a lot of lullabies to put babies to sleep and has upper-class airs . . . I'm off! Not even going to take off my mass-veil. You head off in the other direction. Don't miss Matías' place, in the Calle de la Concepción Jerónima; that's where all the she-asses looking for suckling babies end up. I've heard tell it's a wet-nurse factory, a real warehouse for those animals. Come, come, my friend, don't just stand there, get *La Correspondencia* and read the want ads where it says 'Nurses for the households of new parents.' See? Now hurry over to the Provincial Government Building, where they give them a medical exam . . . If you find one, don't go by appearances . . . ;

take a doctor along. Pick out a boorish one, ugly, mannish. Long dark breasts. Careful with the pretty ones, they're usually the worst . . . Be sure to examine the milk, and check for good teeth. I'm going off the other way; I'll let you know what I find. G'bye."

The solicitude of the good lady brought me hope. Where should I go first? No time for hesitation: I ran to Manuela's house, thinking of Irene, her hastily scribbled letter, and kept seeing the image of her trembling hand filling out the lines, and coudn't rid my mind of the vision of the governess, imperiled by who knows what ferocious monsters. Meanwhile, my pupils were going without class that day; the topic of my lecture was to have been *The Inner Content of the Good.*

I found Manuela in desperate straits. With my godchild on her lap, her mother and sister on either side, she was the most pitiful, pathetic figure in that portrait of desolation. Maximín was bawling like a calf; Lica kept trying to get him to suck from the bottle; he kept pushing away that cold, disagreeable thing; and all the while, the three scatter-brained women were calling on all the Saints in the courts of Heaven. Messages had been delivered to the homes of several friends, asking for help to find a wet nurse; but, dear me! the family was relying principally on me, on my rare goodness and humanitarian heart.

XXXIII

A CURSE ON YOU, MY HUMANITARIAN HEART!

Y OU WERE AN AUXILIARY pressed into universal service, a little machine enrolled in the assistance of others; you were, more properly, a priest of what we call *altruism,* a religion very little practiced. If you produced blooms, you hastened to arrange them in the vase of generosity, where all might help themselves; if thorns, you stuffed them into the pocket of egotism and suffered the stabs alone. That's how I was thinking as I walked to the Provincial Government Building, a place I could count on for finding what my little godson needed. Earlier I had tried to see Augusto Miquis, a young and respected doctor friend of mine. He wasn't in; but his companions told me that perhaps I might find him at the Provincial Government. As luck would have it, he was in charge of examining the wet nurses. This happy coincidence gave me great encouragement; I considered Maximín redeemed already, and wasting no time I presented myself in those paternal offices, which give a fine example, with many others, of the proven and universal vigilance of our Administrative Branch and of how wretched we should all be if it weren't there to care for all our needs, bearing us in its loving arms from the cradle to the grave. Let it suffice to say that in a desire to give us all things it even breast-feeds us.

I had some acquaintance with government-as-doctor, government-as-teacher, and many other varieties of this provident institution; but I had yet to meet the government-as-wet-nurse. I was aghast as I went into that great room, not very light or clean, and saw the mammiferous squadron, lined up on fixed benches against the wall, while two doctors—one of them was Augusto—performed their examinations. The disagreeable herd was revolting in the extreme, and my first thought was a consideration of the horrible perversion and baseness of those women. At first glance one could tell the difference between those who had taken on this work as a regular calling, and those who had ended up in such indignity through a combination of misfortune and poverty. Some were accompanied by greedy parents; others by their

164

husbands or their *gallants*. Very scarce indeed were pretty faces, and ugliness dominated the ranks, an ugliness tinged with cunning. They were the scum of the cities mixed with the dregs of the villages. I saw chunky necks with coral beads, blackish earlobes with filigree earrings; ever so many red printed calico shawls which failed to conceal the roundness of the *merchandise;* black broadcloth skirts, rounded ones, hollow ones, inflated ones which seemed to be concealing a lottery drum; black stockings, sandals, high shoes, bare feet. All that was lacking, as wall decorations, were the coats of arms of the towns of Pas, Santa María de Nieva, Riofrío, Cabuérniga, and Cebreros.* As an ornamental inscription it might have been nice to have the hendecasyllable of that learned poet, who having nothing else to sing of, sang of the wet nurse and called her *the lieutenant of the maternal nipple.*

People kept coming in, seeking, as I was, relief for a baby, and one could hear dealings and bargainings. There were even *lieutenants* who praised their product the way wine-vendors do the contents of their wineskins. Explorations were made which anywhere else would have outraged modesty, and there was a curiosity about hard tissue so as to distinguish the adipose from the muscular. Just as at a sale of horses, people said *let's see the teeth,* and closely observed the bearing and step, the raising and lowering of hooves. Would to God that I had not seen you in such profusion, O flaccid udders, appearing shamefully in one place from among well-wound gauze, plopping out suddenly in another, like a rubber ball, from behind a red shawl! Would that I had not had to watch you being squeezed by the experienced fingers of the doctor or the midwife! At one end, one doctor was examining areolae; at the other, Miquis, after looking for symptoms, took samples and looked against the light at the precious substance of our life spread in a liquid film between two pieces of lab glass.

"This one's all water," he'd say, "this one, so-so . . . , greater number of lacteous globules. Hi, Manso my friend, what are *you* after in this neighborhood?"

"I've come for one of them . . . and in a rush, Miquis my friend. Give me the best you have, any price is all right."

"Have you got married or taken on somebody else's children?"

"Rather more like the latter . . . I'm really in a hurry, Augusto; they're waiting for me . . ."

---

*These are the towns traditionally thought by Madrilenians to furnish more wet nurses than any others.

"This is no trifling matter; just wait, old chum."

He looked at me, without removing the accursed instrument from his right eye. He did so with such rascally maliciousness that he made me laugh, me who was in no mood for jokes.

And while he was preparing his receptacle for the introduction of a new liquor, he made as if to squirt it at me saying:

"Stay right there in front of me!"

Damn Miquis! Always had to be funning, not taking account of the gravity of the situation.

"Dear old top, I'm in a hurry!"

"I'm in a greater one. You think it's pleasant, this daily trip through the *Milky Way*? I'm about ready to drop this stuff and let somebody else take over. We still have to do a chemical analysis with the lactobutyrometer. Because there are fakers, my friend. You see? Some of them are bags of poison, and here we keep a sharp eye out for the health of our infants. But in spite of our efforts, the next generation will see some awful things, yes sir. The people of the twentieth century are going to have plenty on their hands. It'll be the century of the lizards."

"Miquis, it's getting late and . . ."

"Sánchez, come over here please." Sánchez, the other doctor, came up.

"Let's have a look at that one, the one we saw before. She's the only beast worth anything. The one from Segovia . . . There she is, the one with an ear missing because a pig ate it off when she was a child."

"Is she good?"

"Pretty good, first-timer, absolutely harmless. She told me she was a shepherdess. She can't remember how she got in trouble, or who *Romeo* was . . . These people are like that. Usually it turns out that the great stupid ones know more tricks than Merlin. There you have her. Regard those never-washed features! I think she'll get you out of your jam. It's for a little nephew?"

"And godson as well."

"Sometimes a godfather is worth more than a father . . . Tell me, is it true that José María is now a man of diversions? . . . I see him every day now. He and I live in the same building."

"He's in *your* building?"

"Yes, I live up near Santa Bárbara. Three days ago a lady moved into our third-floor flat . . ."

166

"Doña Cándida!" I muttered, feeling Miquis's malice seep into my heart like deadly poison.

"My wife says she saw the lady move in with a young lady in tow. Her daughter?"

"Niece."

"Very pretty. Your brother visits there every afternoon . . . Or so I've heard. When I meet him on the stair, he pretends not to know me, and doesn't speak."

"My brother has his quirks."

And as I said it I felt very grim, and my eyes fell to the floor in dull melancholy, and my spirits were so paralyzed that I no longer saw the examinations, nor the distasteful herd, nor the doctors . . .

"Here she is," Dr. Sánchez said to me in a very kind voice, presenting to me a human beast encased in a greenish-black skirt that made her look like a spinning top. "She's good. Pay no mind to the ear business. A pig chewed it off when she was a little girl. Otherwise, good blood . . . good teeth. Hey, girl, let's see your tools! There aren't any signs of infectious disease."

And hardly looking at her, I prepared to take her along. She croaked something, but I couldn't understand it. Like a villager yanking the halter on a young animal he's bought at the fair, I pulled at the woolen blanket she had over her shoulders, and said: "Come along."

"G'bye, Manso."

"G'bye, Miquis, thanks very much."

On the way out I noticed that the halter was pulling along with the beast some others of the same species, namely: a father, also wrapped in black broadcloth like a bear in its fur and wearing a round hat and leather sandals; a mother, set at the hub of a wheel of green and yellow and black skirts, rolls of hair at her temples; two little brothers the color of dried acorns, dressed in serge embroidered with mud, filthy little savages, one with a leather cap and the other with a sort of basket on his head.

And in the street the venerable rustic who was acting the father stopped and barked:

"Hey, gennleman, how much'll you give my dear girl?"

"We're decent folks, y' know," regurgitated the wild mamma. "My Regustiana won't go just any old place."

"Mister . . . ," roared one of the boys, "want me for a servant?"

"Say, mister," added the author of Regustiana's days, "is it a big house?"

167

"Big enough to have nine balconies on the street and more than forty doors."

Five mouths dropped wide open.

"And whereabouts is it? And how much are you going to give my dear girl here?"

"She'll be well paid. Wait till you see what a nice mistress she'll have."

"A good lady, is she? Take us there, take us quick . . ."

"Right away. I'll take you in a carriage." I opened the carriage door, and thought of the fumigations which the vehicle would have to undergo after carrying that rustic cargo . . .

"No, only the girl and her mother will go with me. You men can walk."

"No, please, mister, take us all" they cried in chorus, in that plaintive tone used by the beggars who prey on diligences.

"My daughter ain't going nowhere without me," announced the father in a great access of paternal dignity.

"Take all of us! . . . I'll get on the back," said one of the boys. "Say, mister, will you take me on as a servant?"

"An' I'll go up front," shouted the other.

"Say, mister, how much'll you pay me?"

They were bewildering me, pawing at me like that, for they spoke more with their front paws than with their mouths. And they were smothering me with their questions and their grimaces. Just to get the thing over with, I finally packed in the lot of them and took them off to my brother's house.

Once inside, I laughed at myself and at what a figure I must have cut, shepherding that flock. I should have liked to say: "Well, that's that" and go off to where my curiosity and anxiety were calling me; but this would have been unseemly, and so I waited to see how little Máximo took to his new mamma and how Manuela got on with Regustiana's untamed parents and little brothers. My sister-in-law was so intent upon seeing to her son's needs, upon seeing whether he would nurse well, that she gave no heed to the retinue the girl had in tow. Sitting in the entry hall, the father awaited with stiff composure the results of the trial; the boys fled down the corridors, terrified at the sight of Ruperto; and the mother, ever at her daughter's side, was scrutinizing everything she saw, in a mixture of terror and joy, suspended, enchanted. It was all so miraculous in her sight that she doubtless imagined she was in the Royal Palace.

And Maximín, blessed be Our lady of Good Milk!, was nursing, and we could all see his fine gastronomical mood and the selfish greed with which he held onto the dark breast, fearful lest it be withdrawn. Lica was happily weeping.

"You're an angel from Heaven, Máximo. Without you . . . What a fine woman you've brought me! I simply adore her! She's got a real charm to her! We'll lose no time getting her outfitted like a queen. And her mother! How good she is! And her father's a saint. And the little brothers? Poor little fellows! I've left word for lunch to be given to all of them . . . Poor things! Makes me so sad . . . ! We must look after them in the best way, yes we must. The mother said they have nothing to eat, no rain this year, nothing to harvest, and they have to go begging . . . Such nice folk!"

That was all fine with me. I wasn't needed there . . . On my way! Corridors, stairs, streets, how long you all seemed!

XXXIV

FINALLY I ENTERED YOUR DOORS,
HOUSE OF MYSTERY!

AND I ASCENDED YOUR nice stucco-plastered stairway, still smelling of paint, the varnish on the doors and handrail still fresh. On the main floor I saw a copper nameplate that said: "Dr. Miquis, Consulting Hours from 3:00 to 6:00"; farther up I met a coal-dealer on his way down, then a baker's boy with his great basket, a milliner's assistant with her sample cases. In my mind I asked them all: "Have you just been *there?*"

And at length I pulled the bell-cord of the apartment, and its vibrating ring startled me. The door was opened by an unfamiliar maid who seemed unpleasant and even, I can't say why, like a bird of ill omen. And there I was in a small bright parlor so new that I felt like the first person who had ever been in it. Its furniture was just so-so, for there were only three chairs and a sofa, but on the walls I saw luxurious hangings, and between the two long windows stood a pretty console with bronze candelabra and a clock. It was easy to see that the furnishings were not complete, or even close to it. And as Doña Cándida told me herself, making a majestic entrance, complete with protective smile, through the large door to the sitting room:

"But, my boy . . . I'm ashamed to receive you in this state . . . Why this is as bare as a dancing school! The upholsterers are surely taking their time! I've had the furniture there since the seventeenth, and it's always 'today or tomorrow.' Wait, do wait—don't sit on that chair, it's broken . . . Careful, careful, not on that one either, it's a bit out of shape."

I headed for the third chair.

"Just wait, please. That one too . . . Melchora will bring you an armchair from the sitting room. Melchora!"

God and Melchora made it possible for me to sit down at last.

"And Irene?" I asked.

"She may not be able to see you. She's feeling a bit poorly."

All my concentration, all my perspicacity, my skill at reading faces seemed insufficient for deciphering the moral hieroglyphics of taut muscles, crossed wrinkles, blinkings, poutings and false smiles with which Doña Cándida covered her Egyptian face. Either I was a complete idiot, or behind the obscure lines on that antique face there lurked some sublime meaning. Wretched me, I couldn't understand what it was, in spite of straining my powers and my subtlety to their very limits, so as to find the key I so much desired.

"Oh, so she's poorly, then . . ." I mumbled, rubbing my hand across my eyes.

My gadfly was about to say something when Irene came in. What a wonderful apparition!

"How are you feeling, my dear?" her aunt asked, obviously displeased.

"Fine," Irene answered curtly. "And you, Máximo, you've certainly been making yourself scarce!"

Damn Caligula! No doubt about it, she was trying to divert me from my purpose, and distract me and get in between Irene and me on any invented pretext.

"Oh!" she exclaimed making a big fuss that left me cold, "did you see what they said about you in the papers? Irene, go get this morning's *La Correspondencia*. It's in there on my dresser."

Irene went out. I observed—for I was observing everything—that she took longer than one takes to bring a paper from atop a chest of drawers. At length she came back in, carrying a newspaper, and put it in front of me. On top of the newspaper was a tiny slip of paper with these words—apparently scrawled in haste and in pencil—written on it: "You're so late. You never do anything on time. I can't talk in front of my aunt. What's happening to me is *really something*. Leave now, saying you won't be back for a week, and then come back after three o'clock."

Pretending to read *La Correspondencia*, I furtively put the slip of paper into my pocket. Irene looked in an awful state. Very pale and very sad; that, together with her round soft countenance, confirmed that it was *really something*. And I, alerted by the little message, talked on about things of no importance to me, about how cheerful the apartment was, its nice view and . . .

"But, Máximo," Caligula abruptly said to me, "haven't you heard that last night there were burglars in the house? Dear God, what a fright?"

"Not really, madam!"

171

"Just as I'm saying, burglars, yes . . . perfectly dreadful! Melchora, of course, sleeps like a log and says she didn't see or hear a thing . . . But *I'll* tell you . . . I sleep very badly now . . . my wretched nerves . . . It must have been about two in the morning when I heard a noise at one of the doors. I got up, called to Irene . . . who claims to have been sound asleep . . . I was so frightened! You can just imagine. At any rate, I roused the whole house. Melchora says I see ghosts . . . Maybe it's my nerves . . . , but I'd swear that in the moonlight . . . I couldn't find the confounded matches . . . in the moonlight I saw a man fleeing . . ."

"Out the window?"

"No, out the hall door."

I looked over at Irene to see what she might say about such fantastic apparitions, but at that moment she was getting up to leave, saying: "The doorbell, Aunt; I think it must be the dressmaker."

"Well, isn't Melchora about? . . . At any rate, it was a real fright, Máximo . . . Poor Irene, when she heard me screaming, came out scared to death. Looking here, there, everywhere for the matches. Melchora laughed and said we were crazy."

"But did you see . . . ?"

"I surely did . . . The lucky thing is that they didn't steal anything. I've searched all around, and there's not even a piece of thread missing . . . , perfectly dreadful."

"And the end result is that the burglars apparently got away only with the matches."

As I said this, my spirit, spurred by its own pessimism, sank into the wildest speculations. My mind completely off the track, I could find no straight path. Could it be true, all this business Doña Cándida was telling about? And if it wasn't, what selfish concern, what malice, what purpose . . . ?

But my first care had to be the fulfillment of the errand sketched, in trembling pencil strokes, by the governess's hand. So I withdrew saying I wouldn't be back before a week had passed, and then spent the hours remaining before my mysterious appointment wandering about the Castellana, the Salamanca quarter, and Recoletos. At three-thirty I was pulling the bell-cord once again, and Irene herself opened the door. We were alone.

"Thank God," I said to her, sitting down in the same armchair that Melchora had brought out for me a few hours before; it was still in the same

172

place. "Finally you can tell me about that *really something* that's going on . . ."

"Oh, and it really is something!"

How her lips trembled, how breathless she was, how deathly pale! What a tone of panic and anguish in her voice as she said:

"If you don't save me, if you don't show your concern for this wretched orphan . . . !"

I simply don't know what happened inside me. The effusion of my hidden affection, expanding and coming out like a compressed gas which suddenly finds a thousand points of escape, was still hampered by that setting of treacherous solitude, by the discretion I believed called for in the circumstances, so that, when the most ordinary rules of romantic behavior demanded that I should go down on my knees and pour forth one of those passionate outbursts which are so effective on the stage, my timidity limited me to saying in the most insipid way imaginable:

"Well, now let's see about that, let's see . . ."

And I said it with my eyes closed and nodding my head, just the way a professor would. Force of habit had won out over my will.

"But, can't you guess? Don't you realize that my aunt is keeping me here against my will to sell me to Don José? It's really *something;* I never saw the like! Who set up this household? Don José. Who bought the furniture for that little sitting room? Don José. Who comes by every afternoon and evening to offer me every sort of present, and nice things, and a future, and maybe even villas and castles? Don José. Who pursues me with his mawkish love, who tracks me down and never lets me draw a free breath? Don José. I've been so terribly unlucky that that man has fallen wildly in love with me, and here I am caught between what I most hate—your brother—and the necessity of killing myself, because I have made up my mind to commit suicide, Manso my friend, and if I don't find a way to get out of this business this very day, I swear—yes, I swear—I'll jump out that window into the street."

Petrified, I listened; and I said in a stammer:

"As I suspected. If you hadn't forbade me to come by here right from the first day, perhaps I could have saved you from a lot of misfortunes."

"It's just that I . . ."

As she came back at me, she had stumbled into a veiled and mysterious notion, perhaps the same one that was keeping me from seeing that whole

173

affair with full clarity. It was then that a decisive line of argument occurred to me.

"Well, let's just consider this, Irene," I said, trying to strike a very paternal note. "Why were you in such a hurry to leave that house, where you surely cannot have feared the advances of my brother? Didn't you realize, using your best judgment, that by setting up this household and bringing you here, Doña Cándida was putting you in a trap? I suspected it, but I could hardly have intruded into such a delicate matter. What *was* your great rush to leave that peaceful and decent job you had?"

"He pursued me there as well."

"But it was precisely there where you had strong defenses against him, whereas here . . ."

"Well, my aunt tricked me."

"Impossible. Doña Cándida isn't capable of tricking anyone. She's like those old actresses past their prime, who can't create the slightest illusion in those who see them on stage. In the dreadful excesses of her own plots this wretched lady has given herself away, almost as soon as she's begun to put on her ignoble act. Her wild appetite for money has corrupted in her even those feelings which are hardest to corrupt. I didn't think you would fall into such a clumsily laid trap. You have jumped right into the abyss on your own . . . And don't justify yourself with complicated explanations; swallow a full dose of bravery and tell me the great, primary motive you had for leaving my brother's house. I don't know that motive for certain, but I suspect what it is. So let's have your statement, or I'll lose my faith in you, and I must have that if I'm to come to your defense. There's nothing more false, Irene, than a half-truth. I cannot espouse the cause of someone who reveals her conscience to me only in vague and partial declarations. I don't wish to keep you from one evil and at the same time stupidly allow you to fall into a worse one. As soon as you entrust your defense to a lawyer, you must reveal all the parts of your case; you mustn't hide anything. By being open, you must provide him with the courage and conviction which he has thus far lacked because of his doubts. Someone who knows you quite well has told me, 'Don't trust her, she's a hypocrite.' Rip out the little roots that these words have sent down into my thinking, and you'll find me ready to serve you as no man has ever served a woman in need."

This is what I said to her; I was eloquent, and even a bit fine and gallant. As I was speaking, I realized that every word was having a profound effect on her troubled spirit, and before I had finished, I could see that she was ill at ease; then upset; and finally, filled with fear.

I thought I might not be on firm ground.

"You must agree," I said in a friendly tone, "that before asking my help in escaping from this trap, you should tell me something—shouldn't you?—something that has nothing to do with my brother? Or let's say, to be very, very clear, something that's worlds apart."

Humbled and pained, she bowed her head, and as if ready to succumb, she answered:

"Yes, sir."

This respectful affirmation wounded my heart, as if it had been rent from top to bottom by an invisible blow. I had a tremendous sinking feeling inside me, like life falling away, my total inner destruction. I had to make an enormous effort to overcome my hurt feelings . . . I did't want to look at Irene, beaten down in front of me, with who knows what suicidal depression and guilty resignation. I weighed and measured my words before saying:

"Since what I need to know isn't and can't be shameful, don't keep me in suspense any longer."

Good Lord, I wish I'd never said such a thing! I saw her suddenly overcome by horrible anguish. Her face was all pain, then shame, then terror. She burst out crying like a Magdalene, got up from her chair, fled away in fright and disappeared from the room.

I couldn't think what to do; I was left perplexed and chilled . . . I heard her wailing in the next room. I puzzled over what I might do, and finally ran into the other room. I found her spread any which way across an armchair, resting her head on the cold marble of a console table, crying her eyes out.

"I don't want to see you that way . . . there's no reason to do that . . ." I mumbled, holding back lest I burst into tears myself. "You are judging yourself much too harshly . . . You may be sure that I . . ."

She was shielding her face with her right hand, and with the left one making as if to push me away.

"Leave me . . . , Manso . . . , I'm unworthy . . ."

"Of what, child?"

"Your protection. I'm the most wretched . . ." And more tears, and yet more.

"But be sensible . . . Let's have a look at things, under the cold light of reason."

175

This idiocy from my lips, as might be imagined, had not the slightest effect. And she tried to push me away with her left hand.

"No, I'm not going to leave. That *would* be something. Now I really *must* stay."

"I'm unworthy . . . I've behaved so badly . . ."

"But, my dear child . . ."

Incapable of assuaging her awful suffering, and unable to get any concrete information from her, I went back to the little parlor, where I paced to and fro, I can't say for how long. As I would turn around I'd see my gloomy face in the mirror, and my folded arms. I was afraid of myself; I don't know what devious track I was treading or what thoughts I was turning over in my head. I must have walked enough to girdle the earth, and thought all the thoughts that the human mind can generate in its infinite gyrations. The wailings kept on all the while, and that agonizing situation seemed just endless. Suddenly the latch made a sound; someone was coming in.

I heard Melchora's voice, in a harsh duet with Doña Cándida's. At last the accursed woman was arriving, she was about to get her just deserts! She came wheeling in . . .

I am not able to describe the astonishment Señora de García Grande felt when she opened the parlor door and saw me. With her rapid and blazing glance, she was shrewd enough, I'm sure, to see how angry I was and to understand that a storm was about to break on her head. For my part, I may say that her Roman-emperor face had never seemed more odious. In its decadence, it was bordering on caricature, so I actually felt less anger as I observed her sharp-bridged nose, her straight eyebrows, her accentuated mouth, and her thick double chin (I thought of Vitellius) which now hung excessively low and shook when she spoke, a veritable bag of dirty tricks. Her first thought and words were:

"What's the matter? Did you forget something?"

I didn't answer. My wrath had muzzled me. Her double chin was shaking and her eyebrows were snaking across her forehead. She went over to the sitting-room door, opened it, saw her niece all upset, and then turned to me. She was scared, so scared that she couldn't speak to me. I kept up my pacing; our silence and the glances we exchanged more than made up for anything we might have said . . . Once past her initial anger, Caligula must have sought strength in her own malice, for she seemed to be taking fresh courage. After a growl, and with a show of righteous rage, she sat down, and without looking at me deigned to say:

176

"Well, I *must* say . . . As if we all didn't know perfectly well what we must do in our own houses; no need for strangers to come butting in . . ."

I could either strangle her or confront her impudence with a strategically ironic and scornful attitude, and I chose the latter. I began to laugh nervously, an easy outlet for the rage that was contracting my heart and my lips, and with supreme disdain I said to my gadfly:

XXXV
"PROXENETES"

WHAT ARE YOU SAYING?"

"*Proxenetes.* I'm saying it in Greek to make it clearer to you."

"Oh, these bookish types! Even when they're insulting us they can't manage to talk like regular people."

"Somebody will come and talk to you in language as clear as running water."

"Who?"

"The judge of the district court."

Neither a silly laugh nor a scornful look could conceal her terror. I kept on pacing. A long pause followed, during which I watched Caligula beating time with her hand on the chair arm . . . Her native wit doubtless suggested to her the comfortable dodge of changing the subject, injecting a completely new one which might allow her to pose as victim.

"You're always so untimely, so . . . philosophical. You come here when you're not invited, and make a fuss. You'd be better off looking after the things that are most important to all of us, and not casting me in a bad light, which is what you've done today . . . Yes, that's right; because if I had known that Maximín had been left without a nurse, wouldn't I have gone flying to Lica's house to find her another nurse instantly? What a sketch you are! As if I weren't there to . . . Why it's actually a lack of respect, yes it is. You know perfectly well that I'm just as concerned as you are, as Manuela herself is . . . Frankly, I'm deeply hurt by this slight. And you, with all your bookish airs as usual! Instead of coming to fetch me and telling me the trouble, you went off to the Provincial Government to look on your own . . . Oh yes, I know all about that family of savages you took to the house . . . As a matter of fact I know a perfectly priceless wet nurse. That's what one gets for trying to help others: insult upon insult."

And I just kept on pacing up and down. I listened as one might to a shower of stupidities.

"And then people are shocked when one turns bitter, with one reverse after another, and on top of that my attacks and nervous ailments: a poor woman is brought to the most wretched state in the world. That's why things end up seeming so different from what they really are. Each of us does in her own house the most proper things she can, within the limits of duty of course, and with the dignity that those of us in a certain class can never forget. Then a nobody comes along who doesn't know the background, and after one look, acts like judge and jury and hangman without really getting the facts. A pampered crybaby of a girl only complicates the question with her nonsense; the egghead gets all hot under the collar, tries to act chivalrous . . . when with just a few words' explanation everything could be settled."

That buzzing was mortifying me in the most unutterable way. I couldn't contain myself.

"Madam . . ."

"What!"

"Will you please be quiet?"

"No respect at all! Will *you* please get out? I'm in my own house . . . I have so much regard for your family, I loved your mother so much, heavenly angel that she was, a matchless creature . . . Oh! You two certainly aren't like her at all, and if she came back to life and appeared to us here, she'd judge me fairly, as I deserve . . . I loved her so much, I can tell you, and her memory sustains me greatly in the face of your rudeness, which is bordering on the inexcusable . . . For it's really wicked, Máximo, perfectly dreadful. There is no name for what you're doing to me. To come and insult me in my own house! With no regard for my poor gray head . . . nor any remembrance of that saintly woman . . ."

Her double chin was shaking so violently that a whole year's store of tricks and lies and frauds seemed to be impatiently thrusting out. At the same time she was struggling to bring on a show of weeping to defend herself, and finally, after great efforts, some tears did appear in her eyes.

"Never," she wailed, blowing her nose very ostentatiously so as to increase the flow of tears artificially, "never would I have believed such a thing of you. At the very least you owe me some respect. And before you make harsh judgments on this unfortunate woman, whom you could easily consider as your second mother, you ought to get all the facts, ask me about things . . . I'm ready and willing to answer every question, and remove your

179

doubts . . . Do you want to know why Irene is crying? Well then don't ask *her,* ask me and I'll tell you. Girls today aren't what they were in my day, all withdrawn and submissive. Why, it's perfectly dreadful! There's no adequate supervision to keep them from getting into all sorts of flirtations and complications. Do you want it in two words? Well she's a false prude. Oh you won't believe it, I know you won't, and you'll just take out all your anger on me. But for me my duty comes first, and the care I take for her. Right there in Lica's own house, where she seemed to be under the same control as in a convent, the rascally child had a—can you believe it—yes, a suitor. Nobody is better at hiding things than these doltish girls. Nobody, not Lica, not you, not I—and I went every day—suspected a thing . . . How could we, in the face of all that modesty and meek submissiveness, that way of hers? But these meek ones are the very devil when it comes to covering up their affairs. A suitor! When we moved here I discovered it, and if you wish me to give you proof . . ."

The rage that suddenly welled up in me was so great that I didn't recognize myself at that moment, for never before had I felt myself so transformed into a brute, a coarse oaf, feeling a base urge to vengeance and all kinds of low, crude things. I don't know how those dregs got stirred up in my soul, even as upset as it was.

"Do you want proof?" repeated Doña Cándida after the manner of a hyena, sensing with clever instinct my momentary meanness, and believing her own permanent meanness might find an opportune welcome in me. "Do you want proof? . . . When we moved, in all the disorder of trunks and things, I found a packet of letters . . . ; no signature on them . . . ; I don't suppose you'd recognize . . . ?"

She gripped the arms of the chair in order to get up. I vacillated a moment. Good Lord! To uncover the mysterious enigma, to know at last . . . ! But not *that* way, no, never!

"Madam, don't move," I shouted spiritedly, back to my normal disposition. "I don't wish to see anything."

"You may perhaps know . . . One of those sly fellows who have access to the house . . . The rascally mulatto girl delivered the letters back and forth . . . But how do these young things manage to throw such a cloak of mystery over their naughty affairs? . . . I'm terrified, surely I'll die from the upset . . . This child, I've dedicated my whole life to her . . . Oh, Máximo, you can't understand this dreadful grief, a mother's grief, for I am a mother

180

to her, an attentive mother who's always making sacrifices . . . And you see how she repays me . . ."

Once again her cynicism was wearing down my patience.

I wasn't looking at her, for her face was painful to look at. Especially disgusting were her shaking double chin and her clear, broad Caesarean forehead. Across it the wrinkles twisted and wriggled strangely, the way worms do when they fall into a fire.

"Madam, please stop talking."

"All right, I'll do my weeping all alone, and my grieving, too. What do you care, you knight in shining armor, you philosopher turned adventurer?"

And at that moment Irene's painful moans were heard again . . . My heart was breaking at that secret anguish, scarcely articulated, which joined itself to another greater anguish deep inside me. I got the idea of rushing in to Irene, who seemed in the grip of a terrible paroxysm; but some unknown repulsion kept me from her. Doña Cándida got up and said in a sweet-sour voice:

"The poor dear is so tormented . . . I've had to scold her . . . I can't hold things in, you see. She'll have to have a cup of linden-flower tea."

She left me by myself. And I just paced back and forth. I was surrounded by the atmosphere of a drama. I foresaw the clash, what in the artificial world of the theater is called the *confrontation* . . . R-r-ring! The bell, the doorbell! My brother!

181

XXXVI
THIS IS *MY* CONFRONTATION

HOW SWIFTLY THEY sped by in my terror, those few seconds it took him to reach the parlor. He came in, and when he saw me . . . No, no man was ever so taken aback. I felt strong and in full command of my faculties, able to do with them whatever I might wish. Whether the "false prude" deserved my ardent defense or not—what did it matter?—I, the champion of right, was preparing to do battle with her enemy, who was my enemy as well. Let's have at him then, and we'd see . . .

Surprise won out over unease in José, and he let escape:

"What in hell are you looking for here?"

I could see that he was making the most strenuous efforts to collect his thoughts, to pretend he hadn't been caught, and to cover the flank of his self-esteem.

"Oh!" he exclaimed, feigning surprise. "What a coincidence! Both of us visiting . . . and meeting here. That's right; I told you I was intending to come."

And the good-for-nothing hadn't remembered that we weren't on speaking terms since our little set-to, and that it was thus impossible for him to have said anything to me about his visit. Seeing that he was caught in his own net, he changed tactics. He started clumsily on two or three topics of conversation (Melchora was just bringing in another armchair, one not being sufficient for the two of us); but as soon as he opened his mouth he got all tangled up and confused. Doña Cándida presented herself at the sitting-room door as upset as my brother, and with her double chin more than with her voice said:

"Both my dear Mansos will have to excuse me; but I'm so busy . . . I'll be back . . ."

And she disappeared like a specter who really didn't want to be called forth again. My brother was so set upon making me believe that this was his

182

first visit to the house that he refused to await the specter's second apparition to shout after her:

"Well, you've finally got me to come here . . ."

"First time."

"Very dreary, this afternoon's session . . . Budget discussion, very dull. Three deputies in the whole chamber. But in the committees we've had an undercurrent. People are falling into line so fast that it would make God's hair stand on end. It's a real scandal, what's going on, and then with that blunder that the Minister of Grace and Justice pulled yesterday . . . The Molasses Committee hasn't issued its recommendation yet. We'll have a special vote for Sánchez Alcudia; he's determined to protect the confectionery trade in his district . . ."

And I didn't say a word. He must have been worried sick. He could doubtless foresee a rough scene, and sought to weaken me with flattery.

"Oh, I had forgotten!" he said, putting on his laughing mask, which suited him about as much as a pair of pistols would befit Christ. "I must thank you, Manuela has told me about it. If it hadn't been for you, poor Maximín would have died on us this very day. I couldn't get home all last night, because . . . it's really too much to bear. I was with the Molasses Committee until 2:30. Then I went with Bojío to have supper at his father's house, you know, the Marquess of Tellería. The poor gentleman had become so sick last night that several of us friends had to stay there with him. I really was sorry to find out this morning when I got home what had happened with that tricky wet nurse! The one you got seems good . . . But look, that's some family I found there! Her father marched right up and tried to wheedle something out of me: 'Hizzoner the marquess is goin' to be a Cabinet Minister, I know. Maybe he'll give somethin' to these poor honest folks.' And he started asking for things. Get this: he doesn't want much, the sweet old fellow. Only this: the village tobacco agency for his oldest son; for the second one, the postman's job; and for himself the job of tax collector and mayor, the octroi accounts, and the administration of town welfare. I was splitting with laughter, and Sáinz del Bardal promised to nominate him for bishop."

José took great pleasure in the amusing story and laughed heartily . . . And I just sat there in silence, very grave. I was impatient, going to pieces, because I didn't want to open fire until the Emperor Vitellius was present. But the sulking old woman had probably made up her mind not to appear, leaving it to *her dear Mansos* to work things out all alone, and to their own liking. All at once José stood up. He had suddenly felt a desire to admire

183

the two large prints that Doña Cándida had hung on the wall of her little parlor.

"Why, did you see this? It's a really splendid engraving. 'Shipwreck of the *Intrepid* on the Rocks at Saint-Malô.' Just look at those waves! They almost splash you right in the face. And this other one! 'Wreck of the Medusa' by Géricault . . . Why, it's nothing but shipwrecks here.

And then the clock struck eleven. It was five o'clock.

"That clock is just like the people in my household," observed my brother sitting down again. "They're all suffering from softening of the brain matter . . . Well, this is a fine way to receive callers. If Doña Cándida doesn't show up soon, I'm leaving."

Farce, sheer farce. He knew perfectly well that something serious was taking place there. My unexpected presence and my somber silence were making him fearful, and that's why he wanted to get out from under.

"You staying?"

"Yes; and so are you."

"That's assuming a lot, my good fellow."

"We've got to talk."

"You have something to say to me?"

"Something, yes."

"Well, a fellow'd hardly know it. I've been here for a quarter of an hour."

"I wanted Doña Cándida to be present, but since the lady is ashamed to appear before the two of us . . ."

José went pale. I resolved to present my case with the greatest possible moderation and not to make violence or blows pass for logic. My adversary was my own brother. A difficult and dangerous juncture!

"Well, get it over with," he said humorously, by dint of pulling his face muscles.

"To put it briefly, you've been making the farcical pretense that today is the first time you've come here, when in fact you've come every afternoon and evening, for as long as Doña Cándida has lived here. Between this lady, whom I shall report to the district judge, and you, the father of a family and a representative of the nation, you've set up a trap . . . not very proper to put it mildly . . . , a trap for that poor decent young woman, who has no father, no relatives . . ."

184

"Don't go any further, no don't," said my brother, trying to appear resolute. "You're acting just like a knight in shining armor. Are *you* a father, brother, husband, or even suitor? And if you aren't, why are you presuming to judge what you don't understand? Are you in this just out of the kindness of your heart?"

"As an impartial observer. The first one who happened by, the man who hears shouts of distress and rushes to offer aid to . . . whoever it is. I speak on my authority as a human being, and that's all one needs to enter a place where suffering is being inflicted, to carry out the first precaution and protection until God and earthly justice take over. That's all I have to say regarding my right to intervene in this affair."

"Well, just a minute . . . , we must put things . . ." stammered José, all ensnared in the labyrinth of his thoughts, and unsure where to begin. "You can't undertake . . . The first thing to bear in mind . . ."

"The first thing to bear in mind is that your behavior has been improper for a gentleman and the head of a family. In your own house you tried to debase the woman who was your children's tutor. You achieved nothing along these lines . . . You great ass, you surely didn't think that all you had to do was . . . But you needed to use certain tricks. Impossible to do it in your own house. You plotted with this wretched woman, enlisted her ferocious greed, and between the two of you set the trap . . . But now you realize that none of it, not your visits or your gifts or your promises or your kindnesses which are as gooey as the Molasses Committee, none of it has helped you achieve your objective. Cornered by you and manacled by her splendid aunt, the victim has found in her own virtue sufficient strength to defend herself . . ."

"But listen, old fellow, let me speak a bit . . . , one must set things out as they are . . . I'll put it this way—you start philosophizing and that's the end of it . . . Perfectly absurd . . . Just hold on and listen . . ."

"Gentlemen don't act this way. If you have passions, overcome them; if you can't overcome them just manage to get along . . . So finally . . ."

"Finally, you don't know what's going on . . . Good Lord, Máximo, you talk that way . . . and you haven't got it right, you haven't got it right . . ."

"Well, what is going on, then?"

He was so stupefied that he couldn't manage to disentangle himself from the web of lies he had wrapped himself in. His mouth was dry, his face flushed, and he smoked one cigarette after another in nervous haste. He offered me one, and I said:

"My dear fellow, are you just realizing now that I don't smoke and never have in my whole life?"

"Oh, that's right; well, let's see . . . I did come here the other afternoon, quite by chance, after I left the Committee. But that's not it. First we must define our terms . . . because if you put things in that elaborate moral framework of yours . . . What's going on here isn't what you think it is . . . I'll start by telling you that Irene . . . It's not that I have a bad opinion of her . . . You just don't know what's going on . . . ; and obviously, when you're not in on the details . . . As for gentlemanly conduct, I assure you that nobody has had to give *me* any lessons yet . . . So let's get to the particulars . . . , for the love of God . . ."

"Particulars, yes, listen to them, José María: once your shameful conspiracy is brought to light, and people realize that you and Doña Cándida put it together with her ideas and your money . . ."

"Easy, easy . . . Just because I help the helpless is no reason to infer . . . Look at it reasonably, old man. I'm no philosopher, but I *can* reason . . . Because you . . . Let's be clear about it . . ."

"Clear, yes. Once the shameful plan comes to light, you won't be able to continue, José. Consider it thwarted. Just think of it as a stock-market gamble and that you've lost the money you gave Doña Cándida. It's all over. There's nothing more to be said. The police have moved in on the illegal game, and putting their nightsticks on the table have said: 'Let Justice rule.' The police is me. I am ready to grant a pardon, if this thing is brought immediately to a close. And I'm ready to proceed toward a punishment if it continues."

"Come, come, now . . . You just don't understand! You're really stubborn . . . Let me explain . . . No reason to put things on such a high plane . . . Come, now!"

"Do you know what weapons I have? Public exposure and scandal are two-edged swords that can wound both you and the woman I'm protecting. But that doesn't matter, she's innocent. God will look after her. So I'm threatening *you* with public exposure, scandal, and also with court action."

"Come on now. It's not that way . . ."

"Oh it's not, eh? We'll just see. Keep in mind what I've just said: the judge . . . "

"In a pig's eye, the judge!"

"But if things change, if you promise never to set foot in this house again, there will be peace; your wife won't find out at all, and you can dedicate yourself calmly to public life."

"I hear you," shouted my brother, putting on a very brave façade and folding his arms, "and I don't know what to think . . . Fine thing indeed! What does this all mean? I've heard you out patiently, but I'm running out of patience. So, it comes down to me being a criminal, a something-or-other, a . . . ? Your philosophizing makes me sick! I suppose all I can do is take it as a joke . . . And at any rate, what does it all boil down to? Nothing, a bit of foolishness. All this uproar and exaggeration and speechifying over a little thing without the slightest importance. You bookish types are really idiots. Suppose I did take a sudden fancy and made a few silly remarks to Irene. For the love of God, my dear fellow! Suppose I made a few more silly remarks to her here, too. For the love of God! Is that any reason to . . . ? I don't know why I'm even listening to you . . ."

"Let's just consider the entire matter over and done with," I said, glad to see him beating a retreat.

"But it never *started,* there's nothing to it, it's all your imagination . . . Frankly, I don't see how your friends can put up with you . . . If you got married, your wife would throw you off the Viaduct and your children would curse you. You're quite the swaggering bully, the height of impertinence and pedantry and nosiness. Really, if I didn't have some knowledge of you good qualities . . ."

"And let's leave it that you'll never come here again."

"You're a fool. As if I had any interest in doing that . . . You can believe me on that score, and if there's anything here that I've spent money on, interpret it more charitably; chalk it up to my pity for this poor family. Answer me this: should one's charities be done publicly or with a certain reserve and privacy? At least I've learned that charity should be practiced in silence. You philosophers have another view of the matter."

"You're a saint . . . I suppose you'll end up asking me to get you canonized?"

"And when I take an interest in helpless people, when I assist them in overcoming the problems of this world, I do the whole job, I don't go just

187

half-way. It doesn't matter very much to me if a slanderer should come along later to distort my deeds . . . I detest slander. As long as my own conscience is at peace . . ."

I couldn't help it. I burst out laughing when I realized that the great humbug was really warming to his role and trying to cast me in the hideous part of slanderer. He was trying to get the most out of his false position; and acting the judge, he said to me:

"And let's just have a look, old chum, who can assure me that with all your chivalry and high-toned airs, *you* haven't come here with some ulterior motive: I think you're the silent Don Juan type. Wouldn't that be something: for the one who had only good and charitable motives to seem like an evil, devious, corrupt man, and the gentleman philosopher, the learned professor of morality to be the *real* threat to the honor of young maidens . . . I must say . . ."

He came right up to me, and emphasized his words by shaking his cane above my head—without touching me, of course.

"I've seen you sneaking into Irene's room, hanging about her on walks, like a young peacock, all puffed up and philosophical. I've seen you next to her, all prim and pedantic and romantic . . . Of course I never thought she could love you . . . You're so disagreeable . . ."

And he went up to a mirror to pull down his shirt collar and straighten his tie, which was a bit off-center.

"Just think if a professor of morals should turn out to be the one who's in love! . . . For the love of God, man! . . . With that priest's face of yours and that respectable look you have, which makes people think Aristotle is behind one spectacle and Plato behind the other . . . and that dullness of yours . . . Holy Mary, Máximo, don't make a fool of yourself . . . You're no good at it, you'll never be a ladies' man."

Even though he had so little right to mock me, he was cutting me deeply.

"I don't understand your ridiculous concern for poor Irene. I'm sure she laughs at you behind her mask of kindness . . . because there's no one to match her at putting on good manners while managing to conceal her naughtiness . . ."

He was walking about the room twirling his cane.

"Look, José," I said, "just do me the favor of getting out of here once and for all. If you insist on being tiresome, I'll insist on being tough. I've caught you in your own noose: you have no defense against me. Just get out;

this little unpleasantness is over, and starting tomorrow we'll be brothers again."

"No, no, I feel no unpleasantness, no spite . . ." he stammered, his very words contradicting the irate expression on his face. "Do you think I care about your foolishness? No, my friend, I pay no mind, my conscience is clear . . . I've been able to help an unfortunate family: we'll see now what *you* do . . . Yes, I'll leave . . ."

"Then do it . . ."

"I leave you in full possession of your role as Don Quixote. Some job you've got, old chum. Not all that glitters is gold. And I don't mean to speak ill of poor Irene. I took an interest in her, not as a wise philosopher, but as a good father, or a brother. What if Doña Cándida *does* come and tell me she's found packets of letters? That's fine, girls do those things! They just naturally fall in love with the first ragamuffin who comes along . . . They just naturally pretend, and cover up and act foolishly . . . What if Doña Cándida *does* say to me: 'Irene is crying; something's going on with Irene; Irene's got into some mess.'? Fine! That's just youth and its fancies . . . girls who read novels do things like that. I attach no importance to all that foolishness. What if I myself observe a certain person hanging about the house in the afternoon, in the evening . . . ? What's to be done? As long as there are coquettes there'll be dandies. I've had the idea of slapping down one of them. I mean calming him down. But that's for you to do now, My Lord of Chivalrous Protection. We'll see whether your volleys of morality drive off the young enemy. Let them see your eyeglasses at close range, and you lecture them on Christ or Socrates. Or something else . . ."

He burst out laughing like a condemned criminal.

". . . One more thing. Bring the judge, bring on that judge you're threatening me with, and tell him: 'Your honor, this man is a suitor of my fiancée; put him in jail, and send me to the crazy-house.' Yes, that's it. I'd like to see that, hotshot."

To tell the truth . . . , I was going to make a reply; but I considered it more dignified not to say anything back to him.

"And I'll leave now. I obey you, little brother. You stay here. Later on you tell me about it and we'll have a good laugh."

I could see he was ready to leave. I thought of something to say, but didn't say it, so that he'd leave once and for all. He went out without saying a word to me, humming a little tune, but with his heart in a fury. I rejoiced in the outcome, for I had achieved my purpose, and knowing José María as I

189

did, I was absolutely assured that he considered the match lost. His fear of scandal guaranteed his defeat and the abandonment of his plans. I had triumphed for the moment, and the best of it was that I had achieved my objective without shouting or violence. No heavy dramatics, which was a happy thing for everybody.

José knew me; he surely understood that if he tried the same thing again I would publish the scandal abroad, and the authorities would intervene, and Manuela would find out. She would probably seek a legal separation and go back to Cuba . . . The favor-seeker, the practical man had no choice but to halt before the threat of these truly terrible dangers. The campaign was won and the battles won—by the early retreat of the enemy, who had been won over rather than defeated! If that's not a sublime strategy I don't know what is.

XXXVII
NIGHT WAS FALLING

D OÑA CÁNDIDA HERSELF brought in a shaded lamp, borne in her own venerable hands. Placing it on the table, she said to me in a hollow, frightened voice:

"He's gone now . . . Lord! I thought we were going to have a real show here . . . But you're both very sensible, and between good brothers . . . The poor girl . . ."

"What about her?"

"She's got a fever, a dreadful fever. We've put her to bed. Do you want to go in and see her? . . . She's a bit calmer now; a little earlier she was delirious, and was saying all sorts of wild things."

"Have Miquis come up."

"We've given her some mallow-flower tea. I think it will do her good to perspire. She must have taken an awful chill last night when we had that burglar scare."

"Have Miquis come up."

"I don't think that'll be necessary. Sit down. You seem to be rather perplexed. While Irene was delirious a bit earlier, she kept saying your name."

"But *do* have Miquis come up . . ."

"We'll call him if we have to . . . Would you like to go in and see her? Oh, I believe she's asleep now. Tomorrow I'll tell her you came by to see her, and she'll be *so* happy. What would become of the two of us without you?"

All that honeyed talk was driving me to my wit's end. I went into the sitting room, which led to the bedroom through a large opening between iron columns painted gold and white, an architectural design which is very stylish in newer houses. I stopped at that entrance. The bedroom was almost totally dark, but I could see the shape of Irene's body outlined by the white bed-clothes. She was like a sculpture whose head had been completed and whose body only roughed out. I saw her from behind; she had turned toward the wall, and there was no sign of her arms. Her breathing was labored and feverish, and accompanied by a whispering that seemed more like prayers than delirium. It made me think of the little sound made by a tiny woodland spring flowing in the grass and mournfully breaking the silence of the forest. I listened hard to catch a syllable or two; but—how strange!—every time I sharpened my attention and my ear, she would stop . . . So I went back; there was no way to understand that music of her spirit.

"The poor dear is very grieved," said Doña Cándida in my ear. "You can just imagine why . . ."

"Of course . . . ; you're not suggesting it's trivial?"

"No, and it's not just the business with your brother . . . She's really quite delirious! She was going on about daggers, poison, and revolvers, no less, as a way to end her life."

I went up a bit closer, step by step; curiosity was pushing me and delicacy holding me back . . . Finally, I could see her close up. Her face was reddened, her mouth half open, her hair loose, in curls and waves, forming a great black halo in two parts, about her head. Up close, her whispering was just as unintelligible as it had been from a distance; a mysterious dialogue between her soul and her dreams.

I withdrew, alarmed, and in the parlor I wrote a short note for Miquis on a visiting card, begging him to come up. This done, I determined to go home to eat, with the idea of coming back later. Caligula read my mind, and all obsequious and sugary she said:

"If you wish, you may stay and have dinner with me. I can't give you the delicious things you'd have at home . . ."

"Thanks anyway."

"Ingrate . . . Well, it's my own fault for caring for you and inviting you. You know perfectly well there's no greater pleasure for me than having you in my house."

I was alarmed by such fine manners. I hadn't counted on that from her.

"But do sit down . . . What's your hurry? . . . You've no idea how happy I am that your tiresome brother has pulled out . . . Now I can speak frankly with you, Máximo. Oh, he had us fairly cornered . . . perfectly dreadful!"

I watched her, simply to take delight in her cynicism and to see how that

192

exceptional quality of the spirit is translated into its own trademarks and nuances on the human face.

"Why, just imagine . . . insisting that the poor child should love him . . . , as if love were a matter of walking through a door . . . But you have no idea of the protestations and agonies and frenzies he went through . . . Hours on end gazing at her like an idiot, giving her the most pretentious compliments . . . And then the gifts started arriving; every afternoon he'd bring something new; a bit of jewelry, a little trinket, a trifle. And every few minutes . . . r-r-ring!—a shop assistant with a couple of dresses . . . ; r-r-ring!—a delivery boy with hats . . . This place looked like the house of St. Anthony Abbot, the one who was so tempted. Poor Irene, unswerving and heroic as she is, has suffered terribly, and so have I, because . . . Well, you can imagine what a difficult position I was in. I couldn't grab José María by the arm and put him out into the street. I'm obligated to him . . . , he's like one of the family. I tell you we've been put through awful suffering. Young Irene would put on such an ugly face to him; lately she's even insulted him. You just don't know; she has the most dreadful temper . . . Well, and the gifts—they've all been cast aside. Some even broken. Of course, because José María has insisted, some things have been delivered, and will have to be paid for, and . . ."

I was watching her, observing her with real delight—it's true, impossible as it may seem. I was like the naturalist who quite by chance, among the dead leaves under his feet, comes upon an unknown type or species of reptile, or hideous insect, or a slimy, repugnant mollusk. Barely touched by the ugliness of his discovery, he thinks only of the rarity of the creature, takes delight in watching it slither through the mud, or in the fetid matter it secretes, or the sharp spines it uses to threaten. He delights not only in all this, but in contemplation of the surprise of other scholars when he shows off his discovery. That's how I regarded Doña Cándida—with the interest of a psychologist—and rather than being horrified at her slitherings, spines, antennae, secretions, shards, or long legs, I wondered at the infinite power and inexhaustible fecundity of Nature. I can't say whether in this spasm of wonderment I moved a hand toward my pocket by a sort of protective instinct, because her now famous double chin shook, announcing a strong burst of laughter. The lady, in the best of humors, said to me:

"Don't be a fool, my dear boy . . . Surely you didn't think I was going to ask you for money! How very amusing! No, calm yourself. Let your soul

193

return to your body. We're not in a situation like that. Of course José María *does* owe me a bit of money . . ."

When I heard that my brother owed her a bit of money . . . , well, I didn't burst out in a hearty laugh, but only because my heart was still in the most troubled state. Still the remark was enough to bring cheer to a cemetery or make a hearse dance.

"Well then he'll have to pay you . . . that's all there is to it."

"No, no; I don't want any trouble. You do understand that it's a family affair . . . I'm in the habit of making these sacrifices . . . Let's not even speak of it. Besides, I don't need it just now. Only if Irene should remain ill . . ."

"I think she'll be over it soon," I said in a loud voice; and to myself: "I can hear you buzzing, gadfly."

"Will she be well tomorrow? Oh, please God! Poor child! When one, two, three days went by and you still hadn't come to see us, I could see how sad she was . . . That's right, once she starts talking about Máximo, she never stops. I'm just the same myself. A man like you, a celebrity . . . , and then all your eminent qualities . . . You're number one among men."

"Oh, thank you! I'm blushing . . ."

"I'm telling you the truth. When Irene finds out what an interest you've taken in her, she'll go crazy, crazy in every sense of the word."

"In every sense of the word; my, my! How perfectly dreadful!"

"You can be sure that if *you* had been the one giving the presents . . ."

Oh, I couldn't bear to listen to any more! I interrupted her. Either she had to shut up or I would strike her. I had to achieve the former, and to do so the best way was to get out of the radius of action of her double chin, and head for the open air. It's an awful thing, wanting to leave and also wanting to, having to, come back. Irene was pulling me back, Caligula was driving me away. There, in one and the same place were my greatest concern and my deepest loathing, my Heaven and my Purgatory . . . I went away thinking of various things, each sadder than the next, past, present, and future. I had never before felt such a blockage in my head. To use a materialistic simile, it was as if there were not enough room in it for all its ideas, and they were coming out through my eyes and ears. That whole tangle was dominated by a single piece of very discouraging evidence, whose truth was a light illuminating my mind and a flame frying my brains. For the first time in my life I invoked a blessing on *illusion,* that unworthy comedy of the soul which brings

194

us bliss, and I said, "Blessed are those who suffer deceit in their senses or blindness in their understanding, for they shall be comforted . . . !"

This piece of evidence had come at its proper, fated, historic moment, as a sort of transformation of earlier states of mind; I saw it, issuing from my own suspicions, like the grain from the stalk and the stalk from the seed. In just that way the tree of doubt produces the flower of certainty. A black flower, a bitter fruit, destined for the accursed palate of the scholar! Once again I must call down a thousand blessings upon the rustic who grows like a stalk and lives rocked in the soft bosom of falsehood . . . Let's investigate. Nature in her prodigality has made it difficult and dangerous to penetrate her laws, and has told us in a thousand ways that she doesn't like to be investigated by man. She seems to desire the ignorance—and thus the happiness— of her children. But they, that's to say men, insist upon knowing more than they ought to; they've invented progress, philosophy, experimental methods, art, and other evil tools they've used to bore holes in the world, and out of a comfortable Limbo they've made a Hell of worries and contentiousness . . . And as a result . . .

I was walking along the street, all absorbed in this sloppy pessimistic philosophizing (admittedly unworthy of me), when I bumped into . . . It was like a violent collision with a hard and heavy object. A purely moral collision, for I suffered no contusion, nor did my body even touch the other one, which belonged to a man younger and taller than I, a man of parts, qualities, and physical attributes entirely superior to my own. I stood there before him, and he before me, neither one of us speaking, both somewhat inhibited. The force of the collision had been as strong in him as it had in me . . . And suddenly there rose to my lips, from my heart, an unrecognizable gall, more bitter than bitterness itself, and I spit it out in these words:

"Manuel! What the devil are you doing around here?"

I looked right through him, feeling myself graced by a superhuman clarity of vision. And I understood all I had heard about wonder-workers and specially gifted people, those who in an unusual combination of events and circumstances can read people's minds. I read the fellow right off, I read him as though he were a wall-poster like those pasted on the nearby corner.

And he, hesitating like anyone unpracticed in lying, answered:

"Well, . . . as a matter of fact . . . I was on my way to Miquis' house for a consultation."

"Are you sick?"

"It's my throat . . . , this old throat of mine."

195

"Oh, it's your throat, is it?"

I grabbed his arm in my hand, thinking of it as a pair of tongs, and said to him:

"Rubbish! You weren't going to see Miquis. He doesn't have office hours now."

"But as a friend, he'll surely . . ."

"Manuel, Manuel!"

I ran him through with another of my looks. (He has since told me that he felt absolutely frozen.) It occurred to me to say something which utterly undid him, and it was this:

"All right, I'm a friend of Miquis too; we'll go together, I'll wait for you, and after he's seen you, we'll go out again. I've got to talk to you."

"No . . . ; but . . . well, all right; well if you really want to . . . Is it that urgent? . . . Let's go then; no, let's not . . ."

XXXVIII
OH, YOU TREACHEROUS TRICKSTER!

IT'S YOU, you accursed young buck, you syrupy orator, you damnable fair-haired boy! It's you, you're the one who's stolen my hopes; by treachery you've gotten the slip on me; you've 'been there and back,' while I'm barely learning to walk! I suspected it, but I didn't believe it; now I do believe it, I can feel it and see it and it still seems hard to believe. You've shattered my hopes, blocked my way, you wretched stripling, and I'd like to throttle you; yes, I will throttle you . . . !"

All this, which would seem natural given my state of mind, and perfectly suited to my desolate situation, I should doubtless have said, making use of the opportuneness and the theatrical traditions inherent in that moment. But in fact I *didn't* say it. When I saw that Manuel's lies were confirmed by his utter perplexity, I treated him with the greatest scorn in the world, and said:

"I don't wish to bother you. Go on alone."

And I went on my way. After a few steps I heard him coming after me, and then his voice:

"Professor, professor . . ."

"What is it you want?"

This was going on in the middle of the Calle de Hortaleza, at the spot where Barquillo merges with it, and we were both nearly struck by an inbound tram.

"What is it?" I repeated after the danger had passed.

"I'm going with you. I have to tell you about . . ."

He took my arm with the same friendly trustfulness of earlier days. I couldn't help exclaiming:

"You hypocrite!"

"Why?" he answered pertly. "We must talk . . . I know where *you've* been twice today; first, this morning; and then all afternoon.

Could I reveal all my spite, my confusion, the miserable state I'd been driven to by my newly acquired evidence . . . ? Impossible. I'd have to pretend, first, to know the whole story, and second, not really to care much about it. Like Cato tearing at his belly with his fingernails, I suffered horribly when I said:

"You're a playboy, a libertine. You deserve . . ."

"Professor, it's time to be frank about this," he said unabashedly. "Who told you about this?"

And with affected serenity—God alone knows what it cost me to pretend!—I replied:

"Stupid, who do you think? She herself."

"Oh, I see . . . The two of us had agreed to tell you our secret. We were arguing about who should do it. She said 'You tell him.' And I said 'You ought to tell him.'"

This closeness, this debate within their amorous intimacy, was making my blood boil. I had to swallow very hard to be able to answer:

"She has shown the noblest trust in me, and has revealed what I already suspected."

"You suspected it . . . Possibly. Nevertheless, professor, we had taken all sorts of precautions to keep everyone from discovering our secret. It's more fun that way . . . "

"What a wrong-headed attitude!"

I had to exercise tremendous self-control to keep from showering him with denunciations . . .

A burning curiosity was kindled inside me, and instead of denunciations, I showered him with innumerable questions . . . ; and how deathly and terrible you were as you appeared to me, you bits of news, bellwethers, small details of that whole affair: in fear I suspected your existence, in terror I saw it confirmed. I heard you from the very traitor's mouth, like versicles from the *Dies Irae,* and as you proceeded to construct the catafalque of my final doom, my soul decked herself in mourning. You, the idea of how that love had begun; you, the realization of what the rascals had done to keep it in deepest secret; and finally you, the image of a vivid passion in *her!* All of you came before my spirit like so many bare and terrifying skulls, alternately frightening me with the deep gaze of your hollow sockets, and setting my hair on end with your dry laughter and clacking jaws . . . As these matters proceeded we reached my house, went in, ascended the stair. Death and materialism! When Manuel told me:

"She's madly in love with me," I gripped the iron handrail so tightly that it seemed to yield like soft wax in my fingers.

And in my study I gazed at my disciple, who had sat down in my armchair, as if expecting more questions from me. He seemed to me the most hateful, the most disagreeable, the most detestable of human beings. Throw him out of my house! No! That would have given my secret away, and I wished to preserve my mask of invulnerability . . . But I *would* throw him out in a well-mannered way.

"Manuel," I said, "I've an awful lot to do tonight . . . The wretched preface to that translation of Spencer . . . I'll have to stay up late . . . Please, I beg you, don't distract me, for if we were to start talking we'd just fritter the night away."

"You're going to work after dinner?"

"I have to."

"You're not going out?"

"No . . ."

"Well I'll leave you alone then . . . Just to finish what we've been speaking of, Manso my friend, this will put an end to the matter; what I mean is that this is not just a passing incident in my life, not just an adventure; it's serious, profoundly serious."

"So then you too . . ." I asked him, feeling some small relief.

He gripped his head in both hands, leaned his elbows on the table, and looked at an open book which was lying there quite by chance.

"Yes," he murmured, "I'm madly in love with her, too."

He heaved a great sigh. The lamplight fully illuminated his slightly pale and unnecessarily abject face.

"I've got to tell you all of it, my beloved teacher. I'll need your advice, your helpful friendship. At first I thought this was just a diversion, but it has grown into something serious, the most serious thing in the world . . . My conscience is all upset and my thoughts are like a volcano . . . I've got to talk to Mother about this . . ."

"A fine idea."

As usual, the cat jumped up on his knees. When you've got to say a difficult thing, one of those things that are hard to get past your lips, there's nothing like stroking a cat to make it easier, to make it come out a bit more smoothly. Manuel kept stroking the dear thing's back. Its tail went stiff and it became excited. It climbed up my disciple's arm and even rubbed its body against Manuel's face . . . And I, making every effort to disguise my burning

199

interest in that affair, felt sorry that the cat hadn't come to play with *me,* because it's *also* the case—you may believe me quite literally—that the mechanical pastime of fondling a cat is also the best way of concealing one's inner turmoil.

"Well, you see . . . maestro . . . It seems impossible for things to lead from one to another; step by step, from one frivolous piece of nonsense to the next, for one to reach the point that seemed so very distant, so utterly impossible . . ."

At a loss for something to do, I started leafing through a book, and then riffling through papers as if I were looking for something I'd lost; and I took to striking the table with my hands . . .

"If I am into this thing more deeply than it appears, maestro, it's your brother's fault. Now I know why that gentleman seemed so disagreeable right from the moment you introduced us at his house . . ."

"Well *you* have a few things to answer for as well," I grumbled, if only because remaining absolutely silent does not make for a very good disguise.

I picked up a piece of paper, and acting as if it were what I was looking for, I began reading it with feigned attentiveness. It was an advertising leaflet from a bootery—I don't know how it had got there.

"Your brother! He's a fine one! Between him and that García Grande woman, Doña Perfectly Dreadful . . . Do you know what the two of them had cooked up?"

"Indeed I do," I mumbled, though it probably came out more like a moan. "I do know . . . , but we mustn't judge people's intentions so hastily."

"What *are* you talking about?! They practically had her under siege, without food! It was just lucky that I . . . Three nights ago I left my house determined to make a first-class row . . . I was beside myself, my dear Manso; I was ready to do the most awful things . . ."

"Theatrics, violence . . . , youthful passion."

These disconnected, meaningless words issued from my lips like bubbles from a boiling liquid. I suppose my face looked like a plaster cast. But I kept the leaflet in front of me so Manuel mightn't see me, and before my eyes, like limping buffoons, there passed lines of print: "Rawhide boots for ladies, 13 pesetas the pair" or some such words.

"That night I took a revolver with me . . . I'd bribed Melchora, the maid. I got into the house, and I hid. If your brother had put in an appearance, I'd have killed him."

I looked at Manuel again, and in his face I could see all his youthful determination, the impulsiveness of love, and all the poetical and novelesque instincts that a man's heart can hold. He looked to me like a Calderonian *caballero* with his sword, slouch hat and doublet; and I by comparison . . . Oh, you muses of inspiration, look away from me, the most dismal and dull figure in the world!

"But my brother didn't appear," I said.

"I was ready and waiting for him. Everyone was asleep. It was a gorgeous night. I slipped noiselessly out onto the balcony. What a night, what a star-studded sky! What peace and quiet up there! . . . and then the half-shadows in the streets, the snoozing noises of sleeping Madrid, curled up on its bed of earth speckled with gaslights. Maestro, there are moments in life when . . ."

I turned rapidly around, like a weathervane impelled only by itself . . . I bent over to pick up a piece of paper that hadn't dropped . . .

"There are moments, maestro . . . It doesn't seem possible that the whole essence of life, God, immortality, beauty, the whole moral universe, pure ideas, perfected form, can fit into a single glass and be sipped . . ."

It was an opening to say something humorous and so soothe my spirit. And I did, with this sharp crack born of my bitterness:

"You're waxing metaphysical . . . and rather tawdrily poetic, too . . ."

I laughed, and I'm sure it was the laughter of a man climbing to the gallows. And pretending to have a terrible itch on my neck I turned around and covered my face as I reached to relieve the itching with my fingers. I think I drew blood as Manuel was saying:

"And the next morning very early, I went back . . ."

"With your revolver?"

"I forgot to take it . . . My strong feelings had upset my good sense. I couldn't see any dangers or obstacles . . ."

Like a talking machine, like the cold metal of the telephone which says what the electrical impulses tell it, I said: "Romeo and Juliet," without knowing where the words had come from, for my brain had gone blank.

"I stayed until first light; everybody was asleep. As I escaped, when daylight was getting brighter, I made a slight noise and Doña Cándida came out screaming:

"Burglars!"

This last part I heard from my bedroom, where I had gone seeking refuge and fleeing an impulse to revenge which was welling up in me . . . I almost broke out in a cry and declared . . . But it would have been to my notorious discredit to reveal a secret which must go with me to my grave! I sweated great, heavy, cold drops like those of the Mount of Olives, and in the darkness of my bedroom, keeping up the pretense of looking for something, I punched myself with my own hands, and shouted in silent agony: "Do yourself in rather than let the secret out!" I think I walked around the dark room a few times, and a space of time went by during which I don't know just what I did, for I had definitely lost my rational thought and self-awareness. I can only remember isolated words, incomplete thoughts poking at my mind, and most likely I said: "Burglars . . . Doña Cándida . . . not finding matches . . ." or some other nonsense like that.

When I recovered my rational judgment I appeared in my study again, looked at Manuel . . . Petra, my housekeeper, was just coming in . . .

"Mischief with the gravest of consequences," I said in a high-sounding voice. "Petra, dinner."

Manuel looked at his watch and I at mine.

"I've got 8:20; I'm fast."

"I've got 8:07; I'm slow. Will you stay and eat?"

"Thanks anyway. What do you advise me to do?"

"It's a very serious matter. Bears some thinking about."

I felt myself calming down a bit. Then he said something that was either pleasant or disagreeable—I don't know which, for the moment was so tense. My ideas were all topsy-turvy, my feelings shuffled into disorder; both were out of phase. A wild anarchy had taken over my spirit, and my reason, all rolled up in a ball, was hiding, out of reach. I was glad to see Manuel in a hurry. I promised him that we'd speak of the matter another day, and he left . . .

XXXIX

THERE I WAS,
ALONE IN FRONT OF MY SOUP

AND I WATCHED, before my very eyes, the orderly troop of round chick-peas parade in, pointed noses and all. And then a redolent braised meat dish, followed by some Málaga raisins, cakes from somewhere and new-wine pudding from somewhere else. As I reach this point I am unable to conceal a fact which then (and even now) seemed most unusual, phenomenal, and extraordinary. I would very much like, as I relate the fact that I ate, to say something usual and customary in such a case, *viz.,* that I lacked appetite and would have sooner vomited up my heart than eaten a single chick-pea. But my devotion to the truth obliges me to make it clear that I *was* hungry and ate the same as any other day. Whether because I'd had a small lunch, or for some other reason, the fact is that I did honor to all the dishes set before me. I am well aware that this sets me at odds with the weightiest authors who've written on matters of love, and even with those physiologists who study the parallels between bodily functions and affective phenomena. But be that as it may, I'm telling it just as it happened, and let each one draw the conclusions he may wish. The only thing that betrayed my upheaval was the distracted way I ate and my failure to realize what was going into my mouth. From this I conclude that there's still a lot to be said on the subject of how the mind affects the digestion. Period, paragraph.

After eating I spent some very sad and burdensome hours in my study. I could find no comfort in reading, nor could any author, no matter how great, succeed in charming my soul away from the contemplation of its own misfortune. It held to this contemplation in burning fervor, like a fanatic to the dogma he idolizes. And there was no way to shift my attention. If by some effort of the imagination I was able to distract it for a moment, kidnapping it

203

off to other spheres, it neatly escaped again and followed the mysterious paths back to its sole object . . . Night was passing, and when it seemed as if the very energy of grief itself was growing weary, I was overtaken by a leveling-off of my nerves and by mental stagnation. Everything turned to funereal sensations, ideas of impending death . . . At dawn, my brain, stimulated by lack of sleep, turned these ideas of death into a real mania and a resultant conviction that I was right. I got the notion that I'd wake up dead, and spent an agreeable time contemplating the surprise my friends would have when they learned the sad news, and the mourning that would be observed by those who really cared for me. And *I* would be calmly watching that mourning and that surprise from the mysterious precincts of death! I felt as if I were completely removed from all I had known up till then, but still knowledgeable about myself within some sphere, region, or space entirely hidden from the general domain of physics. I don't know what it was—a morbid meditation, a fever of emptiness, or what!

Next I thought of the phrases the newspapers would use to impart the news of my unexpected demise. Among other things, after having tossed in my direction that standard brand of readymade incense that seems bought in a shop like the dried herbs used by the lower classes for fumigation, the papers would say something like this "This sad occurrence surprised Señor Manso's friends all the more because he had spent the previous day at his customary duties, in a state of perfect health, and had returned to his home at the customary hour and eaten a good meal . . ."

Stop right there: the good appetite which I had unfortunately felt was out of tune with the lugubrious scene being sketched in my mind at an early morning hour which lent itself so well to delirium and feverishness. On my desk they would find some sheets of the preface to Spencer I had begun to write . . . My panegyrists would call the uncompleted manuscript *his swan song* . . . When I thought of this, and of the literary observance to be celebrated in my honor, complete with poems and speeches, I felt a strong desire *not* to die (or to come back to life if I was already dead), just so that no extra luster could be gained at my expense by Sáinz del Bardal and the rest of the poetasters, two-penny orators, and other ceremonial henchmen . . . No, no, let's stay alive!

All of this finally put me into a deep sleep. Blessed sleep! How it restored my physical and moral powers, and put in tune again all that was inharmonious! What an equilibrium it brought back, and what balance and refreshment it gave my whole being! I rose somewhat late, but my head felt clear, lucid, and well-stocked with moral strength. To use a lovely figure out of the mystical writers—though it's a bit shopworn from all its use by poets and theologians—I'll say that some angel had come down and comforted me as I slept. And yet I couldn't remember having had any dreams . . . At the very least, I had the slightest sensation that *wakes* were being held in my honor.

Moral strength and a certain Herculean robustness I was aware of in myself, provided me with physical strength, agility, full activity. I went to class; I felt like lecturing, and mounted my lectern with the inner confidence that I would do well. A thousand clear and vigorous ideas came rushing into my mind as if in competition to be verbalized first. Good, good—I should like to have preserved that day's lecture. I felt fertile and possessed of a facility in speaking that left one amazed.

Man is a microcosm. His nature contains, in an admirable compendium, the whole organism of the universe in its various orders . . .

And not just in the overall development of his life does man prove to be a reduction of the universe. This phenomenon can be seen palpably also in a single action, one of those actions that occur every day and in their apparent insignificance scarcely merit attention.

There exists a perfect alliance between society and philosophy. A philosopher is acting constantly upon society, and metaphysics makes up the moral air breathed by people's spirits without their knowing it, just as their lungs breathe the atmospheric air.

Sometimes an isolated, ordinary fact, properly analyzed, offers a reflection of the universal synthesis, just as even a tiny mirror will reflect the grand dimensions of the heavens. A philosopher acts upon society in a mysterious way. He is the inner, hidden engineer of the whole scene. His mission is to be constantly at work investigating truth.

The philosopher uncovers truth but does not take pleasure therein. The Christ is the august and eternal image of philosophy: he suffers persecution and dies, although for only three days, in order then to come to life again and continue in the dedicated governance of the world.

The man of thought discovers truth; but the man who takes pleasure in it and makes use of its heavenly gifts is the man of action, the man of the world, who lives in the midst of particularities and contingencies, in the hurly-burly of everyday deeds.

Taken as a whole and a unity, philosophy is the triumph, slow or swift, of reason over evil and ignorance.

After all, things happen as they ought to. The right reason of things wins out over all else.

From the obscurity of his retreat, the priest of reason, deprived of the delights of life and of youth, controls everything with his hidden powers. He has the wisdom to yield to the men of the world, the frivolous and mentally lazy ones, all superficial and transitory riches, and keeps for himself the eternal and the profound.

Consciousness is creative, tempering, and restorative. If one compares it to a tree, one would say that it produces the loveliest of blossoms, whose fragrance transcends all outdoors. Its fruit is not the bitter apple of selfishness, but a rich banquet shared with all who hunger.

These flowers and this fruit fill the gap left in society by the lack of an organizing principle. For present-day society suffers from the evil of individualism. There is no synthesis in society. Total ruin would soon be upon us without the existence of the reconstructive and vigilant principle of consciousness . . .

And I talked so much that I ended up feeling slightly perplexed. I noticed that some pupils were yawning; but others were listening very attentively. Some of these latter ones, little pedants who want to learn everything in one day—they're hard to shake off with all the annoying questions they put to the teacher—some of these told me on the way out that they hadn't entirely understood. I answered, only half-seriously, that the chosen ones among them *would* understand, even if I had to beat it into their heads, and if they weren't *chosen* they could get along fine without understanding it. By *chosen* I meant the ones with skin thin enough to profit by the slaps, pinches, and cuffs given by the watchful schoolmaster. The others, those whose souls are wrapped in leather like that of a rhinoceros, will not have the slightest bit of knowledge even *whipped* into them.

XL
NOT TRUE, NOT TRUE!

I SAY THIS BECAUSE my narrative now includes things so stupendous that nobody will believe them. And not because they have even a grain of the miraculous, nor because in the telling of them there is any more artifice than is necessary to bring forth the truth in an agreeable and coordinated fashion. On the contrary, it's Truth herself, like our crazed imaginations, who arranged a series of events apparently contrary to her own laws, and this put me through the tortures of even greater confusion. The whole business started with me having that untimely appetite, so at odds with all the rules of the ideal, of finesse in matters of eating and even of good taste. Then there was the question of my eloquence in class. Then something very strange happened. Doña Javiera showed up in my house to tell me that she had broken off all relations with that provisional and temporary husband called Ponce. He was, in her words, common, vice-ridden, and a spendthrift. She had been fed up with him for quite some time, and at last everything had come to an end. Most contrite for that lengthy distraction (in such bad taste), the lady now proposed to consign it to oblivion by living a very proper life, of unassailable appearance and conduct. The future of her son, who was making his entry into the world surrounded by high hopes, demanded no less. The butcher shop had already been sold, and—so great is our power to forget—Doña Javiera herself no longer remembered ever having weighed out a veal chop. The world and her acquaintances followed suit.

There is nothing that passes more rapidly into history than a mercantile past which has left money in its wake. I observed in my friend quite obvious attempts to compose her speech, to speak softly, to choose elegant words and eschew a too low-class tone of voice. Her attire went along well with this plan for regeneration, which had begun by torment of tongue and labor of larynx. I thought it all very fine.

Completely open with me, the lady told me that part of her capital had been used to buy a house, a lovely building over in the spacious quarter next

207

to the Retiro Park. She would reserve for herself the main floor and the mews, and rent the other stories.

And she would be very unhappy if I were unwilling to accept the cutest little third-floor flat she had picked out for me and decided to rent to me at the same rate as I was paying in the Calle del Espíritu Santo.

"Thank you, thank you so very much. How can I possibly repay . . ."

The good lady had something else to tell me.

In those recent days, finding she was so much by herself, she had passed the time making lamp-screens out of feathers, pretty, showy things, and was *so* pleased to offer me one.

"Oh, thank you very much indeed! It's just lovely! What nimble hands you have . . ."

There was even more. Sitting confidently in the armchair across from the bookcase crowned with Wise Old Owls, Doña Javiera expressed her feelings of unlimited gratitude toward me for having opened up, by my teaching, such a brilliant pathway for her son.

"Madam, for Heaven's sake . . . I . . . Please speak no more of it."

And indeed, it seemed to be the case that as many people as made Manuel's acquaintance entered into competition to raise his status and open the way for him. Not even envy, as strong as it can be, worked against him. All the academies and societies were bidding for him. From now on there would be no *evening* which could be assured of full brilliance without him, and people were already talking about getting an age exemption for him so that he could get into Parliament. Pez and Cimarra had offered him a certain constituency; there was no question that Manuel would soon be a parliamentary orator of the very first order, and become a Cabinet Minister after a few years. Doña Javiera intended to establish her new household on the basis of the greatest elegance and luxury, because . . .

"Well you can just imagine, Manso my friend, that my son will have to give teas, and any day now he'll probably marry a title . . . I don't like a lot of show and all that, and I'm no good at *ronday-vooz*. I'm just a plain person; but, like it or not, I'll have to go against my own nature so's my son won't come off looking badly."

All of that seemed just fine to me, including the person of Doña Javiera, who was, as the society columnists say of ladies of a certain age, lovelier with each passing day. And in her case the hyperbole was true. It did seem as if the years passed her by, and the years that really did pass were negative ones, marching backwards compared to everyone else's, and leaving her ever younger.

This lady, who was never done sharing confidences with me, gave me the assignment of looking into Manuel's situation to see if I might discover the reason he'd been so withdrawn those last days, spending most if not all of the night away from home. I was to find out why he was so melancholy and sour, and why he'd lost his appetite.

"Naturally, he's not putting a *thing* over on me . . . Either this is love or I'm so stupid I don't understand anything . . . I've heard that at your brother's house and other houses where my Manolo goes the young girls are crazy about him, from the daughters of dukes and marquesses right on down . . ."

There was still one thing my neighbor had left to say; and it was that if there was anything I needed . . .

"Just send me a quick message. To tell the truth, my friend Manso, you don't have very good domestic service. That Petra is a good woman all right, but she's rather clumsy, and couldn't ever understand how to serve in the house of a real gentleman. You need better servants, another style, another . . . I'm not sure I'm making it clear."

"Madam, my means . . ."

"Means be hanged; you deserve better. Such a well-known man, one of the nation's glories! You can't live that way . . ."

And no doubt fearful of proceeding too far in her delicate, solicitous concern for me, she left, not without first having invited me to dinner the next day, which was Sunday.

What I have just related is one more thing on the list of things that seemed just as improbable as my appetite on the preceding evening. But there was one even more strange phenomenon, and that was to find José and Manuela together at home, behaving like a pair of turtledoves. One would have thought, God be praised, that not the slightest cloud had ever darkened the sunlight of harmony between husband and wife. She was in a happy humor; he was festive, although I thought I could detect a bit of worry and anxiousness under that cloak of joviality. He treated me with a sweetness he had never used toward me before. He ran to close a door for fear that I might catch cold from the strong draft that was blowing in. That day everything was milk and honey. The wet nurse was behaving herself.

The family doctor had pronounced her an excellent source of milk, and although her big family were all still living in the house, eating their way

209

through it, no unpleasantness had happened so far. In their zeal to outfit Regustiana in proper wet-nurse livery, the three ladies did nothing but pick through yard-goods, select trimmings, and debate whether it should be red or blue. However things might turn out, my acquisition, once rigged out, was going to bear a striking resemblance to the beribboned cow who won the first prize at the Livestock Exposition.

While we were alone for a moment, Lica said to me:

"I don't know what's come over José María—he's become like putty in my hands. It's nothing but 'my darling wife this and my darling wife that.' Now he wants us to take a trip to Paris. Really, the only joy it will give me is to be able to bring you back some present, maybe a complete gentleman's toilet set like one I saw yesterday; all the pieces had the horn of plenty painted on them. I don't know, I just don't know; some good angel has touched José María's heart. How agreeable he is, and how kind! But I still don't believe it'll last, and I'm always on pins and needles when I see him so softened up . . . "

After this improbable development comes the greatest and most phenomenal one of that whole day. I am certain that no one reading this will have a sufficiently large gullet to swallow it. But I declare it, and testify with all my strength to the truth of its incredibility. Let him be astonished who has any strength for astonishment left! The absurdity is that Doña Cándida got money out of me. It is possible to understand that her singular cleverness should have found the wiles and her audacity the cheek to ask me for it. But that I could have given it to her! I was reluctant to believe it myself, although it was eloquently demonstrated by the emptiness of my depressed pockets! I don't know how it happened; a sort of ambush, a trap, a kidnapping. I forgo any detailed description of the act; the particulars may be filled in by the good judgment of those who, upon reading of it, may come to the hair-raising realization that they could be subjected to the same sort of ordeal.

When I departed the night before, that fatal night, I had promised to come back. I did not do so, because Peña's confidences had produced in me a certain repugnance toward that house and its inhabitants. When I *did* go back it was as the result of a strong impulse from within my conscience. I suffered a great deal when Irene appeared; seeing her brought back my former confusion. But by then my spirit had great strength within it, and I could hide my feelings. She looked in a very bad state indeed. Her fever had passed, but she was still suffering its effects, and I wondered confusedly: "Do weakness and suffering enhance beauty or almost totally destroy it? Is she highly fascinating

210

now, as the conventionalities of plastic art demand, or is she utterly devoid of poetic value?" My mental turmoil made me see her first in the one light and then in the other. When she greeted me her voice was shaking and I could hardly hear what she said. Ashamed and inhibited, she sat down beside me and began going through the contents of a sewing basket while I learned whether Miquis had come by and what he had prescribed. Doña Cándida was hovering over the two of us with the most ferocious amiability. Using the tartness which she deserved so well, I said:

"Now you will be kind enough to leave us by ourselves. Stay in the other room as long as you like, the longer the better."

"My, my, just listen to you! G'bye, g'bye . . . You two don't want to be disturbed . . ."

And she went off laughing. Irene and I were left alone in the tiny sitting room, where many things were in disorder, and others sort of pushed into corners as if condemned. I took it all in at a glance, and then raised my eyes to the window panes and saw a canary in a pretty, picturesque cage.

"He's a special gift from Don José to my aunt," said Irene, trying by means of small talk to keep talking without getting upset.

"And you, how are you feeling?" I asked her the way doctors do.

"So-so . . . , just fine . . ."

"And how is one to take that? So-so *and* just fine?"

"He's a lovely canary . . . , you should just hear him sing . . ."

"I can easily imagine . . . It's *you* I want to hear sing . . . If you would do me the kindness of sitting down in that armchair and answering two or three questions for me . . ."

"Right away, Manso my friend. Just let me go get something I was sewing for my aunt. It's a wrapper she took apart, put together again, and then undid again for another remake. This is the third edition of that wrapper. But wait . . . I have all my sewing things here!"

XLI

THE RASCAL SAT DOWN WITH HER
BACK TO THE LIGHT

S HE HAD HALF-CLOSED the inner wooden blinds to soften the clear brilliance of daylight and by so doing had left her face in the shadows. This whole procedure was a good demonstration of her skill in the arts of dissimulation.

"Well let's see: when did you see Manuel Peña for the first time?"

Her head was bent over her sewing so that I couldn't get a good view of her as she answered me in the humble voice of a schoolgirl: "One night, when he came into the dining room with you to get a cool drink . . ."

"Did you speak with him during those days?"

"No, sir, one afternoon . . . I was coming in from my walk with the little girls, and he was on his way out, going down the stairs . . . I don't know how, I tripped and fell."

"One afternoon . . . Where was *I* that afternoon?"

"You'd stayed down at the street entrance talking with a professor friend of yours."

"And give or take a few days, when did this happen?"

"Before Christmas . . . Then I saw him again when I was going out with Ruperto. He followed me, and insisted on conversing with me. He said a lot of foolish things. I was so flustered, I didn't know what to do . . . The next day . . ."

"He wrote you a letter, doubtless a long one. He sent it to you with the mulatto girl. These mixed races are awful! At midnight, shut up in your room, you read the letter."

"That's true," she said without raising her eyes from her sewing. "How did you find out?"

"And on other nights as well you spent long hours reading Manuel's letters and answering them. You'd go to bed very late."

212

She delayed her answer a long time, and it was only a humble "Yes, sir."

"And on the nights when there were great gatherings here the two of you used to see each other on the sly, in the corridor, in the dimly lit places."

With a faint smile she answered in the affirmative. And lo and behold, I was converted into the kindliest and most fatherly man in the world, like one of those old problem-fixers who appear in old-fashioned plays, whose sole mission is to scatter blessings and solve all the conflicts. Without having any good idea of the inner motives which led me to fulfill such a role, I allowed myself to be moved by my kindness, and said to her:

"We're dealing here with a good friend and student of mine whom I care for very much; but I cannot forgive him for being so secretive about this matter. Perhaps it was you who insisted more strongly upon keeping your love wrapped in shadows . . . You're very secretive. I've known about this for some time . . . I haven't been *completely* deceived. I could observe in you some signs of upheaval, and I was certain that there was something going on in your life that was beyond the ordinary routine. And to prove that the schoolmistress didn't deceive me, I'm going to help her make her confession, the way old priests do with timid children who go to confession for the first time. You saw Manuel, who is one of the most likable young fellows who could come into the sight of a passionate young woman. You liked each other, and with mutual delight offered each other the gift of glances and then went on to communication by letters, that epistolary commerce in which each soul is given to the other. And your soul, which is what we're talking about now, absorbed little by little that dewy sweetness which comes down from Heaven . . . (Please don't consider that poetic.) I continue. Letters; a short chat or two, all the more intense for their shortness; furtive glances, all the more impetuous for their scarcity. And it all sustained in you both the initial passion, which I'm bound to admit—and gladly do so—was all tenderness, chasteness, nobleness; the purest and most legitimate purposes of the human soul . . . Manuel's fine qualities must have awakened in you effects of another sort, for since he is a young man with such a brilliant future and already occupies such an excellent rank in the world, you must have felt your own self-esteem enhanced, and felt some stimulus of ambition . . . Why not admit it openly? A love-struck woman would be glad to set the picture of her amorous dreams in a materialistic frame . . . ; yes, just as I'm saying it . . . , let's be very clear, and add to our ideals another very beautiful thing, which is

213

to be the wife of a rich and well-known man who's surrounded by others just as eminent in a wordly way . . . "

I saw her move her head closer to her sewing, so close that she almost put the needle through her eyes. They shed a tear which fell to refresh the seventh edition of Caligula's wrapper. Irene said not a word; but her silence emboldened me to go on:

"Your spirit had not yet become settled about the matter; you loved him but you hadn't yet reached that exalted passion which brooks no contradiction and usually leads to the statement of a dilemma: *victory or death.* Days passed, and what with the little notes, the glances and a spoken word now and then, your passion was fed, but without getting out of hand. But the crisis had to come, the moment when you were to fall head over heels, as they say, and that crisis, that moment came on the night of the charity benefit, that memorable night when you saw your idol surrounded by all the prestige his talent brought him, basking in the light of glory . . . That night Manuel signed the pact with his destiny and flung wide the gates of his brilliant future . . . How beautiful, Irene, how infinitely blissful to imagine yourself joined forever to the hero of that occasion, the eminent orator, the man who would soon be in Parliament, a Cabinet Minister . . . !"

This time I cut her right to the quick, and it wasn't a single tear but rather a torrent which gushed forth to flood the metamorphosed wrapper. Irene put her handkerchief to her eyes, and said in a choking voice:

"You know . . . more than God."

"Let's agree: it was *that* night you fell head over heels in love," I added jokingly. "Now let's continue. Beginning at that moment my friend Irene was disquieted by a love now indomitable and overwhelming. Her soul now longed with thirsty fury for the satisfaction of her most burning desire. The person she loved had left the realm of ordinary human beings and become supernatural. Your heart, your mind, your projected fantasies were all involved. Manuel was the angel of your dreams, the rich and famous husband. I think I'm making myself clear . . . I seem to be reading a book, and yet all I'm doing is generalizing . . . Be patient, I'll speak for a moment longer. Then you felt the desire to leave my brother's house . . . Am I mistaken? You needed to settle quickly on a solution for the future. Manuel would declare himself even more in love after his successful speech and would probably urge his beloved to become independent. You felt the spur to act. Your womanly instincts, your heart, your wit, would not allow you to remain in a merely passive role. You had to take some initiative and stretch out your hands to grasp the treasures being offered by Providence . . . But now we're at a very special point. Is it Providence or is it the Devil who, by permitting the trap set by my brother, makes it possible for you to get what you so ardently desire, namely, to leave the house, become free, and communicate easily with Manuel? After all, the two of you must feel some gratitude to José María, who set up this house and Doña Cándida with it; and she, in league with him, brought her niece here to reproduce the text of the temptations of St. Anthony. You entered the mousetrap without suspecting what was in it. You also believed the hoax about my gadfly's change of fortune . . . Well, you achieve your goal; you talk with Manuel, who bribes the maid and gets into the house. The overtures of my brother present a momentary stumbling-block. To get past that you call me in. I intervene. I get rid of the great obsta-cle. Manuel, offstage, wins all down the line. And now, what's left to do? That's for you and Manuel to decide."

These last words I fairly screamed, for the canary began to sing so loudly that my voice could scarcely be heard. Irene got up, quite upset; she didn't know what to do . . . She turned to the bird and told him to be still, and in view of his disobedience, said to me:

"He won't shut up until I cover the window."

And as she said it she closed the blinds so tight that we were in virtual darkness. What the rascal wanted was to be in the shadows so that I couldn't see how deeply she was blushing. Instead of going back to her sewing, which was only a pretext for not looking me straight in the face, she sat down on a stool in one corner of the room, and continued weeping.

I was not willing, for the moment, to ask her any more questions. My method of interrogative and deductive confession could be used only very delicately for what still remained to be confessed. Actually, nothing remained hidden now. I could see the whole story with perfect clarity, as if I had read it in a book. The story had a sad and complicated ending. Or rather, it had *no* ending, and stood like a case on trial waiting for the judge's sentence. The sentence might be happy or dreadfully wretched. Was it up to me to take part in it, or on the contrary ought I gingerly to escape and let the criminals sort things out as best they might? Poor Manso! Either I am totally ignorant about human suffering, or Irene was expecting me to be a savior, a providential aide. A long time passed before she said to me, still weeping:

"You know everything. You're like a seer."

This exaggerated praise led me to an observation about myself. I do not wish to hold it back, as it is very interesting, and it may explain some apparent

215

contradictions in my life. I, who had been so awkward in that whole business with Irene when all I had before me were isolated, individual facts, had just shown great perspicacity when I scrutinized and judged those same facts from the higher perspective of general truth. I had been unable, except by vague suspicions, to perceive what was going on between Irene and my disciple. And now, with certain knowledge of only a small piece of that train of events, I saw and understood it all, down to its last details, and was enabled to present to Irene an image of her own feelings and even to uncover her own secrets for her. That lack of worldly ability and this overabundance of generalizing skill derive from the difference existing between my practical reason and my pure reason; the one, incapacitated, as in the case of a person living removed from active life; and the other, most expeditious, as in one who cultivates studious pursuits.

Everything that I told Irene as I received her confession—and it astounded her greatly—was spoken theoretically, using as a basis my academic knowledge of the human spirit. She called me a seer, when in reality I had demonstrated only a good memory and a good use of my talent! Spirit of divination it certainly was not, when it existed in this wretched thinker of things thought first by others! This theorizer who with his subtleties and method and timidity had been playing ideological charades around his idol, while the *truly* human being, disorderly of spirit, willful in affections, a stranger to method, but gifted with an instinct for facts, a stout heart and a sense of drama, had aimed straight at the mark and hit it! Observe then in me the armchair strategist who's never sniffed gunpowder in his life and sets about with methodical sluggishness to study the coordinates of the fortress he proposes to conquer. Observe in young Peña the raw recruit who's never picked up a book on tactics, and while the first fellow is making calculations, the second jumps into the fortress armed with his sword, attacking it and taking it by storm . . . This is one of the saddest . . .

Irene drew me out of my reflections by stopping her crying and offering me more flattery. It was this:

"You are priceless, the best person in the world . . . Manuel respects you so much, that there's no authority greater than our friend Manso. If you told him right now it was night he'd believe you. He does only what you tell him to."

"I can see what you're up to, little fox," I thought, smiling inwardly. "Now you want me to get you married . . . You have some fears, and you're right. There'll be problems . . . First, Doña Javiera will be against it; second,

Manuel himself . . . (these raw recruits are like that) . . . after his triumph and taking the fortress with such verve, may not be too eager to hold onto it. He belongs to the Bonaparte school . . . I can see, my little Irene, that you don't miss a trick. So then, I should be a mediator, a diplomat, a fixer and a matchmaker? That's all I need!"

I said this all to myself, which is how one says certain things. And at that moment I thought I heard a noise at the door leading to the parlor. One more proof of my abilities as a seer. Doña Cándida was behind the fragile wood listening to what we were saying. To be certain, I opened the door. Disconcerted at being caught in the act, the lady pretended to be cleaning the door with a great feather-duster she had in her hand.

"There's no way you'll escape us today, Máximo!" she said.

"What, madam, are you going to lock me in a cage?"

"No; what I mean is, today you must stay and dine with us."

From the corner where she was, Irene made affirmative signs with her head.

"Very well," I answered.

"You won't have the delicious things you eat at home . . . Tell me, do you like squab? Because I have some."

"I like everything."

"Someone gave me an eel yesterday. Do you like them?"

"You're the biggest eel of all."

No; as before, I said this to myself. Then she touched her pocket, which clanked with many keys. I shook like a head of wheat on its stalk.

"I have to go out for some things . . . Look, Irene will make you a pastry you'll like very much."

I looked at Irene, who was gagging her mouth with her handkerchief, dying of laughter, with tears still running down her pale cheeks. Oh, pastry of laughter and tears, how bitter you tasted!

XLII

HOW BITTER!

I'VE GOT TO GO OUT. Melchora will be here soon," said Caligula on her way back in. "But, what's the matter with you, child? Why are you crying? Have you scolded her, Máximo? Well, it's just foolishness. Go to the kitchen and that'll take your mind off of it. Are you going to make the pastry? Look, Máximo will help, he knows about everything . . . Do you know what else you can do? Get out the china, the tablecloth, the napkins; it's all there in the big trunk. Here are the keys. Look sharp, silly . . . What is it? Oh, Máximo, just by hearing you say you'll stay on, this young lady-philosopher gets all flustered! Of course you wouldn't like a boiled dinner, Máximo. I'll give you a French-style meal. Wait till you see how good it is! Just dreadfully good! Say, Irene, the stove is lit. It'll all be fried and roasted food, nothing stewed or boiled. You see, that way our young friend here will be used to it, and come back another day. G'bye, g'bye. See to it, Irene, that everything's ready by the time I get back."

"My aunt says some really strange things," Irene said as soon as we were alone. "She'll starve you to death. There's nothing here, not even forks . . . What my aunt calls *china* are a few unmatched plates still packed in trunks. And the dining room! There's no table that can seat three people. Up till now we've been eating off a little iron night stand that's minus one leg and we have to prop it up with a biscuit-box . . . You'll have a good laugh . . . I swear to you, I'd a thousand times rather eat in the mess hall of a poorhouse than live any longer with my aunt."

I shall never forget the expression of horror and revulsion I saw on her face.

"Well, you've come here by your own choice . . . As I said before."

"Yes, but I thought I had only come passing through," she answered with a decisiveness I couldn't remember having seen in her. "I came the way one goes to a railway station to catch the train."

And then, haughty and insolent, as I had never seen her before, showing a force that astounded me, she said:

"Believe you me, I'll get out of here soon: either married or dead."

It left me cold . . .

"But, after all, Irene, we must help Doña Cándida. If we don't, it's more than likely we'll have to go and eat at an inn after we get up from the table."

And she burst out laughing. She beckoned me to follow her. She showed me the dining room, which was a precinct worthy of study. An old bookcase, with the glass gone from the doors, and green curtains, made do for a sideboard. But let no one think the *china* was there, unless that word could be applied to two stuffed birds, two copper ink-stands, a wooden head of the kind wigmakers use to display their wares, a porcelain dog, two or three plates of dubious value, an Arab slipper, a sword-hilt, a mousetrap, and other junk, representing what the lady had been unable to sell from her ancient furnishings.

"This is my aunt's museum," said Irene mockingly. "Now feast your eyes upon this sumptuous *salle à manger.* She says it's in Renaissance style because of that pair of little carved chests and that hunting scene. They're both in such bad shape that nobody will give her anything for them . . . Get a look at the new style in furniture. Sitting on chairs to eat has gone out of fashion. Here we sit on trunks and boxes and set our table, where do you suppose? On days of high ceremony, we use a night stand we bring in from the sitting room. On ordinary days, we eat off a board we put across the arms of that chair. Today is an occasion of grand sumptuousness, and I'll bring in the table from the kitchen. Don't worry about it being needed there. The kitchen is hardly used in this house, and today I think cold meats will be our menu. This place operates on a high-class basis, my friend Manso . . . Take a lesson so that when you get married . . ."

I could understand perfectly well Irene's disgust at her aunt's house, and her vigorous declaration: "Either dead or . . ." She took the thought out of my mouth and stressed it like this:

"Now do you understand why I said what I did a bit earlier? Is this *living*? And if I don't try to save myself, to open up a way, who will?"

"You're right, you're right!"

"I've thought so much about it, I've turned it over and over. It's hard to open up a way when you're in my situation. A poor girl, alone, no parents, no adviser . . ."

219

I was very pleased to see her talking so openly.

"And now, if you please," she added, "we'll bring in the kitchen table. We must work, my friend. Otherwise . . ."

She led me to the kitchen, which surprised me in two ways: it was very clean; and outside of one pot steaming away redolently on the fire, there was no sign, symptom, or indication of any edible thing.

"It's true," Irene observed, "one must give credit to my aunt. She spends the whole day scrubbing the kitchen. All right, Manso, grab it there."

"I'll take it myself. I can manage it fine . . ."

"No, no, I want to get some exercise. I like doing this. Just obey . . . grab that end."

We lifted the table, and with me walking backwards, inch by inch, she laughing and I too, we bore our burden into the dining room.

"All right. Now, tablecloths, dishes . . . We'll have to open up those trunks. You try the keys; only my aunt has the hang of the thing. The trunks the movers brought still haven't been unpacked . . ."

"Let's have those keys . . . we'll get things open."

After a number of not very easy tries, we opened the three trunks and found the one where the crockery was. In order to extract it from the depths, we had first to take out *The Christian Year* in twelve volumes, some quilts, an embroidery frame, and I don't know what else.

"Well, well . . . now we have plates . . . ; the soup tureen, which is precisely what we don't need. But let's have it. It's not so bad after all. It's in the cutlery department where we're short of things. My aunt and I get along with a couple of forks, but I don't know whether our guest . . . Oh yes! In the other trunk, the one with all the papers about my aunt's former real estate property, and all the old documents and certificates, there must be some place settings. And if not, there's a dagger in the museum. Said to be from Toledo."

I couldn't hold in my laughter. Finally the table was set and didn't look so bad. The clean cloth, newly bought, and some new glassware gave it a fine appearance.

"Now for the main part," said Irene. "We'll see how she wiggles through this one. It'll be an amusing comedy, *really something* . . . Just notice what she says on the way in . . . I can hear it now . . ."

Weary from her work, she sat down on one of the chairs I had brought from different corners of the house. She rested her bare elbow on the table and her forehead on her fist, making a study of the stripes in the tablecloth. I was standing at the other end of the table looking at her wrapper, light-colored, summer weight and so heavily starched that wherever she went the stiff cloth produced strange vibrations and a kind of music that . . . But let's not continue in that vein.

"Do you really think that this life, this house could make anybody want to continue here? Isn't it only fair for me to get free, no matter how? And the strangest part is that I've been brought up this way. But my own nature is so different, I'm so at odds with this disorderliness, this poverty, as though I'd spent all my life in palaces . . ."

"You have plenty of ways of getting free, for you are a worthy young woman. You shouldn't get the idea that you can get free only by taking the wrong road."

"Roads, my friend Manso, are put before us, and one must take them. I don't know if it's God or who it is that opens them up to us. Let me explain to you . . ."

And now not just one elbow, but both, were on the table. Turning to me, face to face, sphynxlike she revealed to me what follows, and I'll never forget it:

"You see, when I was a little girl going to school, do you know what my dreams were and what I thought about? . . . I don't know if this was the result of seeing the other girls study so hard, or of loving my teacher so much. But my dreams were to learn a very great deal, learn about everything, learn what men know—how silly! And I applied myself so diligently that I took on a certain gloss—*really something*! The calling to be a teacher lasted until I graduated from normal school. Then it seemed as if I were on the threshold of the world, looking at it all, saying to myself: 'What can I do here with all the learning I've got?' No, I had no calling to be a teacher, though it might have seemed otherwise. When you spoke to my aunt to get me to go and teach Don José's little girls I accepted happily, not because I would enjoy the job but so as to get out of this awful jail, to put this behind me and breathe a fresh atmosphere. I could rest there; I was at least calm. But my imagination was not at rest . . ."

The worst kind of mistake! I had judged by appearances and considered her to be controlled by reason, and with few fantasies in her. I had seen her as the woman of northern Europe, steady, balanced, studious, serious, without caprice! But let's listen now.

"I've always been very much turned in on myself, Manso my friend. So it's hard for people to tell what I'm thinking. It's such a pleasure to be all alone with myself thinking my thoughts without anybody butting in to find out what's going on in my head! At Don José's house, I performed well in my duties as a teacher, I earned my keep. But, oh my friend, if you only knew how I suffered in overcoming my sadness and my reluctance to teach. . . . What an utterly boring job! Teaching grammar and arithmetic! To struggle with other people's children, to endure their tiresome ways. You've got to be a tremendous hero, and that's more than I've been . . . But I was full of things to teach, I trusted God and told myself: 'Just hold on, hold on a little longer, and God will take you out of this and lead you where you ought to be . . . !'"

Error! Crass, stupid wrongheadedness! To think that I had considered her . . . But hush, and let's hear more.

". . . and I was so grateful for the interest you'd taken in me! But since I held back from telling you my thoughts, you didn't understand me very well . . . You saw and admired in me the schoolmistress, and yet I hated books; you can't have any idea of how much I abhorred them and still do . . . I'm talking about the Grammars, Arithmetics, and Geographies. *Really something*!"

And all the while I thought . . . ! And this, dear God, is the good that study does us! To be mistaken about everything individual or having to do with the heart. I listened to her and was amazed at the magnitude of my own mistakes. But I prefer not to articulate them or to confess my stupidity. On the contrary, at *that* moment I was behaving very perceptively, since with the actual data, the facts I had just obtained, I could philosophize again to my heart's content, as I had done so lucidly only a few hours earlier.

"Look here, Irene," I said to her in that tone of certitude that never fails me when I speak in general terms, "I'm not very surprised by what you've just told me. Without understanding too well what you were thinking, I was aware that the inner reality was quite different from the superficial one. I'm not entirely new at this; I'm sure you know that. So you were fooling everybody but me . . . Your distaste for schoolbooks was not as well concealed as certain other little secrets of yours that were *really something*, more or less. And I'm so convinced of this that I believe I could trace and chart the evolution, we might call it, of your thinking, without making any mistakes. You were born with delicate tastes, with the instincts of an aristocratic lady, with aptitudes of the kind I call *social*, that is, the art of pleasing, living well, conversing well, paying and receiving compliments, all with exquisite grace

222

and delicacy. There is, here, a lack of atmospheric conditions for the development of those instincts and those attitudes; and their very absence causes you to wish for them, aspire to them, dream of them . . . , and just look by what unexpected means Providence has provided them to you. True, you fulfill fatally the law which rules youth and beauty: you fall into what used to be called the net of love . . . a very natural thing. But besides being very natural, it turns out to be most opportune, because . . . Let's speak plainly. If Manuel marries Irene, as I believe he will, and is duty-bound to do, Irene will have what she desires. She will be—just make a list: the wife of an important man; the mistress of a splendid house where she can put on all the airs she wants; mistress of a thousand conveniences: a carriage, servants, a box at the theater . . ."

"Be still, be still," she said, turning red and bursting out laughing as she covered her face.

"No, no, this doesn't mean you're going down the wrong road. Quite the contrary; the greater the cultivation that exists in one's life, the greater the advantages in the moral sphere. You'll be an excellent mother, a good wife, a lady of charitable good works, most distinguished, a model for others . . . You will shine . . ."

"Be still, be still."

And the perspicacity for understanding her which I had lacked at an earlier time came to me then and I could clearly see the full extent of her bourgeois ambitions, so at odds with the ideal I had forged for myself. At the heart of all that itch to get out and be sociable there was so much that was ordinary and run-of-the-mill! Irene, as she was revealing herself to me then, was a person of the sort we might call distinguished in no remarkable sense, one more *lady* cast in the common mold, conformed to the model of mediocrity in her taste—even in her honesty—which is the stuff of present-day society. How much higher, how much more noble had been *my* image of her! The Irene I'd seen from the heights of my general ideas; that model who came from a childhood dedicated to serious study and was led into an essentially practical, didactic womanhood; that present-day Minerva in whom everything was proportion, balance, truth, rectitude, reason, order, hygiene . . .

"What I can assure you of," she said, "is that my desires have always been the noblest ones in the world. I want a happy life the way other women do. Is there anybody who doesn't want that? No. Well I've seen other women marry young men of merit and good position. Why shouldn't I be the same?

223

I've asked God about it, Manso. I've prayed so hard to God and to Our Lady!"

Sanctimonious to boot! That was all I needed for a complete disillusionment . . . She hates studying; she's ambitious to cut a figure in the overpopulated ranks of ordinary aristocracy; she has a secret enthusiasm for trivia; an unhealthy devotion consisting of requests to God for a carriage, a house set in a garden, and a safe, steady income; a wild passion, a weak spirit, and an elastic conscience. *This* is what appeared in her gradual revelation. And towering over all her other imperfections, protecting them and shielding them from an outsider's gaze, was an uncomparable skill for *faking* things, an art which had allowed my friend to present herself before me with a character absolutely opposite to the one she possessed.

What had happened to that contentment with her lot, that serenity and temperateness of spirit, that pure conscience, that precise eye for seeing life the way it really is? What had happened to that repose and marvelous equilibrium of the North European woman I had seen in her? In those fine qualities, as in others, I had got the notion that she was, among all the creatures I had seen on earth, the most perfect. Oh, those perfections were in my books, they were the product of my penchant for thinking and synthesizing, and of my too-frequent dealings with an idea of unity and with the great laws of that deadly gift for perceiving archetypes and not persons. And all of it only so that a doll made by me should then break in my own hands, leaving me grossly disconsolate . . . ! I don't know where these inner lamentations would have led me if Doña Cándida hadn't appeared when we least expected her . . .

"Oh, my little dears! I see you've done your work well . . . the table's set . . . Lord, how luxurious! But, Máximo, is it true you're really staying to eat with us? I thought . . . Since you're so odd, and have never consented to sit down at my table . . ."

Irene was stifling a laugh. I don't know what I said.

"It's not that I'm without food to give you. In case you *did* stay I've brought home . . ."

From a large kerchief she began to take out several things wrapped in paper: a bit of turkey with truffles, a large plain pastry, pickled tongue, boar's head and other cold meats . . . When Caligula went to the kitchen for plates on which to put her acquisitions, Irene said to me, half-disdainfully:

"There's my aunt for you . . . As soon as she gets a bit of money she buys cold meats and won't eat anything else. She says she can't lose her habit

224

of eating well, and only when we're in economic misery does she put a pot on the stove . . ."

A moment later Irene and I stepped into the window opening. It would be necessary to wait a while for dinner to be ready and we didn't know how to pass the time, for neither she nor I felt much like talking.

"Tell me, Irene," I asked her with profound interest. "Suppose Manuel got a bad impulse now, and he . . ."

She didn't let me finish. She answered with a great transformation of her expression, presaging grief and shame, and then she said to me:

"You are killing me even by suggesting that . . . If Manuel, oh! . . . I'd die of sorrow."

"And supposing you didn't die? . . . There are cases . . . "

"I'd kill myself . . . ; I have the courage to kill myself and then kill myself again in case I wasn't all dead . . . You don't know me."

How true! But I was indeed beginning to know her.

Doña Cándida surprised us, appearing all of a sudden to tell me:

"I've got a bottle of champagne I received as a gift last year. It's for you. Wait till you see how good it is. We'll eat soon. Melchora has come now, and in a moment she'll fry the meat and make the omelet."

"Omelet for dinner, Aunt!!"

"What do you know, you silly? I don't like slumgullion . . . , I detest pot food. Don't you agree, Máximo?"

"Yes, madam, whatever you say."

"You can come to the table very soon now. What time is it?"

All that was lacking were the two things that make for an agreeable meal: happiness and food. First Melchora served us a bad-tasting omelet; I really don't know how I got it down. Then came a meat course, scanty and dried up, to which Doña Cándida gave the resounding appellation *filet à la Maréchale.*

"It's simply delicious, Máximo. You have here a dish that nobody in Madrid knows how to prepare any more, except me . . ."

"It's as I say, our culinary traditions are disappearing!"

Irene was winking at me and making the most amusing faces and contortions to make fun of her aunt's dinner and its slim offerings, for the promised squab and eel put in no appearance, not even in effigy.

"Here's some turkey with truffles," declared Caligula, "made especially for me by Señor Lhardy . . . After that I'll give you a French dish that you'll like very much . . . Come, come, uncork the champagne . . ."

225

"But madam, this is cider, and not the best kind either . . ."

"I tell you it's authentic *Duc de Montebello*. You may know about philosophy, but you don't know about wines."

"But what's this—are we going to have another omelet?"

"It's the little dish I was telling you about—*haricots à la sauce proven-çale* . . . Melchora perpares it marvelously well."

If you'll allow me to be frank, madam, I'll tell you it looks like a mustard plaster; but we'll get it down after all . . ."

"You ingrate! Try the pastry . . . Irene, aren't you eating? She's like this every day. She lives on air, the way chameleons do."

Indeed, Irene scarcely ate a thing except for bread and a little of the famous *filet à la Maréchale*. In view of her abstemiousness, *I* went back to reflecting on my eternal theme.

"Who knows," I asked myself, "whether a completely cold and careful critique might lead you to affirm that what you thought of as a series of resounding, fine-grained perfections, if they came to life, would be the most imperfect state of affairs in the world? That business of the woman-as-reason that made you so enthusiastic, couldn't it just be a stupid trick of your mind? There are puns on ideas, just as there are on words. Plant your feet squarely in reality and do a serious study of woman-as-woman. What seems to be defective now, couldn't it all be natural manifestations of the age, the environment? Where did you get that northern model, cold as ice, not made of passions, virtues, weaknesses, and differing gifts? You got it out of chapters in books and pages in an encyclopedia! Pay heed to reality in the raw, and don't come around with your grumbling, professorial morality and label as defects things that are just human accidents, parts and modes of the natural truth which is made manifest in all things! Passion is the fruit appropriate to youth, and the art of dissimulation which sets your hair on end is a trait of character acquired in the state of loneliness in which that poor child has lived, without parents or any real support. A powerful instinct for self-defense has provided her with that art, and it enables her to fill the gap left by having no natural family support. That dissimulation has been her great weapon in the struggle for life. She has defended herself from the world with her reservedness. And her ambition, which so displeases you, is only a product of the abandonment in which she has lived. She has succeeded in learning to count on herself for everything, and thus she feels the itch to take all the initiatives on her own. Dragged on by passion, she has shown regrettable weaknesses. Her wit and prudence have been overcome by her temperament . . . One must make allowances for the extraordinary nature of the seductions she has had to resist. Very much in love, she was drawn toward the suitor of her dreams. In poverty, she was drawn to the wealthy young man. Thus, love was fulfilled and poverty relieved. Who is immune to the attractions of these two great forces? The utilitarian spirit of contemporary society could do no less than to make its influence felt in her. Here we have a poor abandoned orphan girl making her way, and her passion conceals a practical genius of the first rank . . ."

I don't know what else went through my mind! I got up from that disagreeable table, sated with cold and unsubstantial food. I rose from the chairs squeaking their threats to come apart, I fled from the knives that were falling out of their handles, and from that unbearable hostess whose pretenses were by now bordering on the miraculous.

Irene went with me into the parlor; we sat down, but didn't speak to each other. Twilight was coming on, and we were surrounded by melancholy shadows. The sadness of having gone all day without seeing the object of her affections had left her mute and sullen. And I felt the same way, for yet another emotional crisis overcame me as a result of what I have said above. My new affliction consisted in having a vision of her bereft of all the perfections in which my ideas had clothed her, and in realizing that I found her more interesting and loved her more this new way. In a word, I reached the point of feeling a burning idolization of her. A strange contradiction! When she was perfect, I loved her in a Petrarchan way, with cold sentimental feeling that might have inspired me to write sonnets. Now that she was imperfect, I adored her with a new and tumultuous affection, stronger than I and all my philosophizing.

That passion of hers which ended up in weakness; that fascinating reserve which led one always to imagine the existence of something more; even her materialistic air; it all captivated me. Even her amusing tag line, that poverty of language which led her to apply *really something* to everything, even that charmed me. Oh, how much better if I had been what Manuel was, a man, an Adam, than what I *had* been, an angel armed with the sword of methodical procedure, defending the gates of the paradise of Reason! . . . But it was too late now.

And in that darkness, pierced by the timid light of sunset and the yellow glow of the streetlamps, she looked so supremely beautiful to me that I was afraid of myself and thought: "I've got to get out of here before my feelings overtake my reason and lead me to say or do things that so far, thank God,

227

I've been able to avoid." And so it was; I noticed that I felt in danger of stepping over into the ridiculous if I let slip out any part of the train of feelings that was moving along inside me. I felt like a stripling, a playboy, even a little flashy . . . I uttered three or four set phrases and left. Because if I hadn't . . . There are cases on record of profoundly serious people who, in an unhappy moment, have fallen headfirst into the sinkhole of foolishness.

XLIII
DOÑA JAVIERA CAME AT ME
IN A FURIOUS RAGE

I T MADE ME SHAKE with fright, for I had never seen real wrath in her before: I had been used to her great charm and affability and the broadest tolerance. The moment I entered her house, at six o'clock on Sunday, she ran toward me with a threatening look, grabbed me by one arm, took me into her sitting room, closed the door . . .

"But, madam . . ."

I simply couldn't understand, nor at first was I able to attach the most appropriate interpretation to her brusque behavior. I thought she wanted to scratch my eyes out; then I thought she was going for her *own* eyes. She was gesticulating like a road-show actress, and breathing very laboriously; she could express herself only in monosyllables and clipped phrases.

"I'm . . . furious . . . I'm dying, choking . . . Manso my friend, don't you know what's happening to me? I can't stand it, I'm dying . . . You don't know? Manuel, that rascal, that ungrateful child . . ."

"But, madam . . ."

"What d'you suppose he's done? . . . It's something bad enough for me to kill him . . . Well, he wants to get married to a schoolmistress . . ."

And as she said *schoolmistress* she raised her voice in a howl of agony, like someone receiving the *coup de grâce*.

"Some little slut half-dying of hunger . . . What an insult, Blessed Mother, Holy Blessed Mother! . . . It seems impossible, a boy like that, so clever, so worthy . . . Oh, this is like turning Barrabas loose . . . or a punishment, yes a punishment from God . . . Señor de Manso, doesn't it make you indignant enough to stamp your feet? Why, you're made of stone, you don't feel things . . . But have you taken in what I said? A schoolmarm? One of those women who teach little brats their ABC's. When I tell you I'm furious! I'm going to have an attack! What did I do to make him turn out that way? And I choked him when he told me . . . He's a ruined man, I tell you! He can kiss his career goodbye, and his future . . . Christ almighty! And you're so cool, not upset at all . . ."

"Madam, let's eat. Calm down, and then we'll talk."

A manservant announced that dinner was ready. Before going into the dining room, my neighbor said to me in the most solemn tones in the world:

"I'm counting on Señor de Manso. You are my hope and my salvation."

"I . . ."

"No, no. You are to my son what they call an oracle. Isn't that how you say it?"

"Yes, it is."

"Well, if you don't shake that silly idea out of his head, you and I will have a falling out."

It was written somewhere that all bad things that befell me during those days would occur while I was eating at someone else's table. And Doña Javiera's table bore scant resemblance to Doña Cándida's, in terms of the good taste of the food and the form in which it was served. A greater contrast is not to be found. My neighbor's table offered a variety of savory and over-wrought dishes, served on shiny new china. It was a feast more appropriate to gluttons than to delicate gastronomes. And the effects of her tantrum could not be noted—either in small or large degree—in the appetite of Señora de Peña, who that day, no less than any other of the year, gave all the signs of not allowing herself to die of hunger. The little she said was directed toward the end of getting me to stuff myself; she told me I wasn't eating anything, and praised her cook and railed at Manuel for speaking too loudly and leaving us bewildered. (He came in after we had finished the soup course.) He was jovial in the extreme. I could tell that he'd seen his victim; but I couldn't think where or how. Probably it had been right in Caligula's house, for it was very easy for Manuel to bamboozle Doña Cándida or even bypass her com-pletely. During the entire meal, Doña Javiera missed not a single opening to scold her son, fulminating against him with the beams of her beautiful eyes and the lightning-bolts of her sharp, wounding remarks. She treated me royally, desiring me to eat some of every dish (impossible), looking after me and pampering me with affectionate good manners. When I departed, after a short talk about the aforementioned conflict, I said to her:

230

"Leave him to me . . . I'll fix him."

And she:

"I'm counting on you. God bless you for your good work . . . Every time I think of it . . . A schoolmarm! I'm red with shame. What will people say! I won't be able to show my face in the public street!"

And when as I left I saw Manuel going into his room, I signaled to him that I would wait for him upstairs in my apartment. Doña Javiera came out to the stairway with me, and in a soft little voice, half-cheery and half-hopeful, said to me:

"That's right; pin his ears back for him. Tell him I don't want teachers or bluestockings in my house. Tell him to think of his future, his career . . . As if he didn't have marquesses' daughters to choose from. And me, I'll just die if he marries that . . . And he'd better not come back whining and sucking up to me. I won't have it . . . "

"I'll fix it; I'll fix it."

XLIV

MY REVENGE

WHEN MANUEL PRESENTED HIMSELF before me, he seemed very eager to ask me:

"Have you talked with Mamma?"

"Yes, your mamma is furious. She cannot get it into her head that you're actually going to marry Irene; and she has every reason for feeling that way. Now that it looks as if you're going to live like aristocrats, a *good* marriage would be more suitable. You must realize that poor Irene . . ."

"Yes, she's poor and humble . . . and I love her."

The cat jumped up on my lap. What a joy to pet it! And in synchronized rhythm with those strokes down the nervous animal's back, how many thoughts flowered inside me, all luminous and heavy with rationality! I traced a plan and put it immediately into practice.

"Tell me frankly what you're thinking . . . But don't hold anything back. I want the truth, the unadulterated truth."

"I need your advice."

"Advice? Let's hear first what you feel, what you want . . ."

"Well, my dear maestro, if you're asking me about my feelings, I'll just tell you with complete frankness that I'm bursting with love and high hopes. But if you're asking me about my intentions regarding marriage I'll tell you with equal frankness that I haven't been able yet to come to any settled ideas about it. It's a serious matter. Everywhere you go all you hear is diatribes against matrimony. And then we're both so young . . . One must think it through and weigh it carefully, Manso my friend . . ."

"Do you have any fears," I asked, making a supreme effort to appear calm, "that Irene, as your wife, might not measure up to your high hopes and your present enthusiasm about her?"

"No, no fears at all . . . Maybe because I love her so much my passion blinds me, or because she is among the most perfect creatures in existence, I feel that I would have a happy life with her . . ."

"Then what . . . ?"

"Besides, you know . . . ; my mother is so much against it. You know Irene, you've had dealings with her at Don José's house. What's your idea of her?"

"The same as yours."

"She's so good, so smart! That does it, Manso my friend! I'll sail away with her!"

"Sure you won't regret it?"

"You make me hesitate . . . Oh, for God's sake—you ask that in such a way and you rivet me with your eyes . . . How the deuce should I know whether I'll regret it or not?! Just consider the times we're living in and the enormous changes taking place in life. Ideas, feelings, law itself, everything is in revolution. We don't live in a stable era. Social phenomena, each more unexpected and surprising than the last, keep occurring with no letup. I'd say society is a ship, and the winds are blowing from the most unexpected and surprising quarter, and the waves are getting so high . . ."

I was in meditation.

"Marriage! What do you advise me to do?"

"Would you be able to follow an order of mine?"

"I swear that I would," he said to me firmly. "There's nobody in the world who possesses as great a power over me as my maestro."

"Suppose I told you not to get married?"

"If you tell me not to get married," he murmured in great confusion, looking at the floor and putting a flourish on his confusion with a sigh, "I'll follow that advice too . . ."

"And suppose that over and above telling you not to marry, I tell you to break off absolutely with her and not see her any more?"

"Well, that's . . ."

"Well that's how it's going to be. I'm not going to advise you to follow any middle course. You can expect from me only definitive decisions. To counsel anything else would be for me to advocate ignominy and to authorize vice."

"But you must realize that to do that—to give up, to pull out . . . You can't inspire me to do something vile."

"Well then, get married."

"If really . . ."

"I concede that, in view of the special circumstances you may be reluctant to be joined to her by bonds that last your whole life long. I agree that

233

you could interpret this marriage as an obstacle to your career . . . You could wait for a time, until your renown were greater, and you were presented with a *brilliant* match, one of these rich heiresses dying to be addressed as 'Madam Minister.' You are very comfortably well-off, but your fortune is not so great that you can aspire to keep up with the demands of modern life, which are greater each day. The general wealth is expanding like soapsuds, and competitiveness in luxury is reaching an incredible level. In ten or fifteen years' time you may think of yourself as poor, and who can say for certain whether the official posts you occupy may not present a threat to your moral integrity? Think it over carefully, Manuel, look to the future, and don't let yourself be dragged down by a caprice of a few weeks' duration. You can count on being in Parliament within three months if they get you that age exemption. Within the year your great oratorical gifts will have garnered you some triumphs. You will shine on committees and in the great political debates. Perhaps after two years' apprenticeship you will be the lieutenant of a party boss or the colonel of a little battalion of dragoons. Surely you'll soon be the chief of a handful of those *faithful men* who are the ruination of the Government. I can see you as an Undersecretary at 26, and a Cabinet Minister before you're thirty. And then . . ., just imagine, marriage to any rich heiress, from Spain or the New World. It would clinch your fortune, and . . . I don't need to tell you what that would be worth to you . . ."

He watched me, attentive and astonished. And I, firm in my intention, went on as follows:

"Now let's examine the other element in the question. Poor Irene. . . . She's a good girl, an angel; but let's not be swept away by sentimentality. The world is full of these unfortunate cases. She who falls, falls, and who can say who pushed her . . . ? Let's suppose that you, taking your cue now from materialistic criteria, were to cut short your novel of love, just close it out slam-bang, like a writer who's fed up and doesn't feel like writing a dénouement. The victim will weep, she surely will; but rivers of tears, after all, dry up quickly in a great drought. If you give the greatest grief one dry summer, you'll see. Everything passes away, and consolation is a law in the world of morals. What is the Universe? A series of stiffenings, chillings, and transformations which all obey the supreme law of oblivion. All right: the young woman withdraws from view; a year, two years pass, and she's a new woman. She's prettier, smarter, more seductive. What's been happening? Simply that she no longer remembers you, nor you her. It is true that her poverty could perhaps impel her toward degradation; but don't let that trouble you, for

234

Providence looks out for the needy, and that discreet, pretty young woman will find a good honest man to come to her aid, one of those hardened bachelors who reach a private understanding with the flotsam and jetsam . . ."

"By all that's holy!" shouted Peña impetuously, not letting me finish. "If I didn't consider you to be the most dependable man in the world I'd think you were speaking in jest. It can't be that you . . ."

What I was saying would have been egregiously treacherous had it not been a mere tactic, which my disciple realized before I had intended. Seeing my stratagem early on, he uncovered what I was seeking to keep hidden. I had no longer any doubts regarding his inner rectitude . . .

"Don't continue," he exclaimed, getting up. "I'm leaving. I can't bear to listen to certain things . . ."

"Manuel, I was expecting from you the reaction you have shown. When you supposed me to be speaking in jest, I realized that you *are* able to judge me rightly. I wasn't sure what track your thoughts were on, and I laid for you a captious trap of argumentation. Now it is my duty to speak from the heart . . . Do you want some advice? Well here it is . . . I don't know how you've come to expect it from me, nor how you've thought you could find norms for conduct outside your own conscience. But to conclude: if you *don't* marry her, we're no longer friends; your maestro will no longer exist for you. All the esteem in which I hold you will turn to scorn, and I shall remember you only to curse the time during which I considered you my friend . . ."

He gave me a hug. In his effusiveness all he could say was:

XLV

"MY MOTHER"

YOU LEAVE HER TO ME. I'll pacify her; I'll get her to see . . . She doesn't know Irene, she doesn't know how worthy she is. I shall tell your mother that the memory of my own mother lays upon me the obligation of taking that poor orphan under my wing, in view of the ancient debts of gratitude owed by my family to hers . . . Yes, I make that public for your consumption and your mother's too. The schoolmarm is now my sister; her misfortune moves me to confer that title upon her, and with it my public protection, which will go as far as need be to save a man's honor and a family's good name."

I was warming to it: every word made me think of other more vigorous ones.

"Your mother's worries are ridiculous. Let's leave family trees out of it, for otherwise you, your mother, and all the Peñas of Candelario would end up the losers.."

"Yes," he shouted enthusiastically, "down with family trees!"

"And let's not talk about stumbling blocks to your career . . . You're getting a prize of a woman; why, your *intended* is capable of pushing you further perhaps than you might have gone with your own lights alone . . . ! Yes! Imagine even *suggesting* that she doesn't have plenty of enterprising spirit! Manuel, pay no attention to your mamma; hold your temper with her. Doña Javiera will give in; leave her to me."

The rest that we said is unimportant. I remained alone, somewhere between sorrow and gladness. I saw that what I had done was good, and this gave me a sufficiently great satisfaction to stifle my grief at times, as I contemplated it.

And although Doña Javiera came up that very night to find out the result of our conversation, I was not willing to be explicit with her.

"I've convinced him, madam, convinced him," was all I said to her.

She kept saying I was badly cared for in my bachelor flat, with just a housekeeper, the way a priest lives.

"You refuse to follow my advice, Manso my friend, and you'll have a bad time of it. This doesn't look like the home of an outstanding professor. What does that Petra give you to eat? Stew from leftovers; and hollow nothings. Weak food that doesn't give substance to your brains. I'll just have to come in every day and prepare your meals! And then you need a better place to live. Oh, my dear sir, in the Calle de Alfonso XII we'll be really well off. I'll take charge of arranging your new flat and fixing it up for you just beautiful! No, no need to say thanks . . . I'm a plain-speaking woman, and you deserve it. It's the least I could do."

These kind offers were repeated on two or three occasions until one day when my neighbor had learned of her son's decision and my advice, she came at me like an African panther, and after rampaging her way through a string of terrifying imprecations, she stood squarely in front of me, made a lot of gesticulations, and brought her hands again and again very close to my eyes. Finally, I was able to understand the following:

"So then you . . . Just get a look at the phony, the trickster, the deceiver! Instead of preaching to Manuel to get that awful idea out of his head, he preaches at him to bring the schoolmarm home to me . . . Señor de Manso, you are a scarecrow."

And with the liberty I was used to taking, in line with her own, I made bold to reply:

"The one who's been a scarecrow is you, Señora Doña Javiera, when you assumed that I could give your son advice that went against his own honor."

"Don't speak that way. I'm furious . . ."

"Well, fume all you want to, but on this subject you won't hear any different answers from me."

"But Señor Don Máximo—surely you can't imagine that my son is out there to be trapped by the first ragamuffin of a girl . . . ?"

"One thing at a time, madam. However high your noble rank, you will not be able to downgrade my protégée—I want you to know that Irene is my protégée, the daughter of a high-born gentleman who did great service to my father. I am indebted, and this orphaned young lady will not suffer the insults of any young whippersnapper as long as I'm around."

"My, my! Here's Don Quixote all of a sudden! You're getting just a bit tiresome, do you know it? My son . . ."

"Is worth less than she is."

"More; more!"

And with every syllable she raised her powerful voice. Her shouting was making me nervous.

"A fine service you've done for me! And as for now . . . out of here by summer, Manso my friend."

"As far as I'm concerned, whatever season you say. The young people will marry, and we'll be at peace."

"I won't give my consent," exclaimed Doña Javiera, hands on her hips.

"Yes you will."

And in spite of the fury of my friend and neighbor, I was calm before her, and couldn't resist the temptation to treat such a serious matter in a humorous vein:

"My, my, just look at the airs this lady puts on! Is your son some Coburg-Gotha?"

"Don't start using foul names, mister. Whether we're goats or not, it's none of your business. And for what it's worth, there's money in having a lot of goats. We may not be a proud family, but we're an honest one."

"So is mine . . . My, my! When you think that the boy is getting a real jewel, a woman without equal, a prodigy of talents, beauty, virtue . . . , the daughter of a royal groom . . ."

"Of a groom!" repeated the ex-butcher-woman, dumbfounded. "One of those boobs who go alongside the royal coach . . . bouncing in the saddle. Well, I must say . . . Live and learn!"

"And any day now—hear me, Señora de Peña—I'll go through the Archives in the Chancellory and I'll get the title of Baroness for my protégée, a real title. Put that in your pipe and smoke it."

"Is that so?' she said, mixing a bit of laughter with her anger. "A baroness . . . Well, water must be worth something if they bless it."

"Yes, madam."

"She may be all of the baroness you say, but when we go into the *ugly* contest, there's no one to beat her. I've seen her only once since she became a teacher . . . What skinny arms! Good Lord! She's a beanpole in clothes. Never saw anything with less charm. Looks like one of those pale Traviata types. I don't know how my boy could've got it into his head . . ."

"He's shown very good taste. The one with perverse taste is you."

"I don't like people with book-learning. A woman with a degree—how disgusting! Book-learning is for the men; wits, for the women."

As she said this, it seemed that her anger had passed somewhat.

"Keep it up," she said, "keep it up, all those praises of your godchild. She's the kind they wean on vinegar . . . If she walks into my house, I'll bet I'll just shudder and shake."

"You won't be that uncontrolled . . . You'll receive her, and after a short while you'll love her very much."

"Oh really?" she exclaimed in a very vulgar tone of voice. "I can see that Doctor Professor is as stupid as they come. You must be cousin to the fellow who roasted a pound of butter."

"Well, what are we to do about it . . . For now, please be so kind as to send your maid up to iron two shirts for me. Petra is ill . . ."

"Oh! Of course, sir," she replied in officious solicitude, rising from her chair.

"One other small favor . . . here's my sack coat, minus some buttons."

"Yes, yes, yes. Let's have it."

She began to pace about the room, as if she were looking for chores to do.

"More little favors. I have some shirts that could stand having new collars on them."

"Of course! Let's have them!"

"And just look at me here today: I don't even know what I'll have to eat."

"Blessed Mother, that's no problem! Come downstairs or I'll send up whatever you like . . ."

"I'll go down . . . But it wouldn't do me any harm today if one of the maids came up here and straightened things up a little . . . Poor Petra . . ."

"I'll come up myself. Anything else?"

"Just that you'll have to give your consent to Manuel."

Laughter, satisfaction, her eager wish to serve me, all were struggling against her inexplicable pride; but it amused me to hear her say, partly in cheer and partly in anger:

"Well, I don't feel like it . . . Really now!"

"Come, come. You shall indeed give it,"

"I'll take these things with me."

She was diligently gathering up my clothes and examining them with the look of a thoroughly industrious housewife.

"I'll be right back up, I'll bring one of the girls to help me. Blessed Mother, just look at this house! But you'll see, you'll see how quick we'll leave it as neat as a pin."

And from the doorway she looked back at me in an odd way.

"And that other business, what about it?" I shouted at her.

"I don't feel like doing it . . . You just want to hear me talk. This good gent is very hard to take . . ."

XLVI
DID THEY MARRY?

YES, OF COURSE THEY DID! How could they *not* marry, since that was the logical and necessary solution? Conscience and Nature were both begging for it with a variety of pleas. I took special pains to bring it about. The turtledove-schoolmarm would have to live her whole life grateful to me, for without the aid of good old Manso it is certain that the desired salvation could not possibly have been achieved. For, indubitably, Manuel Peña was indecisive that night when I admonished him, and if his love was powerful, so too were his perplexities and worries, not to mention the influence exercised on him by his empty-headed chums and his doting mamma. Thus, I take pride in having resolved that difficult struggle on the side of good, and with just a few words aimed straight at the heart. I don't like to praise myself, so I'll continue my narrative . . . But not wishing to scramble the events, I'll backtrack just a bit to say that not twenty minutes had gone by since Doña Javiera had left, making that remark about my being *hard to take,* et cetera, when the doorbell rang.

A maid: "Madam says will you come down to look at some furniture."

"All right, I'll go down, I'm just finishing dressing."

A little later, ting-a-ling.

"Madam says will you please come down to look at some curtains."

Explanation: Señora de Peña was busy buying things to furnish her new home, and couldn't make up her mind about selecting anything without first consulting me. For her I was the sum of all human wisdom concerning everything God had created, or failed to create. Most particularly in matters of taste, my merest whims had the force of law.

I went downstairs. The whole parlor was filled with luxurious furniture, bought in well-known shops, and a French *tapissier* was showing samples of curtains, portières, and assorted yard goods.

"What do you think, Señor de Manso? Come, come, you decide. These heavy chairs, don't you think they're too big? All right for the Pope, maybe! The things they invent nowadays! And what about these others that look like they're made of wire? If I sat down in them, it'd be good-bye to the money they cost! . . . And nothing matches. It's all different shapes and colors. I like things that match . . . These curtains, Señor de Manso, look like they're made out of chasubles; but fashion gives the orders . . ."

I gave an opinion on all of it, and Doña Javiera, very satisfied, refused to buy some things of doubtful taste which I had vetoed.

"Maybe you'd like to go through the new house, Don Máximo my friend," she said later. "I don't know *what* the painters will do if there's nobody with good taste to tell them . . . well . . . I *did* tell them to paint lots of hares on the dining-room walls, along with some dead quail and a dead stag or two. I don't know what they'll do. I hear tell that now they decorate dining-rooms with plates stuck onto the ceiling. Plates *used to be* for eating off of. I don't understand these new styles. You'll have to advise me. Best thing would be for you to go right to the house and supervise everything according to your taste . . . That's the answer: settle things at will and put in or take out what you like . . . I suppose it's the style now to hang the chairs from the ceiling in drawing rooms, too . . . and put the chandeliers on the floor . . . Say, Señor de Manso, I've just had an idea. You have nothing to do this afternoon. Shall we go over to the new house? Today they're going to deliver the new carriage I've bought. I—we—will try it out today. You can tell me if it's in good taste, if the seats are nice and soft, if the horses are nice and handsome . . . Wait till you see the house, even though it's all torn up and full of plaster and trash. Blessed Mother, those painters and plasterers couldn't care less! You can see I've had to bring all the furniture in here, and the parlor is so chock-full, you can't take a step in there. So, shall we go over there?"

I acceded to everything. The lady went to dress. After a short while she had me sent for so I could see a wrapper the seamstress was fitting on her.

"It looks very nice, madam. It's as if it were . . ."

"Made with me in mind, yes. I knew that already. Everything looks good on me. Right, Manso m'dear? I can still leave a lot of these young hussies eating my dust behind me."

And as she took off the wrapper that was being fitted, the lady was left a bit less dressed than is usual and customary, especially in the presence of gentlemen from outside the family.

"Hey! Don't leave . . . We're close friends, close ones. Everybody knows by now I'm no prude. What can you really see of me? Nothing. You already knew that *in my neighborhood* . . ."

As she said *in my neighborhood,* she ran her hands over her lovely, white, curved shoulders. And she continued the sentence like this:

". . . bags of bones are not in style. That's left for certain toothpick-women I can think of . . . What skinny arms! Oh well, I mustn't lose my temper."

And she dressed quickly.

"As for hats," she said looking at me as into a mirror. "I don't intend to wear one. My face doesn't need any roof-tiles. Let's have my mantilla, Andrea. Look sharp, girl, the professor's waiting."

Determined to please her, I went along, using the brand-new carriage for the first time, both of us putting on great airs along God's own streets. I laughed and so did she. On the way, the conversation provided me an opening to speak of the now famous *consent,* and she got angry when I mentioned it, though not as much as before when she had raised her voice to me.

"Come, now, you're trying to make me angry . . . And I *can* get angry. If I hear any more talk about the schoolteacher . . . Suppose I just order the driver to stop here so I can drop you right in the gutter?"

In the new house I saw horrors. Doors painted blue, ceilings with deer running across them, gilded baby angels on the wainscoting, stained glass all over the place, green foliage-patterned wallpaper with an amaranth border, silver acorns on the doorjambs, rose windows with emaciated or swollen nymphs, swans swimming in ferrous sulfate; and a thousand heresies more. To uproot them all it would have been necessary to organize a great *auto-da-fé.* It was very late in the game, and I could only arrange to have limited remedies and corrections put into effect. I still gave my neighbor courteous compliments on the decoration of her sumptuous dwelling.

We also went to look at the one she had destined for me, and I thought it quite pretty. Doña Javiera made the first assignment of rooms, getting in ahead of my own tastes and desires.

"Here, the study, the bookcases at this end; over there, Señor de Manso's bed, nicely protected from drafts and away from the noise of the stairway; the washstand here. I'm going to install one with piping and a faucet, for greater convenience . . . Let's look outside. Now that's what you call a view. When your head gets weary from all that studying, you can stick it out the windows and take in the whole Retiro Park in one glance. From here my Mister Professor can make love to the hermitage of Los Angeles; you can see it there in the distance. And you can have a roaring good debate with the lion in the Retiro Zoo."

To tell the truth, I was deeply grateful to my affectionate and provident neighbor. And I couldn't help showing it. But as soon as I would touch, even from an angle, on the fearful question, she turned instantly into a basilisk. Still, the next day I found her more tame. She had stopped saying *schoolmarm,* and called Irene *that poor young woman* . . . That afternoon, while Doña Javiera and her maids were straightening up my flat, I charged forward again; and she said to me without invitation:

"You are really hard to discourage! If *you* can't get your way with that push, push, grind, grind, *nobody* can! But no, I'm not letting myself be coaxed . . . No more talk about it. If you do, I'll really blow up."

"But, madam . . ."

"Be quiet. If I get angry, I'll pick up the feather duster . . . and it's out the door and into the street with you."

She was threatening to throw me out of my own house. And she did seem to have taken possession of it, looking at it as hers, arranging things according to her own whims. I couldn't complain, because with the excuse of Petra's illness (she was half crippled) Doña Javiera and her maids had rendered my house shining and spotless. I had never seen so much neatness and cleanliness around me. It was a joy to contemplate my clothing and my modest furnishings. In several places throughout the house, on the mantelpiece and the washstand, I came upon articles of luxury and utility which were not my own. Señora de Peña had brought them up from her house, making me discreet gifts of them.

As her amiability gradually provided me with new opportunites to do pleasing things for her, she was less frequently on the verge of being *furious* regarding her consent, and at length I achieved such a wily technique for pleasing her and making her content, first by direct attentions to her initiation into luxurious living and then by letting myself be cared for and waited on, that one afternoon she said to me:

"Just so I won't have to listen to you any more, Manso m'dear . . . , let 'em get married. There's nothing you can't get me to do . . . You're almost like God when it comes to protecting young girls."

244

XLVII
SHE WOULDN'T GIVE ME
A MINUTE'S PEACE

A THOUSAND BLESSINGS on my affectionate neighbor, who had doubtless set herself the task of making my life pleasant and reconciling me to the human race. O Law of Compensation, thou art unknown to those who eke out an arid life on the steppes of studious effort! But, ah, those who have even once set foot upon the fresh meadows of reality! Down with metaphysics, and on with the story!

I was a bit weary one morning when . . . ting-a-ling. It was Ruperto, who looked blacker than usury to me.

"My mistress . . . please go there now . . ."

"Something for me to do. What's the matter? I'll go immediately."

I found Lica very alarmed because for the long space of three days I had not gone to her house. It was indeed an unusual thing. I made excuses about my work and she called me down for being ungrateful and unappreciative.

"Well, here's why I've sent for you today, dear. You must go with Don Pedro . . ."

"And who is Don Pedro?"

"Oh, you're so out of things. He's Regustiana's father, such a nice gentleman . . . You've got to get him a ticket so he can see the Natural History Museum."

"He and his whole family are a Natural History Museum!"

"Don't be so dreary. He's a good fellow. Go with him to see Madrid, the good man hasn't seen anything. One of the boys must be given a *situation* . . ."

"We'll *situate* them all . . . right in the street."

"Tiresome! She's a very good wet nurse . . . Máximo, you chose well. There's no one like you!"

245

"How's José María?"

"Him? Back to the same things. No sign of him around here now. Apparently the marquess business is all settled."

"My compliments to ya, marchioness!"

"For me, that's all a . . ."

Notwithstanding her modesty and simple goodness, the idea of a coronet pleased her. Humanity was made in a certain way, or has made itself that way. Nobody can bend it out of shape.

"I just want my peace and quiet," she added. "José María is getting more and more sugary-sweet, but he's away so much, my dear . . . He's finished up with the Molasses Committee and now it's the Brown Sugar Committee."

Shortly thereafter we saw my brother come in, and the first thing he said to me, in a very bad humor, was this:

"Look, Máximo, you're responsible for bringing that savage tribe in here; let's see if you can free us from them. This has turned into a plague like locusts or phylloxera; I can no longer deal with it. They're driving me crazy. You get some crazy ideas yourself . . . The old man wants tickets and tracks me down at Parliament. The mother asks me to find jobs for her two wolf cubs . . . Anyway, *you* take charge of getting rid of the plague—you brought it here."

"Poor things," murmured Lica, "they're so good . . ."

"Well, put them out in the street," I suggested.

"No, no, his milk won't be taken away like that," Manuela cried in terror. "Speak softly, for Heaven's sake; they'll hear you."

Speaking softly, I sought to impart a piece of sensational news, and I announced the upcoming marriage of Manuel Peña. Manuela crossed herself several times. My brother, his face changed in the most dreadful way, said only:

"I knew about it already."

He was only moderately successful in concealing his wrath as he took up a newspaper and lit several cigarettes. Later, as a result of having stumbled into the great Don Pedro in the corridor on his way to his study, and of having the said Don Pedro (cap in hand) ask him for some favor, he went into a terrible fit of temper, unable to contain himself:

"Listen, Don Scarecrow, do you think I'm here for the purpose of listening to your stupid remarks? All of you, get out of here; into the street with

246

you; get out of my house this instant, and take your whole drove with you!!"

Good Lord, what a row! Pedro, only Uncle Pedro really, since my sister alone called him *Don,* said he had no need of anyone; his worthy spouse averred that she was as much a lady as Madam herself; the boys went hurtling down the stairs and Regustiana began to cry her eyes out. Lica was paralyzed with fear, and almost knelt to beg me to calm those people down and thus free my godson from another and very grave danger. Meanwhile, we could hear José María stamping his feet in his study; he was accompanied by Sáinz del Bardal, whom he was calling an idiot for some carelessness or other in the drafting of a letter.

"He's finally getting what he deserves," I thought, and had no recourse but to soothe Don Pedro and his wife, telling them all sorts of kind and courteous things, and taking them that very afternoon to see the Natural History Museum. For the boys I had to buy boots, hats, tobacco pouches, and cakes. Lica gave a nice present to the wet nurse's mother. At night, I took her Hottentot father to a café. And finally, the next day, midst gifts and favors without number, we managed to pack them all into the train, paying for their tickets and sending along an opulent lunch to be eaten during the journey.

XLVIII
THE WEDDING TOOK PLACE

I T WAS ON A TUESDAY. Since I don't take much pleasure from speaking of the matter, I'll drop it for now. There are some things that happened before the wedding which deserve to be recorded. For example: Doña Cándida, upon learning about the plans from Manuel himself, saw the heavens opening, and in them the image of a delightful, parasitic future in the Peña household. After all, my gadfly couldn't contradict the laws of her own character, which called for the most exaggeratedly farcical behavior on that very gratifying occasion. Thus, it was really something to see her and listen to her the day she went to Lica's house, "to unburden her griefs and seek consolation in the bosom of friendship . . ."

For the very idea of living apart from the innocent child filled her with anguish. What would become of *her* now, at her age, deprived of the sweet company of her cherished niece . . . , the only one of the García Grandes left on earth? But the Good Lord surely must know what He's doing by taking away from her that pleasure, that moral support . . . We are born to suffer, and suffering we die . . . Of course she was capable of rising above her grief and even smothering it, considering the good fortune of the girl. Oh, of course! The main thing was for Irene to marry well, even if her aunt should die of sorrow at losing her companionship . . . And just think how the *poor child* would weep at being separated from her aunt to go off and live with a *man*! She was so shy, so namby-pamby! One thing my gadfly didn't like was Peña's less-than-gentle origins. She recognized Manuel's fine qualities, his talent, his brilliant future, but oh! that butcher background! Flesh, to put it plainly, was one of the three enemies of the soul. A woman *cannot* get used to certain things, no matter how much people say about our enlightened age, and equality, and the aristocracy of talent . . . In short, it was perfectly dreadful, and the great lady, who out of kindness and tolerance would treat Manuel as her son, was determined not to swallow Doña Javiera, for, really, there are things that are beyond human endurance! The boy, . . . all right; but his mother . . . impossible! If at least she weren't so common! Faugh! Caligula just simply could not overcome her scruples . . . or if you prefer, let's say her *concern.* Her nerves were too delicate and her sensitivity too exquisite to endure brushing up against certain persons . . . No, each one in his own house and God in the house of everyone . . .

For the rest, it goes without saying that all Señora de García Grande's possessions were for her niece. Even the loveliest, rarest, most artistic objects, those she had kept as family heirlooms, she intended to pass along to Irene. She still had *wonders* locked up in her chests, things that would give great distinction to the newlyweds' home. And whatever was left over from her income, that also was for them. Good Heavens! Her niece would need more from her than she from her niece, and the time would surely come when the great lady would help Irene out of a tight spot.

As Lica listened to all this, she became sad, and *Niña Chucha* wiped away a tear. Doña Cándida stayed for lunch, and from that very day resumed her string of daily visits to the house, thus entering a period of parasitism which will come to an end only with the end of the baneful existence of that monster of intrigue, that crocodile of purses.

I had determined not to see Irene again, since by not seeing her I could remain more at peace. But one day Manuel insisted on taking me over there, and I couldn't avoid going. She who had been a teacher of young girls and then *my* teacher in certain ways, was glad to see me and made no secret of it. But her joy belonged to the order of brother-sister feelings, and couldn't have been suspect to young Peña, who also joined in it after his own fashion. We talked for a long while about a variety of things: she demonstrated clearly to me the range and the magnitude of her imperfections, kindling within me, as I saw each defect, the sharp grief which filled my soul . . . She spoke of a thousand amusing trivialities, and each one was like a sharpened arrow piercing me through and through. Her frivolous joy was dripping a drop at a time, like poison, on my heart . . .

I had felt a keen smarting sensation ever since my famous discovery; I suspected and feared that Irene, gifted as she doubtless was with great perspicacity, was aware of the passion and madness I secretly felt for her. That, together with my being silently rebuffed, must have made me appear to her in the most ridiculous light in the world. This distressed me and made me feel nervous. From time to time I would wonder: "What can I do to get that idea out of her head? For there's no doubt she *has* that idea . . . She's sharper than a whip, and smarter than all we bookworms put together. Utterly

249

impossible for her not to understand my . . . And if she understood it, how she must now be laughing at poor Manso, how the two of them must be laughing in the intimacy of their delightful private moments! If only it were possible to wrench that idea loose from her, or at least to sow the seeds of other ones that might choke and stifle it as they grew . . ."

And when she would speak to me, kind almost to a fault, she looked at me with eyes that seemed to reach the furthest and most hidden corners of my being. And then there were her lips, with their ironic little smile that confirmed my fears and made me even more troubled. When she looked at me in that way, I thought I could hear her inner voice saying: "I can read you, Manso; I can read you as if you were a book written in the clearest of languages. And the way I'm reading you now is the same way I read you when you made love to me, philosopher-style, you poor man . . ."

Thinking these thoughts, and feeling all the blood rush to my brain, was all one sensation. I was seeking an opportunity to destroy, albeit with sophistries, that idea (*really something!*) that my friend had about me. And finally . . . I don't know how the conversation took such a turn, but I think young Peña said *I* ought to get married. She supported the idea. I glimpsed the merest thread of an opportunity, and I seized it.

"Me, get married? I've never even thought of such a thing . . . Those of us who devote ourselves to studious pursuits take on a hard shell, right from childhood . . . I mean, we discover that we're priests without having suspected it . . . The routine of bachelorhood ends up creating a permanent condition of indifference to everything but the calm bonds of friendship."

Not very certain of the idea, I had a hard time finding the words as well.

"For . . . we reach the point of not experiencing any feelings but those of friendship . . . It's just that study claims for itself all of our power to love, and we get passionate about a theory, or a problem . . . Women pass beside us like a problem belonging to another world, another branch of learning which is of no interest to us. I have sought at times to change the constitution of my spirit, urging it to drink from those wellsprings which gush for others with so many life-giving currents, but I have not been able to do so . . . I don't want to and I don't need to. I count myself a member of the phalanx of the eternal human priesthood. The celibate man is human, too, and in all ages has served to show forth the excellences of the spirit."

Did I get anywhere with this rigmarole? Seeking a stronger effect still, I mentioned to Irene the period when she gave lessons to my little nieces and spoke of the fatherly affection she had summoned up in me. It's easy to see . . . , we were in such similar professions, it was a comradeship . . .

No, no, it wasn't working at all.

I saw her looking at me and I'd swear she was saying to herself: "Nobody believes you, my dear little Manso; nobody. Let the record show that you fell head over heels like any young student, and now not even with all the philosophy in the world are you going to get me to believe anything different. We schoolteachers are wiser than metaphysicians: the only people they fool are themselves."

XLIX
I FELL ILL THAT DAY

WHAT A COINCIDENCE! . . . I'm referring to the day of the wedding. I chose not to attend. Let's just say that I was confined to my bed with a heavy cold. It was raining hard. A gray sadness was dropping in cold threads from the sky, and whispering as it struck the ground. Through Doña Javiera, who came up to see me once everything was over, I learned that nothing unusual had happened beyond the obligatory ceremony, the blessing in Latin, the curiosity of the guests, the lunch at the new house, and the departure of the blissful pair for I don't know where . . . I think it was Biarritz, or Burgos, or Bordeaux. Some place beginning with a B. *Where* they went doesn't really matter. I got up at once, fully recovered. This astounded Doña Javiera, who told me she'd decided to live in the new house beginning the next day. We spoke of Irene, and my neighbor admitted that she was beginning to find her easy to get on with; and that I had perhaps been right to praise her; and that if her son was happy she couldn't be too concerned for much else. She told me that all the girls looked at Manolo in envy of Irene . . . A mother's vanity hurts no one! After lunch the pair had gone to the station alone, in her new carriage, all nicely tucked into fur rugs . . . Manolo was so handsome! So much better than *her*! *You could set your watch by Manolo*! That rascal of a schoolteacher must have had more tricks up her sleeve than Merlin, for she'd hooked the best-looking, most worthy boy in all the Spains.

Blessed Mother, Doña Cándida just wept and wept! My brother José had also caught cold that day, and couldn't attend. M'lady the Marchioness (I mean Lica) *was* there, along with her mamma and sister, and besides them, a lot of other notable persons. I wasn't much impressed with all that notability, and said so bad-humoredly to my neighbor. She insisted on classifying as eminent all the people who came; we disputed the point, and I ended up asking her:

"And I'll just bet little black Ruperto was there, too?"

"And mighty handsome he was, too; he looked like a person served up in the blackest squid sauce . . . Go right ahead, make fun of him. In time, Don Máximo, you'll see great people come to my house, when Manolo begins to make a splash, and we give tea parties . . . It'll be a regular crush of folks . . ."

I don't remember how much longer her *impromptu* lasted, but it was tireless and miles long. To comfort herself in her loneliness, she began that very day to arrange the move to the new house. Taking the opportunity provided by two days I spent in Toledo on a junket with several friends, Doña Javiera herself completed the transfer of all my furniture, books, and other effects with such diligence and care that when I returned I found the move completed, and without the slightest inconvenience I occupied my new dwelling. To tell the truth, I had no way of repaying all those favors and that growing loyalty which seemed by now to be overflowing the normal bounds of friendship. And since, unfortunately, my old servant remained paralyzed in one leg and not very well in the other, my house continued in the hands of Señora de Peña, who attended to everything with extreme solicitousness, all of which gave rise to gossip among malicious friends and neighbors. I laughed at such naughty speculations, and one day I mentioned them openly.

"You just let them talk," she answered me with less flippancy than usual for her—indeed she seemed a bit troubled. "Let's just laugh at the world. You don't get the honor you deserve, and people don't appreciate you for what you're worth . . . Well, I just feel like doing it, and I'll give my friend Señor Don Máximo the royal treatment. It's justice, no more than justice; I'd almost say it would *indemnify* you, is that the way to say it? These fancy words always put me on edge for fear I'll let out something awful . . ."

My neighbor's words had a profound effect, and produced in me many thoughts and feelings; they've remained etched in my memory forever. Did her regard for me come from that secret, inexplicable admiration that a studious man is apt to awaken in ordinary folk? I have seen rare and most noble examples of this. Doña Javiera had put into circulation a strange aphorism: *Wisdom is to men what wit is to women.* Whatever the meaning of this commonplace might have been, I attributed my neighbor's compliments to her somewhat overwarm temperament and her whimsical sensitivities, which took on new strength as she confirmed her esteem for me. That's why I told myself: "She'll get over this, and the day will come when she doesn't even remember me." But it didn't turn out that way, not at all. Quite the contrary, I could see that she was still seeking intimacy and appropriating more and more what had been mine alone, especially in matters of morality and domestic life, these being the very keys to familiarity. And accustomed by then to her easy company and her diligent cooperation in all that was important in my life, I came to feel that if the fervent friendship of my neighbor were ever to disappear, I should miss it very much. That is why I let myself be pulled down the slope all unawares, without worrying about where I might end up.

I mustn't fail to recount the return of Manuel and his wife after they'd had a splendidly diverting time on their lovers' junket. In the version Doña Javiera told me, they were just unbearably mawkish and lovestruck. The *moon* had been filled with so much *honey.* I honestly wished for the longest possible duration of that sweet state of affairs. Irene looked prettier and more filled-out to me, with good color and in excellent health. Doña Javiera, who held nothing back, told me one day:

"It seems there's a grandchild in the offing. If she has a lot of kids, I'll move to another house. I don't want nurseries all over my place."

Irene always treated me with the most exquisite consideration. Although nothing ought to have surprised me by then, I marveled at seeing her so conformed to the general model, to see her changing all the time, farther and farther—Good Lord!—from the ideal . . . Indeed, was it not she who set about organizing, with other ladies, charity functions and raffles, and money-raising parties for those dear little hospitals that never seem to be done a-building? I also saw her presiding in the street at a table of ladies who were gathering funds for something, and her husband told me that she spent some of his money on novenas and ecclesiastical celebrations. To make everything complete, one Sunday afternoon I saw her charmingly turned out in a black mantilla, high comb, and carnations. She was on her way to the bullfight, and when I asked her if she enjoyed that savage *fiesta,* she replied that she'd taken a liking to it, and that if it weren't for the sad spectacle of the wounded horses, she'd generate more enthusiasm in the bullring than anywhere else.

Final pronouncement: she was just like all the rest. The age, the race, the milieu could not fail to crop out in her. I could have predicted it with certainty: since her marriage she had not picked up a single book.

But let's be fair to her. In her home, the ex-schoolmistress displayed remarkable qualities. Not only had she introduced into the Peña household a hitherto unknown level of taste—and in the process sustained more than one controversy with her mother-in-law; she had also succeeded in showing great gifts as the mistress of a household. With these gifts and her superb tact (alter-

254

nately giving in and resisting), she managed little by little to conquer the affections of her mamma-in-law. No doubt about it: she had enormous gifts for social intercourse and a marvelous art for dealing with people. In the evenings Manuel began to receive, in the drawing room, several notable persons and others who aspired to notability.

The way Irene treated different people; the way she attracted important ones; how she hoodwinked fools; the way she made everything work to her husband's advantage; it was all a wonder to see. I watched it astounded; and Doña Javiera was frightened.

"She's the very devil," she said to me one day. "She knows more than you do."

And it was a truth larger than life, larger than the whole of life! The most amusing part is that Doña Javiera, who had always dominated everyone who lived in her home, was coming under the sway of her daughter-in-law, a little at a time . . . One might almost say that she bore her a certain respect akin to fear. When the two of us were alone, Doña Javiera and I would discuss Irene's receptions, and simply marvel at them.

"She was born to play an important role . . ."

"Manolo's made a fine acquisition; didn't I tell you?"

"If she continues like this and doesn't make any *blunders* . . ."

"Oh! She's so good! She's an angel . . ."

And at times we took mutual comfort in timid meanness:

"We'll see how long she lasts. I don't like all these tea parties and receptions, all this show."

"Well, neither do I . . . Would to God that . . ."

"The things one sees . . ."

And our little snottiness was just simply reprehensible! For they loved each other tenderly. Love, youth, a social milieu filled with appetites and flattery and vanity, were all cultivating *ambition* in those happy souls, nurturing it according to the modern form of that sin, *i.e.,* confined within the limitations of home-style morality and an appropriate demeanor. This was as natural as sunrise, and I would do very well to save for another time my professional grumblings, which are not applicable to the case and would have achieved nothing except to make me look like an impertinent pedant. Purity and refinement in morals appear almost comically inappropriate in the lives of these people. And I'll say nothing about political life, which Manolo entered sure-footedly from the moment he received from the electors his certificate as a Member of Parliament. My disciple, with the consent of his enemies and

255

the secret enthusiasm of his wife, was entering a sphere where the devotee of the Good either acquires immunity by putting on a mask of hypocrisy, or else falls flat on the floor, dead of asphyxiation.

L

LET THEM LIVE!
LET THEM ENJOY LIFE!
I'M GOING AWAY

FOR THEM: life, youth, wealth, contentment, friends, applause, delights, delerium, success... For me: premature old age, monotony, sadness, loneliness, obscurity, torment, oblivion. Each day I put a greater distance between myself and that radiant focus of happiness down on the main floor, which I considered an inappropriate setting for my sickly spirit. I was suffocating there. Moreover, every time I saw young Señora de Peña before me (the wife of my disciple, herself more my teacher than another disciple), I experienced such anguish and depression that I felt I couldn't go on living. And if by chance, in conversation, I should find another little defect in her, the discovery heaped coals on my inner fires. The less perfect, the more human she was; and the more human, the more divine she seemed to my crazed spirit, which had become permanently unhinged from its bearings by that idolatrous fanaticism, that barbarous worship of a fetish with a soul. Every day I thought up excuses for not going downstairs to dine, for not attending their gatherings, for not going for a stroll with them. Because just to see her was equivalent to feeling transformed and overcome with foolish weaknesses. The influence of this turmoil was powerful enough to form a new pattern within me. I was no longer *I*, or at least, I didn't seem to be myself any longer. I was, at times, the disfigured shadow of Señor Manso, like those shadows cast by daylight, or by the sunset, which stretches bodies out like a rubber band.

"But what's wrong with you?" Doña Javiera said to me one day.

"Nothing, madam, nothing. For that very reason I'm going away. If I'm choosing between two empty places, I prefer the other one."

"You look as white as a candle."

"That means that the hour has come for me to disappear from among

257

the living. I have borne my fruit and am not needed now. Everything which has fulfilled its purpose disappears."

"Well, I don't see any fruit of yours, Manso my friend."

"That may be. What is seen, Señora Doña Javiera, is the least important part of what exists. All great things, all laws, all causes, all active elements—invisible, all of them. And our eyes, what are they but microscopes?"

"Shall I call a doctor?" the lady said, very alarmed.

"It'd be like calling a gardener every time a flower fades and rots. Take a pair of scissors, and cut me off. Light, water, air, they no longer affect me. I'm ready for the insects to take over."

"You ought to go and take the waters."

"I'll soon be in the eternal waters."

"That does it! I'm calling a doctor."

"No need to, I can already feel the effects of the great narcotic; I'll strike the right posture . . ."

Doña Javiera burst into tears. She loved me so! Miquis came that very day, accompanied by a famous psychiatrist who asked me a number of questions I didn't answer. When I saw them leave, I laughed so hard that Doña Javiera became even more frightened and made a candid declaration of her strong affections (with which she did me great honor). I listened to her as if I were hearing my own funeral eulogy delivered from up in the pulpit overlooking my bier. And my yearning for rest was so great that I never got up again. My neighbor spared nothing in the prodigality of her tenderest care, and one morning, when the two of us were all alone, in the midst of a great silence—she was terrified and I serene—I died like a little bird.

The same perverse friend who had brought me into the world took me out of it, repeating the same magic words he'd said way back then, and also the diabolical sorcery of the bottle, the drop of ink, and the burnt paper which had preceded my incarnation.

"My dear fellow," I said to him, "will you please have done with me once and for all and take back this mortal flesh you've put me into just for your own amusement? It's not the least bit amusing to me . . . !"

As he let me slip from between his fingers, the serenity I felt made me realize that I was no longer a man.

The wails of sorrow uttered by Doña Javiera when she saw that I had departed for good woke up everyone in the building. Some neighbors came up, Manuel among them, and they all agreed that it was a pity that I could no longer be counted among the living . . . But I was getting on so well in my

258

new being that I had more pity for them than they for me; I even laughed at seeing them so hard-pressed by my absence. Those poor people! Family and friends mourned me, and some of the latter went to the newspaper offices, where they wrote *heartfelt words* in memory of me. As soon as Sáinz del Bardal found out, he grabbed his pen and rammed his way through—oh my!—an elegy for me, a piece which has provided me and my colleagues here in Limbo with great amusement.

My brother, Lica, Mercedes, Doña Jesusa, and Ruperto remained in grief for a number of days, I don't know how many. Manuel turned so yellow that he looked sick. Irene shed some tears and spent two weeks in a sort of fright, thinking she saw me appearing in doorways, raising curtains, and passing like a shadow through all the dark places in the house. She would rather be killed than go into her room alone at night. Superstitious, in addition to all the rest!!

But they all gradually got over their grief. The last one to do so was my Doña Javiera with her great good heart, so straightforward and so spontaneous. According to information that has come to my notice, she has gone more than once to visit the place where there lies buried what was my body, under a slab with a plaque on it saying that I had been very learned.

Of Doña Cándida I know that she heard several hundred masses, and that whenever she went to the Peña house (that was every day, and she descended like a locust on fertile fields), she mentioned my name with a sigh, so that the memory of my virtues might remain alive. I have also heard, through some seraphic grapevine or other, that an incalculable amount of money has been given to her to pay for masses applied to my eternal repose; so much money, indeed, that if it were applied to other souls Purgatory would be empty by now. I need hardly say that all of us here look with approval upon Caligula's fecund wit.

And as time passes, they gradually forget me, and that pleases me. The most singular part of it is that of all my teaching and writing there remain scarcely a few vestiges, and in these regions we all get enormous amusement from hearing a devoted friend or fervent disciple refer at a public meeting to the *unforgettable Manso*. For if one were to seek a place where there exists any memory of our wisdom, one would find no trace or shadow of it. Oblivion is complete and it is real, even though the unthinking use of readymade phrases might lead one to believe the opposite. On different occasions I have descended into people's brains (we are granted the precious faculty of paying visits to the thoughts of those who are still alive) and, inserting myself into the

259

heads of many who were students of mine, I've looked there for my ideas. These encephalic inspections have uncovered but little, and that not the best; indeed, to find even that mediocre bit I've had to rely on the help of other intruding spirits to excavate through layers of new deposits of the strangest ideas, the most recent ones, laid in day after day by reading, study, and experience.

In Manuel Peña I have found a copious amount of knowledge gained from experience. What I taught him can hardly be distinguished beneath the hodgepodge of new acquisitions, as luminous as they are practical, he's made in Parliament and in the combat of political life, *i.e.*, the life of pure action and gymnastics of the will. Manuel is achieving marvels in that art we might call civic mechanics, since there's nothing like it for recognizing and manipulating forces, for seeking practical results, for overcoming dead weight, for combining matter, and for taking risky, stupendous leaps. I've also taken a stroll in the vast interior of a certain person without finding anything special beyond the development and maturity whose existence I already knew of. On one occasion I came upon the shred of a thought of mine, I don't know what, and was so frightened and upset that I fled like a varmint taken by surprise in an empty attic. Later I came to realize that it was only a simple cold memory, mixed in by arithmetical calculation. On the telephone we have out here I heard this sentence:

"No, Aunt; no more masses. That whole business is over and done with."

Only infrequently did I make any excursions to the place where my brother's thought resides. All I found there were commonplace, conventional, routine ideas. Everything bore the mark of recent and incomplete acquisition, ready to disappear again when the next shipment came in, the insipid products of conversation or last night's reading. Like the label on a bottle of elixir, one read there the slogan *Morality and Economy.* José thought no further and was unable to talk of anything else.

As if he had discovered the Philosopher's Stone, he's still stuck on that supreme point of human wisdom. Morality and Economy! With this prescription he's gathered about him a group of somnambulists who consider him outstanding; and the funniest part of it is that among the public who get involved in these things without understanding them, my brother has gained ardent supporters and a level of prestige which is sending him straight down the road to Power. Will he be a Cabinet Minister? I'm afraid so. To arrive more quickly, he's founded a rag of a newspaper which is costing him lots of money and has no readers except for that group of sleepwalkers. Sáinz del Bardal is the Editor-in-Chief and writes practically the whole thing, which makes obvious the fact that said newspaper is the most tiresome, boring, soporific sheet one can imagine. As a result of the enormous gluttony indulged in by the miasma-ridden poet to strengthen him for his task, he contracted an illness which brought him to the gates of these spaces where I live. When we found out about it, there was a great commotion here, and all of us residents mutinied, making a pact to keep him out by any and all means within our power. God in His infinite goodness disposed that Bardal's earthly life should last some time longer. So our fury was calmed and the folk here rejoiced. It is in the nature of omnipotent wisdom to keep everybody happy.

One day when I fell asleep on a cloud I dreamed I was alive again and was dining at Doña Cándida's house. What a morbid aberration of my spirit, still not free from terrestrial influences! I woke up very upset, and it took quite a while for me to regain the placid composure of this blessed existence, which allows one to acquire slowly—until reaching complete possession—a haughty disdain for the actions and difficulties and anxieties of those beings who have not yet finished the great *boring wait* which earthly life really is. Those things make up the huge waiting room of *our* life, and do so with no small annoyance to us.

Oh, happy state and regions even happier, these from which I can look at Irene, my brother, Peña, Doña Javiera, Caligula, Lica—and all the other wretched little figures—with the disdain of a mature man looking at the toys which helped him pass the time when he was a child!